Catering on the Move

# Picnics

## A Cookbook and Guide

*Pat Nekola*

ISBN Number 0-9660610-0-4

Library of Congress 99-90596


Photographs by Bill Paulson
Illustrations by Catherine Baer
Back cover photograph of Pat Nekola by Nick Patrinos

Printed in the United States by
Palmer Publications, Inc.
Amherst, Wisconsin

# Dedication

I would like to dedicate this book to my husband, Steve and also to my mother and father, Mary and Howard Evans. My mother and father said, "You can accomplish anything you want to if you take the time and put in the effort."

# Contents

# Acknowledgments

I would like to thank all the personal and business friends, neighbors and customers that have spurred me onward and used my professional catering services.

I would also like to thank Sue Schmitzer, who spent time helping me outline the book to get me started, and gave invaluable advice; and Sonya Bice, who edited the entire book for me. Thanks also to the staff of Palmer Publications for their hard work and assistance.

# Introduction

Picnics are popular events. Most folks think of picnics as eating and playing games outdoors. People watch meats and vegetables cooking over hot coals, and the smell from the grill teases hungry picnickers. The steam from the corn on the cob, sizzling butter, and a patchwork of calico beans start picnickers thinking of eating immediately. The smoky aroma from the onion-seasoned hamburgers, all-American quarter-pound hot dogs, spicy Italian sausages, juicy bratwurst, barbecued chicken, teriyaki beef with vegetable shish kabobs, and garlic herb tenderloin make picnickers' mouths water. Roast pig, lamb, and a side of beef arouse the picnickers' anticipation of sampling cooked meats. An assortment of simple snacks with old-fashioned country lemonade and freshly brewed iced tea puts picnickers into a munching mode. Picnickers ask questions about ingredients used in common and unusual salads and applaud the assortment of tempting dessert displayed on the buffet table.

Through my travels I have picked up many tips for food and decorations. I had an opportunity to tour the kitchen facilities of a cruise ship. It was fascinating to see how the staff operated, preparing gourmet cuisine for large crowds.

I have experienced foods cooked over an open pit. I enjoyed the elegant Hawaiian Spanfurkel. The roast pig, mai mai fish, fruits, vegetables, poi, and desserts, along with elegant decorations on the buffet tables, set the mood for an upbeat and exotic picnic. Hawaiian dancers entertained guests in the open air, too.

I have always enjoyed entertaining in my back yard, and I used the grill to make steaks, chicken shish kabobs, salmon, and fish. Friends and neighbors would say to me, "You do such a nice job, and your food is delicious. You should become a professional caterer!"

I decided to do just that and began my catering business. As a professional caterer, I discovered picnics were great fun. I catered picnics for many large groups on any one given day and witnessed guests laughing and enjoying the outdoors. Picnickers took part in eating summery foods, listening to and watching the entertainment, and playing games. I especially enjoyed observing children as their faces were full of sunshine, joy and excitement. Parents and grandparents were content to relax and sit in the shade and watch family activities.

Entertainment at picnics consisted of clowns, magic shows, line dancing, singing, guitar playing, and storytelling. Picnickers would get involved in gunny sack races, egg throwing and pie eating contests, volleyball, baseball, or horseshoes. The children especially enjoyed the penny scramble, face painting, balloon sculptures, and the magic show. While the kids were being entertained, dads took the liberty to become involved in a water balloon throwing contest with the moms. I always did say dads were the big kids attending the outdoor event! Many picnickers felt welcome just to visit and enjoy the fresh air. No matter what the activities were, most picnickers indulged in great food and fellowship.

There is a difference between home cooking and catering picnics professionally off-premises. Quantity cooking is easy to do with proper instructions and some practice. You basically are changing the serving size of a recipe to feed more people. Quantity recipes are designed to make tasty dishes successfully.

Because I am a schoolteacher, I have a tendency to over-explain a recipe. It is important to be exact when working with recipes. As my catering service grew I added to my staff and had other people cooking for me. I made sure the recipes they used were exact so that the dish would always taste the same.

Chapters 8 through 11 are designed to explain the steps needed to operate and own a catering business. You can be a great cook, but there is a big difference between cooking for fun and running a successful catering business. You need to understand the financing, keep good books, set up shop, organize the operation, transport food safely, execute a party, and practice commonsense business techniques.

You must select dedicated personnel that you can trust to help you develop and run a successful business. Catering is a people business. You cannot run a catering company alone. Your chef must be a company person that can run your kitchen for profit. He/she must be dedicated and committed to working any scheduled hours needed. Because social catering is a cyclical business, there will be down times, especially in January, February, March and the first part of April, at least in the northern states. (Catering services in other states where the weather is very hot in the summer will tend to do less business then.)

Interacting with people to make them feel important is a big part of being a successful catering company. I found that saying all the right words to the host and guests, displaying an attractive buffet, and serving good food are the three necessary components for a successful catering business. Networking and marketing will make your business grow.

You need to understand that you will be working on weekends and holidays. When people are having fun, you are serving them to enable them to do so. You need to be organized to work under high stress and pressure. You must be flexible and able to adjust to change in the blink of an eye. If a problem arises, you must handle it quickly and calmly. The show must go on with grace and ease.

Consider all aspects of catering before investing your capital outlay and time. If you have a good business sense, people skills, and quality and quantity food service experience, you are a perfect candidate for running a catering service for profit.

Use this book as a guide for catering know-how, or as a ready reference for picnic buffets for fun or profit. Anyone can cook for a crowd with proper ingredients and average cooking ability. Have fun tasting while cooking for your favorite group picnic!

# Life Is a Picnic

A person that desires to do cooking in quantity for family parties or for professional catering will find this book most helpful. Recipes, menus, portions, quantity buying, decorating tips and buffet layouts will help you cater parties for fun or profit.

This book is designed for the cook or professional chef looking for ideas to entertain a crowd. The recipes are simple and easy to make. The majority of ingredients used in the recipes are common and accessible at your local grocery store or wholesale dealer.

What is a picnic? *Webster's Dictionary* states a picnic is "an outing in which the people involved eat a meal outdoors, brought along for the occasion; the food prepared for this population; something easy or pleasant to do or experience." The cavemen cooked out centuries ago, enjoying their favorite meats. I can picture the cavemen smiling as their food roasted over the open fire, anticipating the tastes as the aroma permeated the air.

Actually, the French are responsible for starting the true picnic. Picnic comes from the French word "pique-nique," which began in the late 1600s. "Pique-nique" came from the word "picorer," meaning to pick, peck, or scratch around for food. Aren't many popular picnic foods picked at or picked up with fingers?

Picnics were very popular, especially in England. There even was a picnic society formed in London in the mid-1700s. Most picnics then were elaborate affairs and included cold foods such as Cornish pasties, salads, hard-boiled eggs, cake, and fruit. Lady Wortley had a romantic picnic with her lover in England, sitting in the sun munching on cold, cooked bird and sipping champagne, enjoying each other's companionship back in 1649. It was a great way to get to know a person, be with a friend, or romance a lover!

Today, a picnic for two may consist of a blanket, picnic basket with sandwiches, six-pack of beer, and a few bumblebees, flies, and ants. It can be at a park or a roadside, scenic campsite, fishing stream, or in a family's backyard. In America, it usually refers to casual foods like hamburgers and hot dogs cooked outdoors.

When picnic foods are cooked on a grill, over charcoal or hickory chips in the open air, it is called a barbecue. The word "barbecue" comes from South America, and this type of picnic is extremely popular in the United States today.

Foods eaten outside often seem to just taste better. There is something about that open air that gets people to eat happily. People play games, visit, and return to the picnic table for munchies and picnic foods. While many people can't really explain it, there is just something special about a picnic.

Today, people are very busy working as a two-income family and can better afford to have a party catered. Many businesses sponsor company picnics at parks in honor of their employees. With a mobile society longing to keep in touch with its roots, family reunions are also regaining their popularity. What could be better then a picnic celebration?

Location can sometimes be a drawing card for a company or family party. In Milwaukee, Wisconsin, for instance, the county parks, the Milwaukee County Zoo, and Brewers' stadium are popular picnic sites. The Milwaukee County Zoo contracts many picnics every year

from May through September. The grounds are neat and will capture the entire family to see all of the animals. Children really enjoy this very special outing. As a caterer, I enjoyed watching children smiling while oohing and aahing over the stuffed animals displayed on our picnic buffet tables. Because the zoo lends itself to a family outing, many companies rent the facilities for their corporate picnics.

People gather in the parking lot at the Brewers' stadium in Milwaukee to party and to enjoy casual picnic foods like bratwurst, hamburgers, hot dogs, Italian sausages, snack foods, beer, and soda before baseball games. Tents are pitched with tables and chairs set up to accommodate large groups, while smaller groups or families use car tailgates or card tables to serve their food. I once did a very fancy picnic at the Brewers' stadium. I set up a mock restaurant and did a lobster boil, and tailgaters came from all over to view our fantastic party. Believe me, that was a very exciting experience! Our crew went home feeling like stars because we had made a whole lot of picnickers happy.

The exciting part of doing a picnic is providing a good time for people. The food selection is very important to create goodwill.

It is plain to see that each state or region has various foods that are local favorites only, while others are readily available nationwide or are imported. Picnics in faraway places offer exotic touches—some of which you may wish to re-create. These foods can be made into fantastic picnic feasts using a variety of recipes for picnic pleasure. Just because you are a Buckeye or a Hoosier should not stop you from trying other regional foods for a gastronomic food exploration. For instance, a caterer in Cleveland, Ohio, may do an Eastern clambake as a specialty party, or may serve up a pig roast with pork, roasted chickens or turkeys, corn on the cob, red-skinned potatoes or yams, potato salad, macaroni salad, rolls, and butter. So get imaginative and create a to-be-talked-about theme picnic when you are hosting or catering your next picnic!

I will share my picnic and other catering experiences with you throughout this book because, to me, they are exciting and informative. While I have already shared many ideas about picnic foods in the United States, I offer foolproof tested picnic recipes and menus I served in my catering business.

Each picnic menu shows how to lay out a picnic and carries out the theme. Decorations and centerpieces accent the picnic such as the Red, White, and Blue picnic. Easy snacks and beverages will kick off the picnic mode. Learn how to roast a pig and grill various meats such as steaks, pork chops and shish kabobs. Try unusual hot vegetables and learn how to prepare large portions of baked beans. Colorful salads will brighten your picnic table. Tempting desserts made in minutes will win the hearts of your picnic guests. *Picnics, Catering On the Move* is a ready reference book designed for the average cook to use as a guide for entertaining picnic parties. Each chapter is well explained and will help you have a perfect party. Remember: picnics are great fun. No matter where they are in whatever part of the country, they share the common interest of good food, the open air, and being with family or friends. Do your next celebration picnic-style!

# 2 ◆ Great Beginnings

# *Great Beginnings*
## *Snacks, Spreads, Dips and Beverages*
### Deviled Eggs

Two deviled eggs are made from each whole egg. Use Grade A large eggs. Figure 1 1/2 deviled eggs per person. Many people will take only one, the deviled egg lover may take three, and the weight-conscious person will pass.

To boil a dozen eggs, place them in a 3-quart saucepan. Cover eggs with cold water, and add 1 teaspoon salt and 1 tablespoon lemon juice. Bring eggs to a boil; boil 3-5 minutes. Remove pan from heat and let stand covered 25 minutes. If eggs are boiled too long the yolks turn green. Undercooked eggs will have a raw center and will cause lumps in the filling. Use a 5-quart pan to cook 25 eggs and a 9-quart pan to cook 50 eggs.

To hard-cook 50 eggs, place eggs in a pot, cover with cold water, add 1/3 cup lemon juice and 1 teaspoon salt. Bring to a boil and boil 5-10 minutes. Remove pan from heat and let stand covered 30-35 minutes.

To test an egg for doneness, spin it on the countertop. If the egg wobbles it is still uncooked. To peel an egg, tap the nose of the egg to break the shell. Remove the membrane with the shell to avoid gouges in the egg.

A 12-inch serving tray will hold 25-30 deviled eggs, and 50 will fit on a 16-inch serving tray. Garnish each deviled egg with paprika and a tiny leaf of parsley.

### *The deviled egg romance that led to marriage.*

My mother-in-law and father-in-law courted for about five years. She was a great cook. They liked to go on picnics for two. She made wonderful deviled eggs. Every time they went for a picnic he reminded her to be sure to bring his favorite deviled eggs. He said he had to marry her so he could continue to eat her tasty deviled eggs. She fooled him; after a year of marriage she stopped making deviled eggs. She got her man. I guess he wasn't too upset. They were married for 53 years before his journey home to heaven.

*Yield — 12 deviled eggs*
- 6 hard-cooked eggs
- 1/4 cup salad dressing
- 1 teaspoon lemon juice
- 1/8 teaspoon salt
- 1/8 teaspoon pepper
- 1 teaspoon sugar
- 1 teaspoon yellow mustard
- 1/8 teaspoon Worcestershire sauce

*Yield — 24 deviled eggs*
- 12 hard-cooked eggs
- 1/2 cup salad dressing
- 2 teaspoons lemon juice
- 1/4 teaspoon salt
- 1/4 teaspoon pepper
- 2 teaspoons sugar
- 2 teaspoons yellow mustard
- 1/4 teaspoon Worcestershire sauce

*Continued on next page*

*Deviled Eggs, continued*

| *Yield — 50 deviled eggs* | *Yield — 100 deviled eggs* |
|---|---|
| 25 hard-cooked eggs | 50 hard-cooked eggs |
| 1 1/4 cups salad dressing | 2 1/4 cups salad dressing |
| 1 tablespoon lemon juice | 4 teaspoons lemon juice |
| 1/2 teaspoon salt | 3/4 teaspoon salt |
| 1/3 teaspoon pepper | 2/3 teaspoon pepper |
| 2 teaspoons sugar | 1 tablespoon sugar |
| 1 tablespoon yellow mustard | 2 tablespoons yellow mustard |
| 1/2 teaspoon Worcestershire sauce | 3/4 teaspoon Worcestershire sauce |

When eggs are cool enough to handle, peel them and cut in half lengthwise. Scoop out the yolks and place into a bowl. Carefully set aside whites. Beat egg yolks until they are fine particles. Add salad dressing and beat until smooth. Add lemon juice, salt, pepper, sugar, mustard, and Worcestershire. Beat until smooth and creamy. Insert a 1E cake tube into a 12-inch pastry bag. (Using a pastry bag gives the deviled eggs a professional touch.) Fill the pastry bag three-quarters full. Fill each reserved egg white half. Garnish with paprika and parsley.

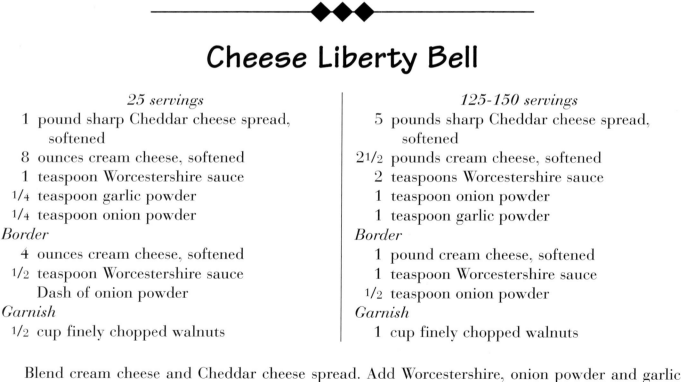

# Cheese Liberty Bell

| *25 servings* | *125-150 servings* |
|---|---|
| 1 pound sharp Cheddar cheese spread, softened | 5 pounds sharp Cheddar cheese spread, softened |
| 8 ounces cream cheese, softened | 2 1/2 pounds cream cheese, softened |
| 1 teaspoon Worcestershire sauce | 2 teaspoons Worcestershire sauce |
| 1/4 teaspoon garlic powder | 1 teaspoon onion powder |
| 1/4 teaspoon onion powder | 1 teaspoon garlic powder |
| *Border* | *Border* |
| 4 ounces cream cheese, softened | 1 pound cream cheese, softened |
| 1/2 teaspoon Worcestershire sauce | 1 teaspoon Worcestershire sauce |
| Dash of onion powder | 1/2 teaspoon onion powder |
| *Garnish* | *Garnish* |
| 1/2 cup finely chopped walnuts | 1 cup finely chopped walnuts |

Blend cream cheese and Cheddar cheese spread. Add Worcestershire, onion powder and garlic powder. Shape cheese mixture into a bell. (For large amounts, make 2-3 bells.) For the border, beat cream cheese with Worcestershire and onion powder until smooth. Using a pastry bag and a number 28 cake tube, pipe border on the bell. In the middle of the bell, using a number 4 writing tip, print "The Spirit of '76"; you can also print the company's or a guest's name. Sprinkle nuts over top of the bell but not on the writing. Serve with crackers. (See diagram on page 18.)

# Onion Dip

### Serves 50

3 pounds sour cream
3 packages (1.2 ounces each) dry onion
   soup mix

### Serves 75

5 pounds sour cream
4 packages (1.2 ounces each) dry onion
   soup mix

### Serves 100

6 pounds sour cream
4³/₄ packages (1.2 ounces each) dry onion
   soup mix

### Serves 150

10 pounds sour cream
7¹/₂ packages (1.2 ounces each) dry onion
   soup mix

Blend sour cream and onion soup mix until smooth and creamy. Serve with potato chips.

# Cream Cheese Onion Dip

### Serves 20

1 package (8 ounces) cream cheese,
   softened
1 pound sour cream
1¹/₂ packages (1.2 ounces each) dry onion
   soup mix

### Serves 50

2 packages (8 ounces each) cream cheese,
   softened
3 pounds sour cream
4 packages (1.2 ounces each) dry onion
   soup mix

### Serves 90

2¹/₂ pounds cream cheese, softened
5 pounds sour cream
5 packages (1.2 ounces each) dry onion
   soup mix

Beat cream cheese until smooth. Add sour cream and onion soup mix. Beat until smooth and creamy. Serve with potato chips or raw vegetables.

## DIP TIPS

◆ In quantity cooking in general, use less salt. Dry onion soup is salty. Larger quantities of dip made require less onion soup mix.

◆ Serve one pound of dip per 10-12 people.

◆ Make dip at least 24 hours in advance to let the flavors blend. Refrigerate up to 5 days in a tightly covered plastic container. Carry the dip to the picnic in a tightly covered container with ice packs.

◆ To keep food costs down, purchase commercial onion soup mix and sour cream at the local wholesale dealer when you are making large amounts of onion dip.

# Avocado Dip

*Serves 12-18 — Yield 4½ cups*

4 avocados
2 packages (1 ounce each) guacamole mix
½ cup sour cream
1 medium tomato, chopped
*Garnish*
1 black olive
½ cherry tomato

Cut avocados in half. Remove pits and peel. Mash avocados in a bowl with a fork. Add the guacamole mix and sour cream and stir until thoroughly blended. Cover and refrigerate 30 minutes to allow flavors to blend.

Just before serving stir in the tomato. For garnish, place olive in the center of the dip. Cut cherry tomato half into 5 strips to form petals; place around the olive to form a flower. Serve with tortilla chips. (See picture on page 13.)

# Black Bean Dip

*Serves 10-12*

1 can (15 ounces) black beans, rinsed and well drained
1 cup sour cream
¼ teaspoon garlic salt
½ teaspoon onion salt
1 green onion, chopped, including green
*Garnish*
1 cherry tomato
½ green bell pepper
½ cup black beans

In a large bowl, mix together black beans, sour cream, garlic salt, onion salt and green onion. Cover and refrigerate.

For garnish, with a sharp knife, peel tomato in one long spiral, starting at the base. Keep peel about ⅛-inch thick, but thicker at the bottom of the tomato to form a base for the rose. Coil peel tightly to form a rose. Place rose on center of dip. Cut pepper into 4 strips and place around tomato rose like spokes. (See picture on page 13.) Refrigerate until serving. Serve cold with tortilla chips.

## How to Heat Restaurant Nacho Cheese Sauce

1 can (6 pounds, 10 ounces) nacho cheese sauce will make fifty 2-ounce servings or thirty-five 3-ounce servings. A 1-pound can serves 10-12 people.

Put 12 cups (3 quarts) hot water into a 9-quart pan. Using a commercial can opener, open the top of the can. Set the can into the hot water. The water should come halfway up the can. (The water will keep the sauce from burning.) Bring the water to a boil. Heat the cheese sauce for about 30 minutes, stirring every 10 minutes. Place the heated cheese sauce into a 4-inch deep hotel half-pan and insert into a chafing dish. Or transfer heated cheese into a 4-quart slow cooker. Stir occasionally.

# Firecracker Chili Dip

| *Serves 25* | *Serves 100* |
|---|---|
| 1 pound ground beef | 4 pounds ground beef |
| 1/3 cup diced onion | 1 large onion, diced |
| 1/3 cup diced green bell pepper | 1 green bell pepper, diced |
| 1 can (15 ounces) chili beans | 4 cans (15 ounces each) chili beans |
| 1 can (15 ounces) diced tomatoes | 4 cans (15 ounces each) diced tomatoes |
| 1/2 teaspoon cayenne | 2 teaspoons cayenne |
| 1 teaspoon chili powder | 3 teaspoons chili powder |
| 1/2 teaspoon ground cumin | 1 teaspoon ground cumin |
| 1 teaspoon black pepper | 1 teaspoon black pepper |
| 2-3 drops Tabasco sauce, optional | 1/4 teaspoon Tabasco sauce, optional |

In a large pan cook ground beef with onion and green pepper. Drain fat from pan. Add chili beans, tomatoes, cayenne, chili powder, cumin, black pepper, and Tabasco sauce. Simmer for 1-2 hours or until chili dip is like a thick soup. Serve with tortilla chips.

To heat bean dip in the oven, stir the ingredients into a bowl, then transfer the mix into 4-inch deep hotel pan or baking dish. Cover the pan with foil. Bake at 350 degrees for 35-40 minutes.

TIP: Smaller batches can be kept warm in a slow cooker on low heat.

◆◆◆

# Hot Bean Dip

*Serves 70*

1 No. 10 can (6 pounds) refried beans
2 pounds thick and chunky salsa
2 packages (1 1/4 ounces each) taco seasoning mix
4 cups shredded Cheddar cheese, divided
16 ounces sour cream
1 teaspoon garlic powder
1 teaspoon onion powder

In a 9-quart pan mix together refried beans, salsa, taco seasoning, 2 cups of the cheese, sour cream, garlic powder, and onion powder. Heat on low for 25-30 minutes, stirring every 5 minutes to prevent the dip from scorching. The bean dip will become bubbly. Transfer the dip into a 4-inch deep hotel half-pan. Top with remaining 2 cups cheese. Cover pan with foil and place pan into chafing dish. Or place dip into a 4-quart slow cooker set on low heat, and stir occasionally. Serve with tortilla chips.

# Layered Cream Cheese Taco Salad Dip

*Serves 25-30*

*Layer 1*
- 2 pounds cream cheese, softened
- 2 packages (1¼ ounces each) taco seasoning
- 2 tablespoons dehydrated minced onions

*Layer 2*
- 2 cups grated mild Cheddar cheese

*Layer 3*
- ½ head (10 ounces) lettuce, shredded

*Garnish*
- 1 bunch onions (7 or 8)
- 1 tomato, diced (about ¾ pound)
- 2 ounces sliced ripe olives

Beat cream cheese, taco seasoning and onion together; spread over one 14-inch tray. Sprinkle grated cheese over layer 1. Spread lettuce over layer 2. Slice onions, using green and white parts. Sprinkle onions, tomato and ripe olives over layer 3. Serve with tortilla chips. This dip can be made with lowfat sour cream, and can be served with baked tortilla chips.

# Layered Mexican Bean Dip

*Serves 50*

*Layer 1*
- 2 cans (10½ ounces each) jalapeño bean dip
- 2 teaspoons ground cumin
- 1 teaspoon chili powder
- ¼ teaspoon garlic powder
- ¼ teaspoon onion powder

*Layer 2*
- 1 cup sour cream
- ⅔ cup salad dressing

*Layer 3*
- 1 can (24 ounces) chopped, peeled chilies

*Layer 4*
- 1 medium avocado, peeled and mashed
- 2 teaspoons lime juice
- ¼ teaspoon garlic powder
- ½ teaspoon salt

*Layer 5*
- 2 cups grated cheese

*Layer 6 (Garnish)*
- 1 bunch (7-8) green onions
- 1 large tomato, diced
- 20 large black olives, sliced

Mix together jalapeño bean dip, cumin, chili powder, garlic powder, and onion powder. Spread onto a 14-inch tray. Mix sour cream and salad dressing; spread over layer 1. Sprinkle chilies over layer 2. In a small bowl, mix avocado, lime juice, garlic powder, and salt. Spread over layer 3. Sprinkle grated cheese over layer 4. Slice onions, using both the green and white parts. Sprinkle onions, tomato, and sliced olives over layer 5. Serve with tortilla chips.

TIPS: To hold food cost down, substitute two 15-ounce cans of refried beans for the jalapeño bean dip. There are about 40 large olives in a 6-ounce can.

# Spicy Mexican Vegetable Chile Pepper Dip

### Serves 16

1 1/2  pounds sour cream
  1  package (1 1/4 ounces) taco seasoning
  2  drops Tabasco sauce, optional
  1  package (1 ounce) dehydrated whole red
     chile pepper, chopped (about 3/4 cup)
  3  cloves fresh garlic, minced
1/2  cup finely diced green bell pepper
1/2  cup diced onion
  1  cup fancy shredded mild Cheddar cheese
*Garnish*
  6  ounces (1/2 of 12-ounce jar) jalapeño
     peppers, sliced and drained
1/4  orange bell pepper, cut into 5 strips
  1  large cherry tomato, halved
  1  large black olive, pitted

Stir taco seasoning into sour cream. Add Tabasco, chile pepper, garlic, green pepper, onion, and cheese. Stir thoroughly. Place one pound of dip into each 6 x 6 x 1-inch serving dish. Lay jalapeño peppers across the top of the dip. Place bell pepper strips over the jalapeño peppers to form petals of a flower. Remove the seeds from the cherry tomato halves. Cut each half into 6 strips. Place 1 tomato strip between each pepper strip. Place 1 olive in the middle of flower. Place the sixth tomato strip into the hole in the olive so end jets out of the middle. Cover and refrigerate. Serve dip cold with tortilla chips. (See photograph above.)

TIP: One 12-ounce jar of jalapeño peppers contains 1 1/3 cups jalapeños and 3/4 cup of juice.

# Taco Refried Bean Dip

*Serves 12*

1 can (15 ounces) refried beans

1/2 cup sour cream

1 cup fancy shredded mild Cheddar cheese

1 tablespoon chopped green onion, white part only

2 tablespoons diced red bell pepper

2 tablespoons taco seasoning

3 drops Tabasco sauce

*Garnish*

1/2 cup fancy shredded mild Cheddar cheese

9 green olives stuffed with pimientos

1 tablespoon diced green bell pepper

1 tablespoon diced red bell pepper

In a bowl beat together refried beans, sour cream, Cheddar cheese, green onions, red pepper, taco seasoning, and Tabasco sauce until blended. Place dip into a 6 x 6 x 1-inch serving dish. Garnish with cheese. Place an olive in the middle of the dip. Place remaining olives around the outer edge (one at each end and one in the middle) to form a border. Top with green and red bell peppers. Cover and refrigerate. Serve cold with tortilla chips. (See photograph on page 13.)

# Snacks

CRACKERS

There are a wide variety of crackers on the market. If you are serving a large number of people it is wise to buy crackers by the case. There are 36 to 40 crackers per sleeve depending on the brand you buy. Some brands have 3 or 4 varieties packaged together. Bulk crackers come in 8-pound packages with 4 varieties (2 pounds of each) or 10-pound packages with 3 varieties, for example, wheat, sesame, and butter crisp. A 10-pound case has approximately 1,440 crackers. Generally, you figure 3 crackers per person. Therefore, one 10-pound case of crackers would serve 480 people.

You can buy crackers individually wrapped in packages, usually 2 per package or 500 per case, but I don't recommend them for most catered events. Generally, the customer at a catered party does not want to be bothered with taking the package wrap off the crackers. When buying crackers, allow for breakage of packed crackers.

Use soda crackers for serving with soups and chili only. Fat-free crackers are also available. A 13-ounce box of wheat wafer crackers contains 68 to 75 crackers while a 9 3/4-ounce box of butterfly-shaped crackers has 3 packs of 26, a total of 78 crackers. Use simple to fancy crackers for serving the Liberty Bell cheese spread. Count the box of any variety of crackers that you choose to serve so that you will know exactly what amount of crackers to purchase.

POPCORN

Popcorn is an inexpensive snack. It is an extra item that can be placed in small roll bas-

kets and set out at the individual picnic tables. For a repeat customer a caterer might offer popcorn at the individual picnic tables at no extra cost. This gesture is often well received by the person paying the bill.

Guests can snack on the popcorn while they are waiting to go through the buffet line. It also helps curb the appetite. It is interesting to see that if there are a variety of snacks on the buffet line popcorn is the snack that people will take last. However, popcorn on the individual tables will be enjoyed because it is the only snack in front of the seated guests. There are a variety of flavored seasonings for popcorn and a variety of gourmet popcorns on the market. Plain old-fashioned popcorn is still a favorite of the majority of picnic crowds.

## POTATO CHIPS AND DIP

One pound of potato chips will serve 12-15 people, if you figure about 12 pieces per serving. Remember not every person in the buffet line will eat potato chips; some will pass on the potato chips due to the high fat content. Although there are fat-free potato chips the consumer should note that they are still very high in calories, and the artificial fat in them can cause stomach distress in some people. If you do serve them, indicate with a small sign that these are fat-free potato chips.

Serve potato chip dip in a small container such as a salad bowl. Use a soup spoon to serve the dip. There are also chip-and-dip bowls on the market. Potato chips can be served in round or square baskets with 2- to 4-inch rims. Place a colored napkin in each basket to match the theme of the party. The napkin also absorbs the salt and grease from the chips.

## PRETZELS

Gourmet pretzels come in a variety of flavors such as dill, onion, garlic, Cajun, Jamaican, or Bavarian style. Various gourmet mustards, such as sweet and tangy or coarse with dill, accent the variety of pretzels on the market. It is more expensive to serve gourmet pretzels with such mustards, but it is well worth it.

It is important to always go the extra mile for the customer. Customers remember the gourmet pretzels and mustards. Many called to inquire where to purchase these great items. Gourmet mustards are also good for sandwiches, soups, and various dips. Pretzels can be served in baskets, wooden bowls, or variously shaped monkeypod bowls. Pretzels can also be served on mirrors with a bowl of gourmet mustard on the center of the mirror.

## TORTILLA CHIPS

One 12$\frac{1}{2}$-ounce bag of bite-sized white tortilla chips contains about 300 pieces and serves 16-19 people. There is a minimum of 1 cup of broken chips per bag. A 14$\frac{1}{2}$-ounce bag of triangle-shaped tortilla chips contains about 80 pieces and serves 12. A 14-ounce bag of nacho cheese chips contains approximately 90 pieces and serves 10-12. Approximately half of the nacho cheese triangles are broken. A 13$\frac{1}{2}$-ounce bag of lowfat mini-triangle chips serves about 15. There are approximately 200-225 whole chips and about a quarter to a third of the bag are broken.

# Picnic Beverages

SOMETHING TO WET YOUR WHISTLE

I once catered a picnic on a summer day when the temperature soared to 105 degrees. I prepared three times the amount of lemonade I would typically make for a picnic. I set up the buffet line and soon realized that no one wanted to eat anything; all they wanted was lemonade. It wasn't long before we were running out and I was running out to the grocery store for more lemonade and ice, enough for two more servings of lemonade per person. It still wasn't enough. I made yet another trip for more juice and soda. I could not keep up with the crowd on the beverages because of the heat. It was far too hot for anyone to eat the hot food; what little was eaten was vegetables and fruits.

On the other hand, I recall one picnic when the weather turned cold. I made double the coffee and had just enough!

THE GOLDEN RULE OF BEVERAGES:
DON'T RUN OUT

How much beverage should you plan per person? There's no simple formula for that. Picnics are outdoor events, and circumstances beyond your control—mainly the weather—determine how much people will drink, as the above stories illustrate.

Normally, 2 to 2 1/2 beverages per person will be adequate for up to a 1 1/2-hour period. If the event is to last all afternoon, figure 3 to 4 drinks per person. (When using soda, buy individual cans so the unused cans can be used at the next party if the customer does not buy them.) Most of the time I figure 2 sodas per person for a 1- to 2-hour buffet.

CHOOSING THE BEVERAGE MENU

In addition to sodas, I also provide lemonade and iced tea, and coffee if the customer requests it. When I first began catering I made regular coffee for every party including picnics. I found out coffee was not well received on hot summer days, so I adjusted to the situation and offered lemonade, iced tea, soda, beer, wine, wine coolers, and only some coffee. My friend in the South tells me that iced tea is more popular there for picnics, whereas Wisconsin folks like lemonade.

Milwaukee people are particularly fond of their beer—it's a local product, after all. But due to increasingly strict laws on drinking and driving many businesses stick to nonalcoholic beverages for company events. In my experience, dark sodas are more popular than light sodas.

Some picnics have wine coolers and wine. In my experience, the red berry flavor wine coolers are most popular. If serving adults at a picnic with beer, wine coolers and sodas, figure that a third of the folks will drink the wine coolers. The majority will drink beer and soda if given the choice. Have light and regular beer at the party. It is my policy not to offer a full bar at a picnic.

ICE: Figure 1/2 to 1 pound of ice per person depending on the temperature of the day.

To ice down a half-barrel of beer, use four 20-pound bags of ice. Ice down a quarter-barrel of beer with two 20-pound bags of ice. Carry one beer tapper for each barrel. Also carry a spare beer tapper just in case one does not work.

BEVERAGE EQUIPMENT: For larger picnics some caterers own or rent a beverage unit—a 6-foot by 7-foot refrigerated box on wheels that holds wine, beer and soda. The unit uses a tapping system. Wine and beer come in quarter- and half-barrels, and soda comes in 5-gallon canisters. A portable beverage unit is handy for company picnics with a crowd of 300 and up.

You can rent a refrigerated portable container to make lemonade in for a large crowd and mix as you go. Rent 2 units and make 10 gallons at a time. It takes only a couple of minutes to make lemonade. Make sure you have electricity

with 3-prong outlets at your party location and 24-foot extension cords packed for a large party.

ICED TEA: Instant pre-sweetened iced tea mix comes in 48-ounce (3-pound) jars at the grocery store. The 48-ounce container makes 15 quarts. Tea bags can also be purchased wholesale. A case contains six 28-count boxes or twelve 3.75-ounce tea bags. In the Southern states fresh-brewed iced tea is a must. Most Southerners drink iced tea year-round.

LEMONADE: Frozen lemonade concentrate also comes in 1-quart cartons. Keep frozen until ready to use. Mix with 4 1/3 cartons cold water. Stir briskly. This makes 1 1/3 gallons of lemonade. There are 12 quarts of frozen lemonade to a case. Three 1-quart cartons of frozen concentrate will make approximately 4 gallons of lemonade. One case of lemonade will make 12 gallons of lemonade. Four gallons will fit into a portable liquid carrying container with a spigot.

You can also purchase lemonade in powdered form in a 5-gallon box from your wholesale dealer. Follow instructions on the box. At your local grocery store you can purchase a 20-ounce can of dry lemonade mix, which makes 8 quarts of lemonade. One pound 14 ounces of dry lemonade mix will make 12 quarts of lemonade. The dry mix is the least expensive; however, I always use frozen lemonade concentrate. I add 2 sliced lemons to every 4-gallon batch. This makes the lemonade taste homemade. I receive many compliments on my method of making lemonade.

COFFEE: Check before you leave for the party to be sure coffee is perked properly. Carry an extension cord and an adapter if you plan to plug in the coffee. If you are at a picnic site chances are you will not have electricity. Transfer the coffee into an insulated carrier with a spigot. Coffee does not stay as hot in this type of container as it will in an electric coffeepot.

Clean out the bottom of the coffeepot, especially the indention where the stem goes. Otherwise, the coffee does not perk properly. Use cream of tartar with water and perk to clean out the pot. There are coffee cleaners on the market but they are expensive. Use the long thin brush that comes with the pot to clean the glass tube.

## COFFEE CHART

The chart below shows how much coffee, how much water, and how long it takes to perk various amounts of coffee. (See diagram on page 18.)

**Strong Coffee**

| | | | | | |
|---|---|---|---|---|---|
| Water (cups) | 20 | 40 | 60 | 80 | 100 |
| Coffee (cups) | 2 | 3 | 4 | 5 | 6 |
| Perk (minutes) | 20 | 30 | 40 | 50 | 60 |

**Regular Strength Coffee**

| | | | | | |
|---|---|---|---|---|---|
| Water (cups) | 20 | 40 | 60 | 80 | 100 |
| Coffee (cups) | 1 1/4 | 2 | 3 | 4 | 5 |
| Perk (minutes) | 20 | 30 | 40 | 50 | 60 |

*Note*: I prefer strong coffee, so that is the way I make it. Coffee tastes vary according to region, so adjust the measurements to reflect local preferences.

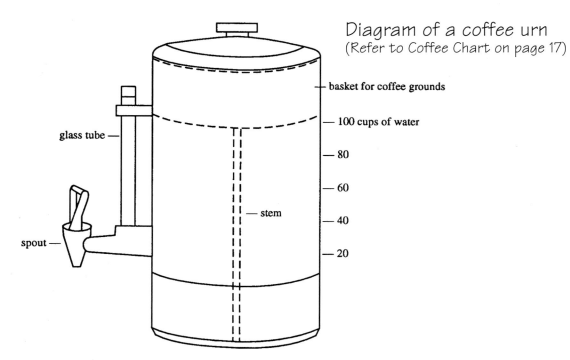

## Diagram of a coffee urn
(Refer to Coffee Chart on page 17)

— basket for coffee grounds

— 100 cups of water

glass tube —

— 80

— 60

— stem

— 40

spout —

— 20

## Cheese Liberty Bell (page 8)

# 3 • Salads

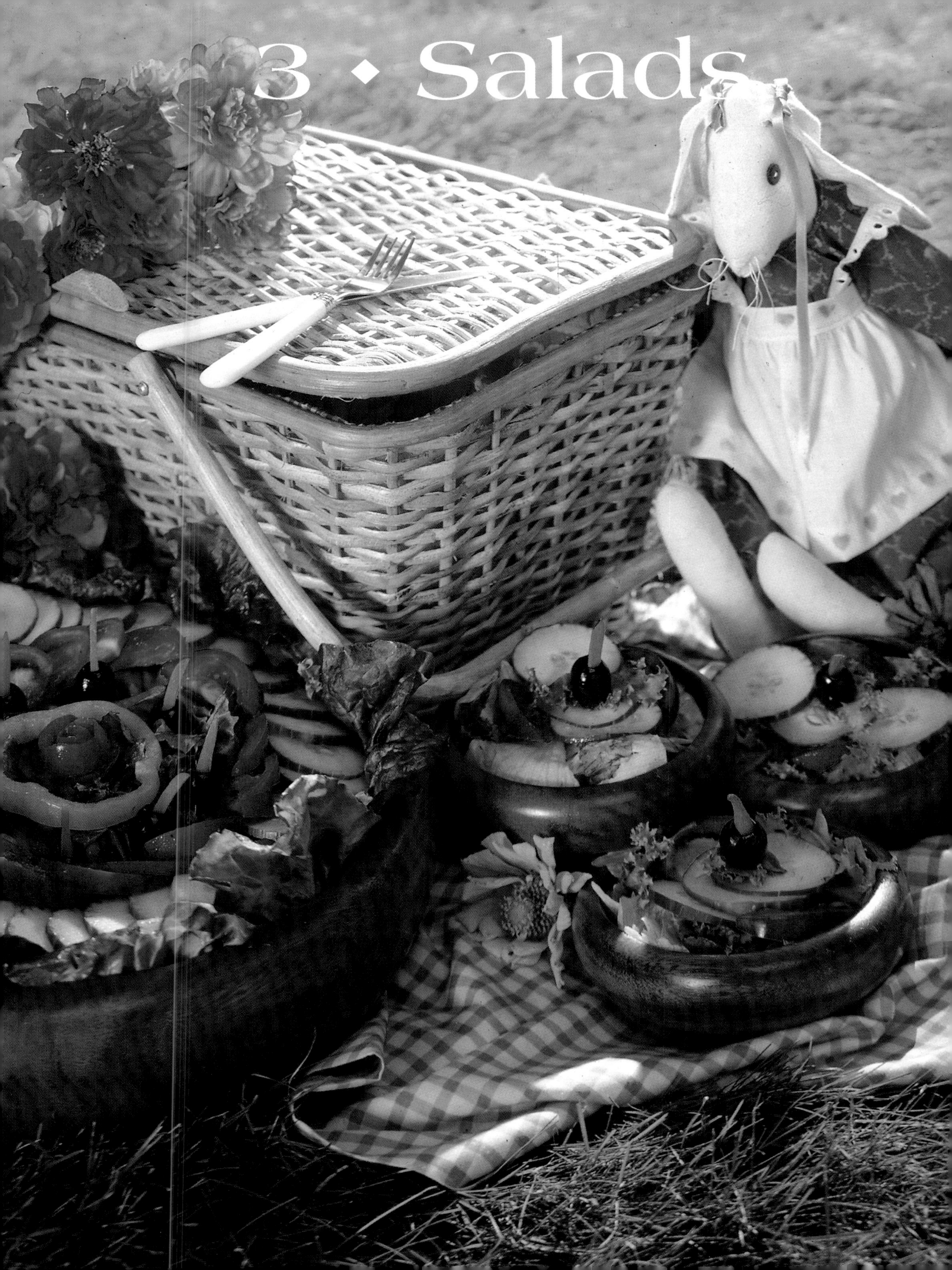

# Salads

Salads are fun to make, good to eat and one of the most versatile of picnic foods. Creativity and innovation abound in the salad bowl. Toss them, tray them or top them; they all reflect what is bright, beautiful and healthy in nature. Salads can be a complete meal or a complement to any menu.

The choices are endless:

◆ A hearty chicken or turkey salad is a main course. Additions of crisp bacon, cubed chicken or turkey, grated cheeses, hard-cooked eggs or seafood to a green or pasta salad all add up to protein and flavor.

◆ Canned fruit mixed with whipped topping can be served as a dessert or a salad.

◆ Flavored gelatin is an old standby and still a favorite.

◆ Fresh fruit is nature's own contribution to the salad lineup.

◆ Raw vegetables and dips together with relishes and pickles are great finger foods and add crunch.

◆ Potato salads and pasta salads have universal appeal. Pasta Shrimp Salad is sensational for the more upbeat Caribbean picnic. Avocados and tomatoes combined with special seasonings accent the Mexican picnic theme.

Coordinate salads with their dressings. Use sweet dressings for fruits and tart dressings for vegetables and greens. Counting fat grams is a part of life today; there are many lowfat and fat-free dressings available.

For picnics, presentation should be casual and simple. Use romaine, kale and red leaf lettuce to line salad bowls and platters. Use only the freshest and finest ingredients. Limp greens, languid vegetables and lifeless fruits will spark unwanted conversations in the buffet line. "Crisp, colorful and savory" is the caterer's mantra.

## POTATO SALAD TIPS

◆ One cup of potato salad weighs 8 ounces. This will yield 2 servings.

◆ There are approximately 3 medium potatoes to a pound.

◆ Buy high-quality potatoes for high yield. (Twenty pounds of poor-quality potatoes will result in up to 3 pounds waste.) Three pounds of cooked potatoes will yield about 2 1/2 pounds of peeled and diced potatoes. The weight loss will be made up by the addition of the celery, onions and hard-cooked eggs.

◆ Many people like using small new red potatoes. Another favorite is the baking potato. It is larger and less labor-intensive to peel.

◆ Boil potatoes in their skins in enough water to cover until tender when pierced with a fork. Or, wrap the potatoes in foil, place on a baking sheet and bake at 400 degrees for 1 hour or until tender.

◆ The potatoes must be peeled and sliced or cubed to allow the dressing to permeate the potato. Potato skins will slip off more easily if peeled while still warm.

◆ Use Grade A large eggs in all your cooking. One dozen large eggs weigh 1 pound 12 ounces. One dozen large hard-cooked eggs will yield 4 cups peeled and diced.

# French Potato Salad

### Serves 4 — Yield: 1 1/2 pounds

**Salad**
- 1 hard-cooked egg, chopped
- 1 pound potatoes, cooked, peeled and sliced
- 2 tablespoons diced celery
- 1 tablespoon diced onion

**Dressing**
- 1 cup mayonnaise
- 1 teaspoon prepared mustard
- 2 teaspoons vinegar
- 2 teaspoons sugar
- 1/8 teaspoon salt
- Dash of pepper
- 1 hard-cooked egg, sliced, for garnish

### Serves 12 — Yield: 4 1/2 pounds

**Salad**
- 2 hard-cooked eggs, chopped
- 3 pounds potatoes, cooked, peeled and sliced
- 3 tablespoons diced celery
- 2 tablespoons diced onion

**Dressing**
- 3 cups mayonnaise
- 2 teaspoons prepared mustard
- 1 tablespoon vinegar
- 1 tablespoon sugar
- 1/2 teaspoon salt
- 1/4 teaspoon pepper
- 1 hard-cooked egg, sliced, for garnish

### Serves 20 — Yield: 7 pounds

**Salad**
- 3 hard-cooked eggs, chopped
- 5 pounds potatoes, cooked, peeled and sliced
- 1 cup diced celery
- 1/4 cup plus 1 tablespoon diced onion

**Dressing**
- 1 quart plus 1 cup mayonnaise
- 1 tablespoon prepared mustard
- 1/4 cup vinegar
- 1 tablespoon plus 1 teaspoon sugar
- 1/2 teaspoon salt
- 1/2 teaspoon pepper
- 1 hard-cooked egg, sliced, for garnish

### Serves 40 — Yield: 12 1/2 pounds

**Salad**
- 5 hard-cooked eggs, chopped
- 10 pounds potatoes, cooked, peeled and sliced
- 2 cups diced celery
- 1/3 cup diced onion

**Dressing**
- 1 quart plus 2 cups mayonnaise
- 3 tablespoons prepared mustard
- 1/4 cup vinegar
- 2 tablespoons plus 2 teaspoons sugar
- 3/4 teaspoon salt
- 3/4 teaspoon pepper
- 2 hard-cooked eggs, sliced, for garnish

### Serves 100 — Yield: 24 pounds

**Salad**
- 10 hard-cooked eggs, chopped
- 20 pounds potatoes, cooked, peeled and sliced
- 1 1/4 pounds (4 cups) diced celery
- 2/3 cup diced onion

**Dressing**
- 2 quarts plus 1 cup mayonnaise
- 1/4 cup prepared mustard
- 6 tablespoons vinegar
- 3 tablespoons plus 2 teaspoons sugar
- 1 teaspoon salt
- 1 teaspoon pepper

**Garnish**
- 4 hard-cooked eggs, sliced, for garnish
- Paprika
- Dehydrated parsley

Place potatoes, chopped eggs, celery, and onion in large bowl. In another mixing bowl (use commercial mixer and bowls for the 2 larger quantities), combine mayonnaise, mustard, vinegar, sugar, salt and pepper. Mix until smooth and creamy. Pour over the potato mixture. Mix until all ingredients are well combined. Refrigerate until ready to serve. Place no more than 8 pounds of potato salad in each serving bowl; top each bowl of potato salad with 1 sliced egg. Sprinkle with paprika and parsley.

### French Potato Salad
*50 to 100 pounds*

Buy precooked, peeled and sliced potatoes. Purchase hard-cooked eggs already shelled and diced. More labor can be saved by buying diced celery and onions. Place potatoes in large mixing bowls, 25 pounds per bowl. Add eggs, celery and onion.

#### Dressing for 50 pounds French Potato Salad
*Yield: 18 cups dressing*

1 gallon plus 2 cups mayonnaise
1/2 cup prepared mustard
1 cup vinegar
3/4 cup sugar
1 teaspoon salt
1 teaspoon pepper

With commercial mixer, mix mayonnaise, mustard, vinegar, sugar, salt and pepper until well blended. Use half (2 quarts plus 1 cup) of dressing in each 25-pound bowl of potato mixture.

#### Variation on Dressing for 50 pounds French Potato Salad
*Yield: 18 cups dressing*

1 gallon plus 2 cups mayonnaise
1/4 cup spicy brown mustard
1 cup red wine vinegar
3/4 cup sugar
1 teaspoon horseradish
1 teaspoon salt
1 teaspoon pepper

With mixer, mix mayonnaise, mustard, vinegar, sugar, horseradish, salt and pepper until smooth and creamy. Use half (2 quarts plus 1 cup) of dressing in each 25-pound bowl of potato mixture.

---

## POTATO SALAD TIPS

◆ Use a heavy duty restaurant-style mayonnaise. It is richer and smoother, and comes in 1-gallon containers. Keep filled bowls on ice on the buffet table on hot days to keep potato salad fresh.

◆ You can use throwaway aluminum half-pans. Each half-pan will hold up to 8 pounds of potato salad. Plan on 1 hard-cooked egg for garnish for each 5- to 8-pound serving bowl.

# German Potato Salad

German Potato Salad is a popular sweet and sour picnic salad complemented by the flavor of cooked bacon. It is served warm. Plan on 1/2 cup per serving.

BACON—There are 15 to 16 slices of bacon per pound. One pound of bacon, cooked, will yield 1 cup of bacon grease and 2 cups (12 ounces) of cooked bacon.

| *Serves 8 — Yield: 2 pounds* | *Serves 44 — Yield: 11 pounds* |
|---|---|
| 2 pounds potatoes, cooked, peeled and thinly sliced | 10 pounds potatoes, cooked, peeled and thinly sliced |
| 1/2 pound (8 slices) bacon | 1 pound bacon |
| 1/2 cup diced onion | 8 ounces (1 cup) diced onion |
| 2 tablespoons flour | 1 cup flour |
| 1 1/2 teaspoons sugar | 1/2 cup sugar |
| 1 teaspoon salt | 1 teaspoon salt |
| 1/4 teaspoon celery salt | 1/2 teaspoon celery salt |
| Dash of pepper | 1 teaspoon pepper |
| 3/4 cup water | 5 cups water |
| 1/3 cup vinegar | 1 cup vinegar |

Place potatoes in large bowl. Dice bacon and cook in skillet until crisp. Remove from skillet and drain on paper towel. Add onion to bacon grease in skillet and saute until golden brown. With wire whip, whisk in flour, sugar, salt, celery salt and pepper. Add water and vinegar and cook over low heat, stirring constantly, until thickened. Pour over potatoes. Add bacon. Mix until well combined. Cover and let stand until ready to serve. Put into appropriate size hotel pan (for 8 servings put into serving bowl). Serve warm.

TIP: For very large quantities, make several batches of German Potato Salad up in no more than 11 pounds at a time. Sometimes flavor is lost when making a large quantity at once.

*Note:* German Potato Salad can also be purchased ready-made. It is available in 6-pound 10-ounce cans and contains 25 to 28 servings. Remove from can and heat, covered, in a convection oven at 350 degrees for 35 minutes. Fry 4 or 5 slices of bacon; drain and crumble over the top for garnish. Precooked bacon can also be purchased, but is more expensive. Imitation bacon bits can be substituted.

# Macaroni Salads

The advantage of serving a macaroni salad is that it's an inexpensive filler salad that goes a long way. The vegetables, usually radishes, onion and celery, add to the cost, but also add texture and color.

Adding chopped green bell pepper is optional; use the same amount as celery. Macaroni salad will serve 5 persons per pound, 1/2 cup per person. This is approximate as the yield will be affected by the type of macaroni used, the amount of swelling when cooked and the amount and number of vegetables and mayonnaise added.

MACARONI—There are 5 cups of uncooked macaroni per pound. One pound uncooked macaroni yields about 2 pounds cooked. Macaroni absorbs more water and will weigh more when cooked in larger quantities.

Overcooked macaroni is mushy as the pasta will absorb water as it cooks. If this happens, throw it away and start over. Otherwise, instead of macaroni salad, you will be serving macaroni paste. Be sure to stir frequently when cooking to prevent it from sticking. Macaroni tests done when easily cut in half; or you can taste-test a piece.

For large quantities, place cooked, drained and rinsed macaroni on 17 x 25-inch baking sheets and chill in the walk-in cooler. Put no more than 8 pounds of cooked macaroni on each baking sheet.

## To Cook Macaroni

| Uncooked macaroni | Water | Salt | Oil | Cooking time | Yield cooked macaroni |
|---|---|---|---|---|---|
| 8 ounces | 1 quart | 1/2 teaspoon | 1 tablespoon | 5-6 minutes | 1 pound |
| 1 pound | 2 quarts | 1 teaspoon | 2 tablespoons | 6-8 minutes | 2 pounds |
| 2 pounds | 4 quarts | 1 teaspoon | 1/4 cup | 8-10 minutes | 5 pounds |
| 3 pounds | 5 quarts | 1 teaspoon | 1/3 cup | 9-10 minutes | 8 pounds |
| 4 pounds | 6 quarts | 1 teaspoon | 1/2 cup | 9-12 minutes | 12 pounds |
| 5 pounds | 7 quarts | 1 teaspoon | 3/4 cup | 10-15 minutes | 16 pounds |

Boil uncooked macaroni no more than 4 pounds per 9-quart stockpot. Use a 41/2- or 5-quart saucepan to cook 1/2 to 1 pound of macaroni. Use a 12-quart stockpot to cook 5-6 pounds. For larger quantities, use a 15- or 20-quart stockpot or two 9-quart stockpots. Add salt and oil to the water and bring to a boil. Add macaroni; boil, uncovered, stirring frequently, for required time or until macaroni tests done. Drain in a colander and rinse with cold water. Chill until assembling salad.

# Elbow Macaroni Salad

*Serves 6 — Yield: 1 1/2 pounds*
*without dressing*

1 pound cooked elbow macaroni, drained, rinsed and chilled (1/2 pound uncooked)
1/2 cup diced celery
1/2 cup sliced radishes
1/4 cup diced onion
1/4 teaspoon salt
1/2 teaspoon pepper
1/2 teaspoon garlic salt
1 1/3 cups mayonnaise

*Serves 12-15 — Yield: 3 pounds*
*without dressing*

2 pounds cooked elbow macaroni, drained, rinsed and chilled (1 pound uncooked)
3/4 cup diced celery
3/4 cup sliced radishes
1/2 cup diced onion
1/2 teaspoon salt
1 teaspoon pepper
1/2 teaspoon garlic salt
3 cups mayonnaise

*Serves 25-30 — Yield: 7 pounds*
*without dressing*

5 pounds cooked elbow macaroni, drained, rinsed and chilled (2 pounds uncooked)
2 cups diced celery
2 cups sliced radishes
1/2 cup diced onion

1/2 teaspoon salt
1 1/2 teaspoons pepper
1/2 teaspoon garlic salt
7 cups mayonnaise

*Serves 45-50 — Yield: 10 pounds*
*without dressing*

8 pounds cooked elbow macaroni, drained, rinsed and chilled (3 pounds uncooked)
4 cups diced celery
2 3/4 cups sliced radishes
1 cup diced onion
1 teaspoon salt
1 1/2 teaspoons pepper
1/2 teaspoon garlic salt
2 quarts plus 1 cup mayonnaise

*Serves 95-100 — Yield: 20 pounds*
*without dressing*

16 pounds cooked elbow macaroni, drained, rinsed and chilled (5 pounds uncooked)
5 1/4 cups diced celery (2 pounds)
4 cups sliced radishes (1 1/2 pounds)
2 cups diced onions (1/2 pound)
1 teaspoon salt
2 teaspoons pepper
1 teaspoon garlic salt
3 quarts mayonnaise

In large bowl(s), mix macaroni, celery, radishes and onions. Add salt, pepper, garlic salt and mayonnaise. Mix well to combine all ingredients. Put into appropriate size and number of serving bowls. Chill before serving.

# Elbow Macaroni Salad with Protein

Sometimes you may want to add protein to macaroni salad. Do this with the addition of such foods as hard-cooked eggs, Cheddar cheese, tuna, ham, chipped beef, chicken, turkey, small salad shrimp or canned salmon. Adding protein will greatly increase the cost. For every 3 pounds of cooked macaroni, add one or more of the following:

Hard-cooked egg: 1, diced = 2 ounces

Cheddar cheese: 3/4 cup, shredded = 3 ounces

Tuna: 1 can (6 ounces) packed in water, drained

Ham: 1 cup, diced = 6 ounces

Chipped beef: 1 cup, diced = 6 ounces

Cooked chicken or turkey: 1 cup, cubed = 6 ounces

Salad shrimp: 1 cup = 6 ounces

Canned salmon: 1 cup = 6 ounces

The amount of meat added to the macaroni salad does not have to be exact. For every portion of protein added, increase the amount of mayonnaise by 1/4 cup. For example, if 3/4 cup shredded Cheddar cheese, 1 cup of meat and 1 hard-cooked egg are added to 3 pounds of cooked macaroni, increase the mayonnaise by 3/4 cup. Do not adjust the amount of salt, pepper, garlic salt, Beau Monde seasoning, lemon juice or sugar. In fact, when adding ham and/or cheese, decrease the amount of salt as these two foods are already salty.

## A Macaroni Story

When I was only 10 years old, I decided to surprise my Dad and make him a macaroni and cheese lunch. I did not know I needed to cook the macaroni in advance. I had practiced very hard to make a great cheese sauce. I poured the perfect cheese sauce over the uncooked macaroni and baked it for 1 hour. As I watched my Dad taking his first bite, I heard a lot of crunching and saw in his face the struggle to swallow. He did not want to hurt my feelings and told me how great the sauce tasted and suggested that I must have forgotten to cook the macaroni first. From that day on, I cooked the macaroni to perfection. I always think of my Dad when making macaroni and remember that experience as a great moment between a father and a daughter.

# Elbow Macaroni Chicken Salad

*Serves 8-10 — Yield: 2¹/2 pounds*
*without dressing*

1 pound cooked elbow macaroni, drained, rinsed and chilled (¹/2 pound uncooked)
1 cup cubed cooked chicken
1 cup broccoli florets
¹/2 cup sliced radishes
¹/2 cup diced onion
¹/2 cup diced celery
¹/2 cup chopped pecans
¹/2 teaspoon garlic pepper
¹/2 bottle (8 ounces) fat-free honey-Dijon mustard dressing

*Serves 15-20 — Yield: 4 pounds*
*without dressing*

2 pounds cooked elbow macaroni, drained, rinsed and chilled (1 pound uncooked)
2 cups cubed cooked chicken
2 cups broccoli florets
1 cup sliced radishes
¹/2 cup diced onion
1 cup diced celery
³/4 cup chopped pecans
1 teaspoon garlic pepper
1 bottle (16 ounces) fat-free honey-Dijon mustard dressing

*Serves 35-40 — Yield: 8 pounds*
*without dressing*

5 pounds cooked elbow macaroni, drained, rinsed and chilled (2 pounds uncooked)
3 cups cubed cooked chicken
3 cups broccoli florets
2 cups sliced radishes
1 cup diced onion
2 cups diced celery
1 cup chopped pecans
1 teaspoon garlic pepper
2 bottles (16 ounces each) fat-free honey-Dijon mustard dressing

*Serves 95-100 — Yield: 20 pounds*
*without dressing*

12 pounds cooked elbow macaroni, drained, rinsed and chilled (4 pounds uncooked)
2 pounds cubed cooked chicken
2 pounds broccoli florets
1 cups sliced radishes
¹/2 pound diced onion
1¹/2 pounds diced celery
1 pound chopped pecans
2 teaspoons garlic pepper
4 bottles (16 ounces each) fat-free honey-Dijon mustard dressing

Mix together elbow macaroni, chicken, broccoli florets, radishes, onion, celery and pecans in a large bowl. Sprinkle garlic pepper over mixture. Pour dressing over macaroni mixture and mix well. Put into appropriate size and number of serving bowls. Refrigerate until serving time.

*Note:* You may substitute slivered or sliced almonds for pecans. I like pecans best in this salad.

# Slenderella Chicken Salad

*Serves 25  Yield: 6 1/2 pounds*

8 cups water
2 tablespoons oil
1 teaspoon salt
4 cups uncooked pasta bows
1 whole chicken (4 1/2 pounds), cooked
1 cup thin tomato wedges
2 cups (1/2 pound) broccoli florets
1 cup diced cucumbers
1 cup sliced mushrooms
   (6 medium mushrooms)
1 cup (6 ounces) diced green bell pepper
1 cup (4 ounces) sliced radishes
1 cup (6 ounces) diced celery
1 cup (4 ounces) julienned carrots
1 cup diced onion
1 teaspoon gourmet garlic seasoning
2 teaspoons Italian Mediterranean spice
1 teaspoon pepper
1/2 teaspoon onion powder
2 bottles (12 ounces each) fat-free herb
   vinaigrette dressing

*Garnish*
   Parsley
   Tomato wedges

In a large pot, bring water to a boil. Add oil, salt and pasta bows. Cook pasta until tender. Drain, rinse and chill. Set aside.

Remove meat from chicken and cut into cubes. You should have about 1 1/2 pounds of cubed chicken.

In a large bowl, combine chicken, tomato wedges, broccoli florets, cucumber, mushrooms, green pepper, radishes, celery, carrots and onion. Add pasta bows.

In a separate bowl, combine garlic seasoning, Italian Mediterranean spice, salt, pepper, onion salt and bottled dressing. Add to chicken-pasta mixture. Combine until all ingredients are well moistened. Garnish with parsley and tomato wedges. Cover and refrigerate.

*Note:* You can substitute cherry tomatoes for the regular tomatoes. Cut cherry tomatoes into quarters.

## PASTA SALAD TIPS

◆ Half the mayonnaise can be substituted with an equal amount of salad dressing. Omit the lemon juice and sugar as salad dressing has a sweeter taste and thinner consistency than mayonnaise. Mayonnaise is preferred as it is more full-bodied.

◆ For the crowd counting fat grams, the low-fat Elbow Macaroni Chicken Salad is a good choice.

◆ For large quantities of chicken, purchase cooked and deboned chicken.

◆ If you can't find Beau Monde seasoning, you can substitute celery salt.

# Coleslaw

Coleslaw is not as popular as potato salad. Many people will pass right by it in the picnic buffet line. However, it is an inexpensive salad to make and works well to fill in the buffet table. In some areas of the country, especially the South, coleslaw is served not as a separate side salad, but as a topping for barbecued pork sandwiches, hamburgers and even hot dogs.

This cabbage-based salad can be very versatile, and can be dressed with many different types of dressing. The coleslaw recipes presented here use either a creamy or vinegar and oil dressing. Investigate and select your own favorite coleslaw dressing. Personalize this salad by adding pineapple chunks, raisins, diced apples or grapes. Experiment with spices and herbs such as dill weed or celery seeds. Add diced green and/or red bell peppers, cucumbers, shredded red cabbage and carrots. Keep in mind that extra ingredients will add to the cost.

COLESLAW—The average head of cabbage weighs 2 to 3 pounds. The outer leaves and core account for 4 ounces of waste per head. One cup of shredded cabbage weighs 4 ounces; 4 cups of shredded cabbage weigh 1 pound. Three heads of cabbage will yield 8 pounds, shredded. Plan on 1 pound of cabbage to serve 5 people. Basic coleslaw will consist of shredded cabbage, shredded carrots and diced onion. Diced celery can also be added. If used, add in the same quantity as shredded carrots. As a general rule, plan on 1 cup of dressing for every pound of shredded cabbage.

PREPARING THE VEGETABLES—To save time, purchase pre-shredded coleslaw mix with grated carrots. This comes in 3- and 10-pound bags. Rinse well.

To prepare the coleslaw vegetables in the catering kitchen, use commercial equipment made for shredding. KitchenAid makes a vegetable shredder, but only a small amount of vegetables can be pushed through at a time. It is a useful appliance for small quantities. There are also attachments for shredding. A buffalo chopper is another piece of commercial equipment for shredding cabbage and carrots, but very few caterers use this.

When serving 20 pounds or more of coleslaw, find a salad vendor with a good reputation and purchase pre-shredded cabbage, or ready-made coleslaw. The price is right and the amount of labor to make large quantities is better spent elsewhere in the kitchen.

DRESSING—For very large quantities, buy the dressing pre-made in half-gallon or gallon amounts. This will be cost-effective. Coleslaw vegetables are very low in calories and fats and can be mixed with fat-free dressings for the weight-conscious crowd. Place a sign in front of the fat-free salad to identify it for the guests.

GARNISHES—Garnish the finished salad with additional shredded carrots, parsley, cherry tomatoes, bell pepper rings or radish roses. A large serving bowl will hold 8 pounds of slaw. TIP: After placing the slaw in serving bowls, garnish and cover with plastic wrap; do not cover with foil as acid from the salad will eat through the foil and go into the food.

# Coleslaw

### Serves 5 — Yield: 1 pound

*Salad*
- 4 cups shredded cabbage
- 1/4 cup shredded carrots
- 2 tablespoons minced onion

*Basic Creamy Dressing*
- 1/2 cup mayonnaise
- 1/2 cup salad dressing
- 1 1/2 teaspoons lemon juice
- 1 1/2 teaspoons sugar
- 1/8 teaspoon salt
- 1/8 teaspoon pepper
- 1/4 teaspoon celery salt

*Vinegar and Oil Dressing Variation*
- 1/4 cup oil
- 1/2 cup vinegar
- 1/2 cup water
- 1/4 cup sugar
- 1/4 teaspoon salt
- 1/4 teaspoon pepper
- 1/4 teaspoon celery salt

### Serves 10 — Yield: 2 pounds

*Salad*
- 2 pounds (8 cups) shredded cabbage
- 1/2 cup shredded carrots
- 1/4 cup minced onion

*Basic Creamy Dressing*
- 1 cup mayonnaise
- 1 cup salad dressing
- 1 tablespoon lemon juice
- 1 tablespoon sugar
- 1/4 teaspoon salt
- 1/4 teaspoon pepper
- 1/2 teaspoon celery salt

*Vinegar and Oil Dressing Variation*
- 1/2 cup oil
- 1 cup vinegar
- 1 cup water
- 1/2 cup sugar
- 1/2 teaspoon salt

- 1/2 teaspoon pepper
- 1/2 teaspoon celery salt

### Serves 25 — Yield: 5 pounds

*Salad*
- 5 pounds (20 cups) shredded cabbage
- 1 1/4 cups shredded carrots
- 3/4 cup minced onion

*Basic Creamy Dressing*
- 2 1/2 cups mayonnaise
- 2 1/2 cups salad dressing
- 1/4 cup lemon juice
- 3 tablespoons sugar
- 1/4 teaspoon salt
- 1/4 teaspoon pepper
- 1 teaspoon celery salt

*Vinegar and Oil Dressing Variation*
- 1 cup oil
- 2 cups vinegar
- 2 cups water
- 1 cup sugar
- 1/2 teaspoon salt
- 1/2 teaspoon pepper
- 1/2 teaspoon celery salt

### Serves 50 — Yield: 10 pounds

*Salad*
- 10 pounds pre-shredded coleslaw mix

*Basic Creamy Dressing*
- 1 quart mayonnaise
- 1 quart salad dressing
- 1/4 cup lemon juice
- 1/3 cup sugar
- 1/2 teaspoon salt
- 1/2 teaspoon pepper
- 1 teaspoon celery salt

*Continued on next page*

*Cole Slaw, continued*
*Vinegar and Oil Dressing Variation*
Serves 50

2 cups oil
1 quart vinegar
2 quarts water
2 cups sugar
1 teaspoon salt
1 1/2 teaspoons pepper
1 tablespoon celery salt

Serves 100 — Yield: 20 pounds
*Salad*
20 pounds pre-shredded coleslaw mix

*Basic Creamy Dressing*
2 quarts mayonnaise
2 quarts salad dressing
1/2 cup lemon juice

3/4 cup sugar
1 teaspoon salt
1 teaspoon pepper
1 1/2 teaspoon celery salt

*Vinegar and Oil Dressing Variation*
3 1/2 cups oil
2 quarts vinegar
4 quarts water
3 3/4 cups sugar
2 teaspoons salt
2 teaspoons pepper
4 teaspoons celery salt

*Garnishes*
Shredded carrots
Bell pepper rings
Radish roses
Parsley

In large bowl(s), mix cabbage, carrots and onion. In a separate bowl, blend together dressing (Basic Creamy or Vinegar and Oil Variation) ingredients until smooth. Pour dressing over cabbage mixture and mix until vegetables are well moistened. Put into appropriate size and number of serving bowls. Garnish with shredded carrots, pepper rings, radish roses and parsley. Refrigerate until ready to serve.

# French Dream Salad

This vegetable salad makes its mark with an unusual dressing combining French dressing, seasonings and prepared whipped topping. The whipped topping mix comes in a 2.6 ounce box with 2 packages (1.3 ounces each) to a box. Each package, when prepared, makes 2 cups of topping. French dressing can be purchased by the gallon or case. Each case contains 4 gallons.

# French Dream Salad

*Serves 25 — Yield: 5 pounds*

**Salad**
- 3 pounds fresh green beans
- 1 pound canned kidney beans, drained
- 8 ounces diced celery
- 8 ounces diced green bell pepper
- 4 carrots, peeled and grated

**Dressing**
- 1 package (1.3 ounces) whipped topping mix
- 1 cup French dressing
- 2 teaspoons chili powder
- 1/2 teaspoon garlic powder
- 1/2 teaspoon onion powder
- 1/2 teaspoon celery salt
- 1 teaspoon salt
- 1 teaspoon pepper

*Serves 50 — Yield: 10 pounds*

**Salad**
- 6 pounds fresh green beans
- 2 pounds canned kidney beans, drained
- 1 pound diced celery
- 1 pound diced green bell pepper
- 6 carrots, peeled and grated

**Dressing**
- 2 packages (1.3 ounces each) whipped topping mix
- 2 cups French dressing
- 1 tablespoon chili powder
- 1 teaspoon garlic powder
- 1 teaspoon onion powder
- 1 teaspoon celery salt
- 1 1/4 teaspoons salt
- 1 1/4 teaspoons pepper

*Serves 100 — Yield: 20 pounds*

**Salad**
- 10 pounds fresh green beans
- 4 pounds canned kidney beans, drained
- 2 pounds diced celery
- 2 pounds diced green bell pepper
- 12 carrots, grated

**Dressing**
- 3 packages (1.3 ounces each) whipped topping mix
- 3 cups French dressing
- 4 teaspoons chili powder
- 1 1/2 teaspoons garlic powder
- 1 1/2 teaspoon onion powder
- 1 1/4 teaspoons celery salt
- 1 1/2 teaspoons salt
- 1 1/4 teaspoons pepper

**Garnish**
- Cherry tomatoes
- Green onion garnish
- Parsley

Cut ends off of green beans and cut into bite-sized pieces. In bowl(s), combine green beans, kidney beans, celery, green bell pepper and carrots.

In a separate bowl, prepare whipped topping according to package directions, omitting vanilla. Fold French dressing into whipped topping. Add chili powder, garlic powder, onion powder, salt and pepper. Mix the dressing with the vegetables. Chill for 2 hours.

To serve, put into appropriate size and number of serving bowls. Garnish with cherry tomatoes, green onion garnish (see diagram on page 63) and parsley.

# Italian Vegetable Salad

This is a popular perfect picnic salad packing a lot of color and crunch. It is easily assembled and uses prepared Italian dressing. You can buy the dressing in your supermarket in 24-ounce bottles. If you make large batches of this salad, buy the dressing from the wholesaler by the gallon or by the case (4 gallons to a case). Use fat-free dressing for a low-calorie version for your clients.

*Serves 25 — Yield: 6½ pounds*
*without dressing*

- 1 pint cherry tomatoes
- 3 pounds fresh broccoli florets
- 2 pounds fresh cauliflower
- 1/2 pound carrots, julienned
- 1/4 pound red onion rings
- 3 cups Italian dressing
  Salt to taste
  Pepper to taste

*Serves 50 — Yield: 12 pounds*
*without dressing*

- 2 pints cherry tomatoes
- 6 pounds fresh broccoli florets
- 4 pounds fresh cauliflower
- 1 pound carrots, julienned
- 1/2 pound red onion rings
- 6 cups Italian dressing
  Salt to taste
  Pepper to taste

*Serves 100 — Yield: 20 pounds*
*without dressing*

- 4 pints cherry tomatoes
- 7 pounds fresh broccoli florets
- 7 pounds fresh cauliflower
- 3 pounds carrots, julienned
- 1 pound red onion rings
- 2 quarts plus 1 cup Italian dressing
  Salt to taste
  Pepper to taste

*Garnish*
  Red and green bell pepper rings
  Black olives

Take stems off cherry tomatoes; leave tomatoes whole. Mix together tomatoes, broccoli, cauliflower, carrots and onions in a large bowl. Pour bottled Italian dressing over vegetables; add salt and pepper to taste. Marinate in the refrigerator for 2 hours. Transfer into serving bowl(s). Garnish with bell pepper rings and black olives.

# Cucumber Salad

Cucumber salad is not a salad every person will help themselves to in the picnic buffet line, but it is relatively inexpensive to make and goes a long way. Normally, 6 thin slices cucumber and 2 small pieces of onion will satisfy the cucumber lover, especially with many other picnic dishes before them. Two favorite dressings are Basic Oil and Vinegar Dressing and Creamy Dressing. Select one style per picnic.

CUCUMBER SALAD—A 1-pound cucumber has approximately 2 ounces of peelings and will yield 60 thin slices. Allow 10 servings to a pound of cukes. For faster slicing than by hand, use a meat slicer.

Yellow and white onions have a strong flavor. Vidalia onions are sweeter.

Dressing recipes can be doubled. Do not automatically double salt amounts. Rely on experience and your own taste buds.

*For those guests with special needs, sugar substitutes can easily be used in the Basic Oil and Vinegar Dressing. Use 4 individual packets of sweetener to replace the sugar in the recipe for 30 servings. Rely on your own taste for the amount of sweetener.

Make Cucumber Salad in small batches to retain flavor. To prevent spilling, carry salad to the picnic in tightly closed containers in a cooler or refrigerated truck. Bring along the serving bowls and garnishes and dish out at the picnic site.

Serve salad with a slotted spoon if guests have only a plate in their service so the salad dressing won't run on the plate and soak into the other foods. If small bowls are used, serve with a tablespoon and let the marinade bathe the cukes and onions.

*Salad with Basic Oil and Vinegar Dressing*
*Serves 30 — Yield: 4 pounds without dressing*
3 pounds cucumbers, peeled and thinly sliced
1 pound onions, thinly sliced
1 batch (30-50 servings) Basic Oil and Vinegar Dressing

*Salad with Basic Oil and Vinegar Dressing*
*Serves 50 — Yield: 6 pounds without dressing*
5 pounds cucumbers, peeled and thinly sliced
1 pound onions, thinly sliced
1 batch (30-50 servings) Basic Oil and Vinegar Dressing

Combine cucumbers, onions, and dressing. Let marinate in refrigerator for at least 3 hours; 24 hours is best.

◆ *Variation on Cucumber Salad with Basic Oil and Vinegar Dressing:* Substitute 2 tomatoes for 1 of the cucumbers. Cut out core and remove bottom. Cut in half. Cut each half into thin wedges (8 to 10 wedges to a half). Add to salad. Green bell pepper strips can also be a nice addition along with the tomato wedges.

*Basic Oil and Vinegar Dressing*
*Serves 30 — Yield: 5 1/2 cups*
1/2 cup oil
2 cups vinegar
3 cups water
1 cup sugar
1 teaspoon salt
1/2 teaspoon pepper
1/2 teaspoon onion powder
1/2 teaspoon garlic powder

In a bowl, mix together oil, vinegar and water. Add sugar, salt, pepper, onion powder and garlic powder. Whisk until sugar dissolves. Refrigerate in tightly closed container for up to 5 days.

# Cucumber Salad with Creamy Dressing

*Serves 30 — Yield: 6 pounds*

*Dressing*

- 2 pounds sour cream
- 1 cup vinegar
- 1 cup water
- 1 cup sugar
- 2 teaspoons dried dill
- 1/2 teaspoon garlic powder
- 1 teaspoon salt

*Salad*

- 4 pounds cucumbers, peeled and thinly sliced
- 2 pounds onions, thinly sliced

Place sour cream in large bowl. With an electric mixer, gradually beat in vinegar. Gradually add water and beat till smooth. Add sugar, dill, garlic powder and salt; beat thoroughly. Add cucumbers and onions to the dressing. Refrigerate, covered, and marinate for 24 hours. The dressing will keep for 4 days.

◆ *Note:* If the sour cream is added to the vinegar instead of the other way around, the mixture will be lumpy.

◆ ◆ ◆

# Broccoli Salad

While this salad is expensive with such ingredients as fresh broccoli florets, bacon, nuts, raisins and red bell pepper, it does do very well at all my picnics. I rarely have any left over. The combination of colors and flavors makes this a standout salad.

BROCCOLI—The major ingredient of this salad is broccoli florets. Two pounds of fresh broccoli will yield one pound of florets. For large quantities, buy the florets in 5- or 10-pound bags to save on your labor costs.

CARROTS—To julienne carrots, use peeled tender baby carrots and cut into matchsticks. For large amounts, buy them already julienned from your wholesale producer in 5- or 10-pound bags.

WALNUTS—There are approximately 5 cups of whole shelled walnuts to a pound; 4 cups chopped. Chopping your own will give you a better quality nut size but is very labor-intensive. One 10-ounce box of walnuts,

chopped, yields 2 1/2 cups.

◆ One pound of salad ingredients (excluding the dressing weight) will serve 4.

BROCCOLI SALAD INGREDIENTS: WEIGHTS AND EQUIVALENTS

Bacon: 1 pound cooked = 12 ounces

Walnuts: 1 cup = 3 ounces

Raisins: 1 cup = 5 1/3 ounces

Carrots: 1 cup = 4 ounces

Celery: 1 cup = 6 ounces

Onion: 1 cup = 6 ounces

Red bell pepper: 1 cup = 6 ounces = one 8-ounce pepper, cored and seeded

Green bell pepper: 1 cup = 6 ounces = one 8-ounce pepper, cored and seeded

Salad dressing: 1 cup = 8 ounces

# Broccoli Salad

## Serves 12 — Yield: 3½ pounds
### without dressing

**Salad**

- 2 pounds fresh broccoli florets
- 4 ounces raisins, plumped in water, drained
- 1/2 cup chopped walnuts
- 1/2 cup diced red bell pepper
- 1/2 cup julienned carrots
- 3 tablespoons chopped onion
- 1/4 cup chopped celery
- 1/4 cup diced green bell pepper
- 1/2 pound bacon, chopped, fried crisp and drained

**Dressing**

- 3/4 teaspoon salt
- 3/4 teaspoon pepper
- 3 cups salad dressing
- 1 tablespoon lemon juice
- 1 tablespoon sugar

## Serves 25 — Yield: 6½ pounds
### without dressing

**Salad**

- 4 pounds fresh broccoli florets
- 1/2 pound raisins, plumped in water, drained
- 1 cup chopped walnuts
- 1 cup diced red bell pepper
- 1 cup julienned carrots
- 1/3 cup chopped onion
- 1/2 cup chopped celery
- 1/2 cup diced green bell pepper
- 1 pound bacon, chopped, fried crisp and drained

**Dressing**

- 1½ teaspoons salt
- 1½ teaspoons pepper
- 6 cups salad dressing
- 2 tablespoons lemon juice
- 2 tablespoons sugar

## Serves 50 — Yield: 14½ pounds
### without dressing

**Salad**

- 8 pounds fresh broccoli florets
- 1 pound raisins, plumped in water, drained
- 2 cups chopped walnuts
- 2 cups diced red bell pepper
- 2 cups julienned carrots
- 2/3 cup chopped onion
- 1 cup chopped celery
- 1 cup diced green bell pepper
- 2 pounds bacon, chopped, fried crisp and drained

**Dressing**

- 1¾ teaspoon salt
- 1¾ teaspoon pepper
- 1½ quarts salad dressing
- 1 quart mayonnaise
- 1/4 cup lemon juice
- 1/4 cup sugar

## Serves 100 — Yield: 25 pounds
### without dressing

**Salad**

- 17 pounds fresh broccoli florets
- 2 pounds raisins, plumped in water, drained
- 1 bag (1 pound—4 cups) chopped walnuts
- 3 cups diced red bell pepper
- 3 cups julienned carrots
- 1⅓ cups chopped onion
- 2 cups chopped celery
- 2 cups diced green bell pepper
- 3 pounds bacon, chopped, fried crisp and drained

**Dressing**

- 2 teaspoons salt
- 2 teaspoons pepper
- 1 gallon salad dressing
- 1 quart mayonnaise
- 1/3 cup lemon juice

*Continued on next page*

*Broccoli Salad, continued*
  1/3  cup sugar
*Garnish*
      Red kale
      Red bell pepper rings

TIP: In larger quantities, using part salad dressing and part mayonnaise keeps dressing from separating.

In large bowl(s), combine broccoli, raisins, walnuts, red bell pepper, carrots, onion, celery, green bell pepper and bacon. (The salad ingredients can be combined in advance and refrigerated.) In separate bowl, mix together salt, pepper, salad dressing, lemon juice and sugar. (Dressing can be made in advance and refrigerated.) Add the dressing to the salad the day of the picnic to ensure that the vegetables stay crisp.

Line appropriate size and number of serving bowls with red kale. Turn salad into bowl(s); garnish with red bell pepper rings. Refrigerate until served.

◆ *Note:* Please notice that in quantities of 100 and up, you do not have to double the amount of bacon, onions, carrots and walnuts. Add extra broccoli florets to increase to the needed weight of salad ingredients. It is less expensive to add broccoli than nuts.

# Fresh Cauliflower Salad

This salad takes second place to the Broccoli Salad, but nonetheless is unusual and will spark conversation. Serve the salad with a variety of dressing choices: Olive Oil Vinaigrette, Sour Cream Ranch, Regular Ranch or even a fat-free Ranch dressing. Try them all and experiment with choices of your own.

CAULIFLOWER—A 2-pound head of cauliflower will only weigh 1 pound after coring and cleaning. Purchasing whole heads of cauliflower involves a lot of waste and a lot of labor to prepare. Buy cauliflower florets from your wholesaler.

◆ Toss cauliflower florets with a mixture of 1/2 cup lemon juice and 2 quarts of cold water to keep the cauliflower's nice white color. For larger quantities, use a commercial whitener. Be sure to pat the cauliflower dry after rinsing in the lemon solution. Excess water will make your salad runny.

# Fresh Cauliflower Salad

## CAULIFLOWER SALAD INGREDIENTS: WEIGHTS AND EQUIVALENTS

| Ingredient | Weight | Volume | Pieces |
|---|---|---|---|
| Cauliflower florets | 2 pounds | 5 cups | 60 |
| Carrots, julienned | 4 ounces | 1 cup | 150 |
| Black olives, drained | 6 ounces | 1 cup | 40 |
| Cherry tomatoes | 6 ounces | 1 cup | 9 |
| Pea pods | 6 ounces | 1 cup | 32 |
| Red onion rings, quartered | 4 ounces | 1 cup | 75 |
| Celery, diced | 6 ounces | 1 cup | 150 |
| Parmesan cheese | 2 ounces | 1/2 cup finely grated | |
| Bean sprouts | 4 ounces | 1 cup | |

◆ For every 6 ounces of pea pods, there is 1 ounce of waste in trimming the ends of the pod. If you are trying to keep down the cost of this salad, you can eliminate the pea pods and bean sprouts and substitute frozen green beans that have been thawed, dried thoroughly and cut into 1-inch pieces. However, it is the pea pods and bean sprouts that make the salad so unusual.
◆ One large red onion weighs 1 pound.
◆ One pint of cherry tomatoes weighs 8 to 12 ounces, depending on the size of the tomatoes.

## Cauliflower Salad Vegetables
*5 servings per pound (weight is with vegetables only.)*

| Servings | 25 | 50 | 100 |
|---|---|---|---|
| **Approx. Pounds of Salad** | **5** | **10** | **20** |
| Cauliflower florets | 3 pounds | 6 pounds | 14 pounds |
| Carrots, julienned | 6 ounces | 10 ounces | 1 pound |
| Black olives, drained | 6 ounces | 10 ounces | 1 pound |
| Pea pods | 6 ounces | 10 ounces | 1 pound |
| Bean sprouts | 6 ounces | 10 ounces | 1 pound |
| Red onion rings, quartered | 6 ounces | 10 ounces | 1 pound |
| Cherry tomatoes, quartered | 6 ounces | 10 ounces | 1 pound |
| Parmesan cheese, finely grated | 4 ounces | 6 ounces | 12 ounces |

As you study this recipe chart, you will see that the vegetables can easily be altered—add a little of this vegetable, subtract a little of that vegetable—as long as the total weight of the salad equals the needed weight for the number of servings required. The flexibility of the vegetables can really help depending on market prices of certain ingredients.

## Cauliflower Salad with Olive Oil Vinaigrette Dressing

| Servings | 25 | 50 | 100 |
|---|---|---|---|
| Bottled olive oil vinaigrette | 2¹/₂ cups | 1 quart | 2 quarts |
| Salt | 1/2 teaspoon | 1 teaspoon | 2 teaspoons |
| Pepper | 1/2 teaspoon | 1 teaspoon | 2 teaspoons |
| Salad vegetables | 5 pounds | 10 pounds | 20 pounds |

*Garnishes*
   Red kale
   Cherry tomatoes
   Parsley

Mix the salt and pepper with the vinaigrette. Pour over vegetables. Line appropriate size and number of serving bowls with red kale. Put salad into serving bowls and garnish with cherry tomatoes and parsley. You can substitute balsamic vinaigrette or roasted garlic Italian dressing for the olive oil vinaigrette.

## Cauliflower Salad with Sour Cream Ranch Dressing

| Servings | 25 | 50 | 100 |
|---|---|---|---|
| Sour cream | 1¹/₄ cups | 2 cups | 4 cups |
| Bottled ranch dressing | 2¹/₂ cups | 1 quart | 2 quarts |
| Garlic pepper | 1 teaspoon | 1¹/₂ teaspoons | 2 teaspoons |
| Dried dill | 2 teaspoons | 4 teaspoons | 2 tablespoons |
| Beau Monde seasoning | 1 teaspoon | 2 teaspoons | 1 tablespoon |
| Salad vegetables | 5 pounds | 10 pounds | 20 pounds |

*Garnishes*
   Red kale
   Cherry tomatoes
   Parsley

Whisk together sour cream and bottled ranch dressing. Stir in lemon pepper, dill, Beau Monde seasoning and salt. Pour over salad vegetables and mix well. Line appropriate size and number of serving bowls with red kale. Put salad into bowl(s) and garnish with tomatoes and parsley.

# Cauliflower Salad with Ranch Dressing

| Servings | 25 | 50 | 100 |
|---|---|---|---|
| Prepared ranch dressing | 3¹/₄ cups | 3 pints (6 cups) | 6 pints (12 cups) |
| Garlic pepper | ¹/₂ teaspoon | 1¹/₂ teaspoons | 2 teaspoons |
| Dried dill | 1 teaspoon | 2 teaspoons | 1 tablespoon |
| Salad vegetables | 5 pounds | 10 pounds | 20 pounds |

*Garnishes*
  Grated Parmesan cheese
  Red kale
  Cherry tomatoes
  Parsley

Combine bottled ranch dressing, garlic salt and pepper. Pour over vegetables. Line appropriate size and number of serving bowls with red kale. Turn salad into bowl(s). Sprinkle ¹/₂ cup grated Parmesan cheese over each bowl. Garnish with cherry tomatoes and parsley. I use this dressing most frequently as it is quick and easy.

*Note:* To reduce the fat in the Cauliflower Salad, substitute lite or fat-free ranch dressing for the regular dressing. Also, try using half cauliflower and half broccoli for a delicious alternative. Add diced red bell pepper for extra color.

# Pea Salad

Use only frozen green peas. They have a brighter color than canned peas and firmer texture. Thaw peas in the refrigerator. Drain in a colander and gently pat dry, being careful not to flatten peas. Very little salt is used in this salad as the Cheddar cheese has a salty taste.

### Serves 12 — Yield: 3¼ pounds
### without dressing

*Salad*

2½ pounds frozen peas, thawed and patted dry
½ cup grated Cheddar cheese
¼ cup chopped celery
¼ cup chopped onion
¼ cup diced red bell pepper

*Dressing*

1¼ cups mayonnaise
1¼ cups salad dressing
⅛ teaspoon salt
⅛ teaspoon garlic pepper
⅛ teaspoon Beau Monde seasoning

### Serves 25 — Yield: 5 pounds 12 ounces
### without dressing

*Salad*

5 pounds frozen peas, thawed and patted dry
1 cup (¼ pound) grated Cheddar cheese
½ cup chopped celery
½ cup chopped onion
½ whole red bell pepper, cored and diced

*Dressing*

2½ cups mayonnaise
2½ cups salad dressing
⅛ teaspoon salt
¼ teaspoon garlic pepper
⅛ teaspoon Beau Monde seasoning

### Serves 50 — Yield: 12½ pounds
### without dressing

*Salad*

10 pounds frozen peas, thawed and patted dry
2 cups (½ pound) grated Cheddar cheese
1 cup chopped celery
¾ cup chopped onion
1 whole red bell pepper, cored and diced

*Dressing*

1 quart mayonnaise
1 quart salad dressing
½ teaspoon salt
1 teaspoon garlic pepper
¼ teaspoon Beau Monde seasoning

### Serves 100 — Yield: 23 pounds
### without dressing

*Salad*

20 pounds frozen peas, thawed and patted dry
4 cups (1 pound) grated Cheddar cheese
2 cups chopped celery
1½ cups chopped onion
1½ whole red bell pepper, cored and diced

*Dressing*

1 quart plus 3 cups mayonnaise
1 quart plus 3 cups salad dressing
1 teaspoon salt
1½ teaspoons garlic pepper
1½ teaspoon Beau Monde seasoning

*Garnishes*

Romaine lettuce
Red bell pepper strips, radish slices or tomato roses
Parsley

*Continued on next page*

*Pea Salad, continued*

Gently mix peas, cheese, celery, onion and bell pepper in a bowl. In separate bowl, combine mayonnaise, salad dressing, salt, pepper and Beau Monde seasoning. Stir dressing into the pea mixture. Line serving bowl(s) with romaine lettuce. Turn salad into bowl(s) and garnish with either red bell pepper strips, radish slices or tomato roses. Use parsley to complete the garnish.

# Seven Layer Salad

This popular picnic salad is casual, tasty, eye-appealing and feeds a lot of people. Everyone seems to enjoy this salad. Make it in batches of no more than 20 servings to a platter for freshness and ease of transporting.

A lot of the preparation can be done the day before the party. Use a meat slicer to shred the lettuce. TIP: Hit the core end of the head of lettuce firmly on the countertop. This will loosen the core which is then easily removed before shredding.

Mix a solution of a commercial preservative called a whitener according to the instructions on the jar. Pour whitener into cold water and shred lettuce into this mixture. (Lemon juice mixed with water will also work, but is more expensive in larger quantities.) Drain the preservative off and pat the treated lettuce dry. The lettuce will stay crisp and fresh. Store in the cooler.

The green pepper and celery can also be chopped and the peas can be thawed a day in advance. Keep all ingredients in separate containers in the cooler until assembly time the day of the picnic.

*Note:* Make sure all the vegetables, especially the lettuce, are dry before assembling the salad, or salad will be soggy.

*Serves 10 — Yield: one 12-inch platter*
**Salad**
1 head iceberg lettuce, cored and shredded
1 cup chopped green bell pepper
1 cup chopped celery
1 cup frozen peas, thawed and patted dry

**Dressing**
1 cup mayonnaise
1 cup sour cream
1/2 teaspoon lemon juice
1/2 teaspoon sugar

**Topping**
1/2 cup grated Parmesan cheese
1/2 cup grated Cheddar cheese
4 strips bacon, fried crisp, drained and crumbled

*Serves 20 — Yield: one 14-inch platter*
**Salad**
2 heads iceberg lettuce, cored and shredded
2 cups chopped green bell pepper
2 cups chopped celery
2 cups frozen green peas, thawed and patted dry

**Dressing**
1 1/2 cups mayonnaise
1 1/2 cups sour cream

*Continued on next page*

*7 Layer Salad, continued*
1 teaspoon lemon juice
1 teaspoon sugar
*Topping*
1 cup grated Parmesan cheese
1 cup grated Cheddar cheese
8 strips bacon, fried crisp, drained and
   crumbled

*Serves 30 — Yield: one full-size hotel pan*
*Salad*
3 heads iceberg lettuce, cored and shredded
3 cups chopped green bell pepper
3 cups chopped celery
3 cups frozen peas, thawed
   and patted dry
*Dressing*
2 1/2 cups mayonnaise
2 1/2 cups sour cream
1 1/2 teaspoons lemon juice
1 1/2 teaspoons sugar
*Topping*
1 1/2 cups grated Parmesan cheese
1 1/2 cups grated Cheddar cheese
12 slices bacon, fried crisp, drained and
   crumbled

*Serves 40 — Yield: one full-size hotel pan*
*Salad*
4 heads iceberg lettuce, cored and shredded
4 cups chopped green bell pepper
4 cups celery
4 cups frozen peas, thawed
   and patted dry
*Dressing*
2 1/2 cups mayonnaise
2 1/2 cups sour cream
1 3/4 teaspoons lemon juice
1 3/4 teaspoons sugar
*Topping*
1 3/4 cups grated Parmesan cheese
1 3/4 cups grated Cheddar cheese
12 slices bacon, fried crisp, drained and
   crumbled

*Garnishes*
Red bell pepper rings
Black olives
Parsley

Place the shredded lettuce on a deep platter (or full-size 4-inch hotel pan for 30 or 40 servings). Layer the green pepper, celery and peas on the lettuce.

In a bowl, using an electric mixer, beat mayonnaise and sour cream. Add lemon juice and sugar. Spread mayonnaise mixture over the top of the salad. Cover the surface and seal the edges. Sprinkle the grated cheeses over the mayonnaise dressing. Sprinkle the crumbled bacon over the top of the cheese. Garnish with red pepper rings, black olives and parsley. Refer to page 24 for bacon information.

TIP: When making larger amounts of this salad, it is best to serve it in hotel pans, 20 servings per pan. I like to mix the lettuce, green pepper, celery and peas together for the first layer when making larger amounts. Water chestnuts can be added for extra crunch.

◆ *Note:* Imitation bacon bits can be substituted for the bacon, but the real thing is much better.

# Three Bean Salad

This is my famous bean salad recipe. The first week of my marriage, I made bean salad. Because it is difficult for me to cook in small portions, I made enough to serve 25 people. After serving it to my husband four days in a row, he told me how tasty it was, but then asked, "Don't you have any friends who like bean salad too?" That was the last time I ever made bean salad for my husband.

This is not everyone's favorite salad. However, it is inexpensive to make and can be a good filler in the buffet line.

*Serves 25 — Yield: 5 1/2 pounds,*
*without dressing*

*Salad*
 2 pounds canned kidney beans, drained, rinsed and drained again
 2 pounds canned green beans, drained, rinsed and drained again
 1 pound canned garbanzo beans, drained, rinsed and drained again
 1 onion (1/2 pound), diced

*Dressing*
 1/2 cup oil
 2 cups white vinegar
 3 cups cold water
 1 cup sugar
 1 teaspoon salt
 1/2 teaspoon pepper
 1/2 teaspoon onion powder
 1/2 teaspoon garlic powder

A day or two before the picnic, combine beans and onion. In separate bowl, whisk together oil, vinegar, water, sugar, salt, pepper, onion powder and garlic powder. Pour over beans. Cover and marinate in refrigerator overnight or up to two days.

◆◆◆

# Seafood Pasta Salad

This upscale pasta salad uses pasta in the shape of seashells. The shells come in 3 sizes: small, large and jumbo. For this salad, the large size are the best. They show their shape nicer in salad bowl than the small size. Jumbo shells are stuffed with a filling and served as an appetizer or main dish.

SEASHELL PASTA—There are 5 cups of large uncooked seashells to the pound. After cooking, the pasta will be 2 1/2 times the dry weight. Care must be taken after cooking to drain shells very well as their shape tends to hold water. After draining, rinse in cold water; drain again. Shake off excess water.

SEAFOOD—Sea legs are an imitation pre-cooked crabmeat. Imitation crab comes packaged in 1/2-, 3- and 5-pound packages, cut and ready to serve. Salad shrimp are small and can be purchased cleaned and cooked. They come in 5-ounce, 1-pound or 5-pound bags. Use in salad or as a garnish. TIP: Both the sea legs and salad shrimp should be squeezed dry before adding to a recipe.

## To Cook Seashell Pasta

| Shells (uncooked) | Water | Oil | Yield | Servings |
|---|---|---|---|---|
| 2 pounds | 1 gallon | 1/2 cup | 5 pounds cooked | 25 |
| 4 pounds | 2 gallons | 3/4 cup | 10 pounds cooked | 50 |
| 8 pounds | 4 gallons | 1 cup | 20 pounds cooked | 100 |

In large pan, bring water and oil to a rapid boil. Add the seashell pasta. Boil 10 to 12 minutes or until tender. Drain and rinse under cold water. Drain again and shake off excess water. Cool before mixing with other salad ingredients.

### Serves 25 — Yield: 6 pounds without dressing

 5 pounds cooked seashell pasta, drained and rinsed (2 pounds uncooked)
10 ounces salad shrimp, drained
1/2 pound sea legs, chopped and drained
 1 can (6 ounces) white tuna packed in water, drained
 2 cups diced celery
 1 cup diced red bell pepper
 2 cups grated Cheddar cheese
1/2 bunch green onions, chopped
 1 cup cashews, whole or halves
 2 cups broccoli florets
21/2 cups mayonnaise
21/2 cups salad dressing
 2 teaspoons curry powder
 1 teaspoon salt
 1 teaspoon garlic pepper

### Serves 50-55 — Yield: 15 pounds without dressing

10 pounds cooked seashell pasta, drained and rinsed (4 pounds uncooked)
15 ounces salad shrimp, drained
14 ounces sea legs, chopped and drained
 2 cans (6 ounces each) white tuna packed in water, drained
 3 cups diced celery
 1 red bell pepper, diced
 2 cups grated Cheddar cheese

 1 bunch green onions, chopped
 2 cups cashews, whole or halves
 3 cups broccoli florets
 1 quart plus 1 cup mayonnaise
 1 quart plus 1 cup salad dressing
 2 teaspoons curry powder
 1 teaspoon salt
11/2 teaspoons garlic pepper

### Serves 120 — Yield: 29 pounds without dressing

20 pounds cooked seashell pasta, drained and rinsed (8 pounds uncooked)
20 ounces salad shrimp, drained
24 ounces sea legs, chopped and drained
 4 cans (6 ounces each) white tuna packed in water, drained
33/4 cups diced celery
 2 red bell peppers, diced
 2 cups grated Cheddar cheese
 2 bunches green onions, chopped
 1 pound cashews, whole or halves
 1 pound broccoli florets
 2 quarts mayonnaise
 2 quarts salad dressing
 2 tablespoons curry powder
 1 teaspoon salt
 2 teaspoons garlic pepper

*Continued on next page*

*Seafood Salad, continued*
*Garnishes*
- Romaine lettuce leaves
- Salad shrimp
- Chopped red bell pepper
- Parsley
- Cashews and broccoli florets, if desired

In large bowl(s) place seashell pasta, shrimp, sea legs, tuna, celery, red bell pepper, green onion, Cheddar cheese, cashews and broccoli. In a separate bowl, mix together mayonnaise, salad dressing, curry, salt and garlic pepper. Mix well. Add to pasta mixture and combine until all ingredients are well moistened. Line serving bowl(s) with romaine lettuce leaves. Turn salad into bowl. Garnish with salad shrimp, chopped red bell pepper and parsley; may also add cashews and broccoli florets, if desired. Refrigerate until serving.

◆◆◆

# South of the Border Avocado Salad

I serve this salad at my Mexican theme picnics to a flurry of "olés." While avocados are expensive, the advantage of this salad is that you can add more or less of an ingredient to reach the needed weight. Do, however, use the recommended amounts of tomato called for in the recipe as the tomatoes release their juice which combines with the seasonings and makes for a delicious dressing.

Make the salad the day of the picnic to retain the freshness, color and texture of the tomatoes and avocados. Use a commercial whitener, per package instructions, (or lemon juice) to treat the mushrooms to maintain their light color.

AVOCADOS—Use only ripe avocados. Their skins will be very dark green or black depending on the variety. The ripe fruit should yield easily to light pressure. A firm avocado is not ripe and will be hard and tasteless. A ripe avocado will peel easily with no pulp adhering to the skin when removed. An average avocado weighs approximately 8 ounces with the pit accounting for 2 ounces.

*Serves 15 — Yield: 3 pounds*
*Salad*
- 1/4 pound fresh mushrooms, sliced
- 1 pound avocados, peeled, pitted, cubed
- 2 pounds tomatoes, chopped
- 1/2 pound green bell pepper, diced
- 1/2 pound onion, chopped

*Seasonings*
- 1 1/2 teaspoon chili powder
- 1 1/2 teaspoons ground cumin
- 1/2 teaspoon salt
- 1 teaspoon pepper
- 1/4 teaspoon onion powder
- 1/4 teaspoon garlic salt

*Serves 25 — Yield: 7 pounds*
*Salad*
- 1/2 pound fresh mushrooms, sliced
- 2 pounds avocados, peeled, pitted, cubed
- 3 pounds tomatoes, chopped
- 2 pounds green bell pepper, chopped
- 2 pounds onions, chopped

*Seasonings*
- 1 tablespoon chili powder
- 1 tablespoon ground cumin

*Continued on next page*

*Avocado Salad, continued*

    1  teaspoon salt
    1  teaspoon pepper
  1/2  teaspoon onion powder
  1/2  teaspoon garlic salt

### Serves 70 — Yield: 14 pounds

*Salad*

    1  pound fresh mushrooms, sliced
    4  pounds avocados, peeled, pitted, cubed
    5  pounds tomatoes, chopped
    2  pounds green bell pepper, diced
    2  pounds onions, chopped

*Seasonings*

    2  tablespoons chili powder
    2  tablespoons ground cumin
    2  teaspoons salt
    2  teaspoons pepper
  3/4  teaspoon onion powder
  3/4  teaspoon garlic salt

### Serves 100 — Yield: 20 pounds

*Salad*

    2  pounds fresh mushrooms, sliced
    6  pounds avocados, peeled, pitted, cubed
    7  pounds tomatoes, chopped
    3  pounds green bell peppers, chopped
    3  pounds onions, chopped

*Seasonings*

    3  tablespoons chili powder
    3  tablespoons ground cumin
    2  teaspoons salt
    2  teaspoons pepper
    1  teaspoon onion powder
    1  teaspoon garlic salt

*Garnishes*

    Lettuce leaves
    Tomato rose(s)
    Parsley
    Green bell pepper leaves

Rinse mushrooms with commercial whitener (or lemon juice diluted with water); drain and pat dry. Mix avocados, tomatoes, green bell pepper, onion, mushrooms, chili powder, cumin, salt, pepper, onion powder and garlic salt together in large bowl. Line serving platter(s) with lettuce leaves. Place salad onto platter(s); garnish each platter with a tomato rose and 5 green pepper leaf-shaped cutouts (see below).

◆ TO MAKE A TOMATO ROSE: Take a small paring knife and, starting at the base of tomato, cut 1/2-inch wide strip of peel in one continuous circle around the tomato until you reach the stem end. Be careful not to cut or break the peel. Take the tomato peel and coil it, working from the inside out, to resemble an open rose. Do this on the surface you are garnishing. Garnish the center of the rose with a sprig of fresh parsley. (See diagram on page 63.)

◆ TO MAKE BELL PEPPER LEAVES: Cut whole bell pepper in half lengthwise. Flatten pepper halves; remove core and seeds. With a small, sharp leaf-shaped cookie cutter, cut out leaves and place around tomato rose.

# Relish and Vegetable Trays

A relish tray is a must at a picnic. People look for little extra munchies to go with their meal. The most common relishes used are carrot and celery sticks, pickles and olives and radishes and cherry tomatoes. Generally the carrot sticks and black olives are the first to go on a relish platter. The radishes are for color and are the least favorite item on the platter. At least five varieties should be used per relish tray. Use a 16-inch tray for 50 servings.

## To Assemble a Vegetable Tray

Drain the pickles and olives very well on paper towels. (Their liquids may discolor the radishes.) Line a 16-inch tray with kale or romaine lettuce; alternate fresh vegetables with pickles and olives. Place the radishes in the middle of the platter. Garnish with fresh parsley.

For platters of 6 to 12 people use a 7-inch plate and serve 1 piece per guest plus 4 extra pieces of each item.

For serving 13 to 24 people use a 9-inch plate and serve 1 piece per guest plus 7 or 8 extra pieces of each item.

For 25 to 35 people use a 12-inch platter and serve 1 piece per guest plus 15 extra pieces of each item.

Cover each relish platter with a damp paper towel, then cover with plastic wrap. Place the covered tray in a bag and tie with a twist tie. (Or use a dome cover instead a bag.) Carry the relishes to the party in a cambro or large plastic box with ice packs to keep the relishes cold.

CARROTS—Cut tops and bottoms off each carrot. Peel carrot and cut into sticks. You will lose one to two ounces when trimming and peeling a carrot. An average trimmed carrot weighs 2 ounces. Peeled large carrots are 3 to 4 ounces. A 3-ounce carrot yields 16 carrot sticks. A 2-pound bag of carrots generally yields 115-120 carrot sticks. Store carrot sticks in cold water in a covered container in the refrigerator. They will keep up to 9 days if the water is changed every other day. While carrots are economical they take labor to prepare. If the party is large it is better to buy prepared carrot sticks in 5- or 10-pound bags. Carrots can also be purchased in bulk, whole, in 50-pound bags and will keep for many weeks if stored in the refrigerator with tops and bottoms intact. Or you can purchase whole baby carrots in bags to save time, as they can be served whole.

CELERY—Cut tops and ends off. One stalk of celery can be cut into three 3-inch pieces lengthwise. Cut each 3-inch piece into 4 strips depending on the thickness of the stalk. The celery heart is more tender than the outer pieces of celery. You can save the celery tops for stock. A 2-pound bunch of celery yields 115 to 125 celery sticks. About 1/4 pound of celery is wasted. Store celery sticks in cold water in a covered container in the refrigerator up to 9 days, changing the water every other day.

RADISHES—There are 30 to 35 radishes in a 1-pound bag of radishes. Cut off the top and bottom of the radish and place into cold water to store. Rinse with 1 tablespoon commercial whitener to 2 pints water (or a mixture of lemon juice and water). Store radishes in cold water in a covered container in the refrigerator for up to 7 days, changing water every third day.

BLACK OLIVES—A 6-pound 3-ounce can of medium sized pitted black olives contains 460 to 475 olives. A 6-pound 3-ounce can of large pitted black olives contains approximately 275 olives. The medium olives are a better buy since you get more olives per pound. Store olives in their brine.

GREEN OLIVES—A 41-ounce jar of Spanish green olives stuffed with pimento contains approximately 116 olives, or 2 1/2 pounds of olives and 24 ounces brine. One 41-ounce jar serves 90 to 100. Green olives also come in gallon jars, 4 to a case. Store olives in their brine.

PICKLES—A No. 10 can (98 fluid ounces) of dill pickle spears contains 75 spears. One No. 10 can serves 60 people. A 1-gallon container of dill pickle slices contains 690 to 700 slices. There are 4 gallons in a case. Dill pickle spears and slices also come in 5-gallon containers.

A 2-quart (64-fluid-ounce) jar of bread-and-butter pickle slices contains 150 to 160 pickle slices and 2 1/2 pounds brine. Store all pickles in their brine.

Mixed pickled vegetables come in 2-pint or 2-quart jars. Pickled vegetables are just an extra filler item.

CHERRY TOMATOES—One pint contains 20 to 25 cherry tomatoes. Remove the stems and wash and dry the cherry tomatoes. Store covered with plastic wrap that has slits cut in it for ventilation. You can store them in their original containers if the containers have been thoroughly washed and dried first.

WHOLE FRESH TOMATOES—Serve tomatoes in wedges instead of slices as wedges are easier to eat. One tomato yields 14 tomato wedges or 7 to 8 slices. The larger the tomato the large the slice or wedge. It is more cost effective to use a small tomato; for example: four 1/4-pound tomatoes would yield 56 wedges and feed 28 people where as a one 1-pound tomato would yield 14 wedges and feed only 7 people. The cost is a great deal of difference.

GREEN BELL PEPPERS—One 1/2-pound bell pepper yields 30-32 strips or 24 to 28 rings.

BROCCOLI—Use the florets. A 1 1/2-pound bunch will yield 3/4-pound florets (about 40 pieces); enough to serve 25 people. Rinse thoroughly and dry well. Store in a 4-inch-deep full-size pan. Cover and refrigerate. Stored properly, broccoli will keep for 5 days.

CAULIFLOWER—A 2 1/2-pound head will yield 1 3/4 pounds of florets (about 60 pieces), enough to serve 35 people. To keep cauliflower white, rinse in a commercial whitener solution (or lemon juice and water). Dry and store cauliflower florets in a 4-inch-deep full-size pan. Cover and refrigerate. Stored properly, cauliflower will keep up to 5 days.

## To Assemble a Vegetable Tray

There is a difference between a relish tray and a vegetable tray. A vegetable tray has all vegetables on the arranged platter while relishes have some fresh vegetables and pickles and olives. Most picnics use relishes.

A typical vegetable tray has carrot sticks, celery sticks, broccoli, cauliflower and radishes or cherry tomatoes. Place the red vegetables in the center of the tray for an attractive presentation.

Carry an extra bag of carrot sticks to the picnic to use if needed. If kept in an airtight bag, extra carrots can be used at the next party. Vegetable trays are usually served with an accompanying dip.

ESTIMATING AMOUNTS FOR
20 TO 100 SERVINGS

For broccoli, cauliflower, celery and carrot sticks, serve 1 piece per guest plus 15 extra pieces. For example, to serve 75 guests, you will need 90 pieces of each item. For radishes or cherry tomatoes, serve 1 per guest plus 10 extra. Offer an assortment of at least 5 vegetables.

## Vegetable Tray Quantities at a Glance

| Servings | Tray Size | | Servings | Tray Size |
|---|---|---|---|---|
| 20-30 | one 12" tray | | 70 | one 18" tray plus one 12" tray |
| 40 | one 16" tray | | 80 | two 16" trays |
| 50-60 | one 18" tray | | 100 | two 18-inch trays |

### Pieces of each item per serving

| Servings | 20 | 30 | 40 | 50 | 60 | 70 | 80 | 90 | 100 |
|---|---|---|---|---|---|---|---|---|---|
| Broccoli | 35 | 45 | 55 | 65 | 75 | 85 | 95 | 105 | 115 |
| Cauliflower | 35 | 45 | 55 | 65 | 75 | 85 | 95 | 105 | 115 |
| Celery | 35 | 45 | 55 | 65 | 75 | 85 | 95 | 105 | 115 |
| Carrots | 35 | 45 | 55 | 65 | 75 | 85 | 95 | 105 | 115 |
| Radishes | 30 | 40 | 50 | 60 | 70 | 80 | 90 | 100 | 110 |
| Cherry tomatoes | 30 | 40 | 50 | 60 | 70 | 80 | 90 | 100 | 110 |

### Pounds of broccoli per serving

| Servings | 25 | 50 | 75 | 100 |
|---|---|---|---|---|
| Broccoli, untrimmed | 1 1/2 lbs. | 3 lbs. | 4 1/2 lbs. | 6 lbs. |
| Broccoli, trimmed | 3/4 lb. | 1 1/2 lbs. | 2 1/4 lbs. | 3 lbs. |

### Pounds of cauliflower per serving

| Servings | 25 to 35 | 50 to 60 | 75 to 85 | 100 to 110 |
|---|---|---|---|---|
| Cauliflower, untrimmed | 2 1/2 lbs. | 5 lbs. | 7 1/2 lbs. | 10 lbs. |
| Cauliflower, trimmed | 1 3/4 lbs. | 3 1/2 lbs. | 5 1/4 lbs. | 7 lbs. |

# Dill Dip

| Servings | 20 | 40 | 60 | 80 | 100 |
|---|---|---|---|---|---|
| Sour cream | 1 lb. | 2 lbs. | 3 lbs. | 4 lbs. | 5 lbs. |
| Mayonnaise | 1 lb. | 2 lbs. | 3 lbs. | 4 lbs. | 5 lbs. |
| Dried dill | 1/2 c. | 2/3 c. | 1 c. | 1 1/3 c. | 1 2/3 c. |
| Worcestershire sauce | 1 1/2 tsp. | 3 tsp. | 3 tsp. | 3 1/2 tsp. | 4 1/2 tsp. |
| Lemon juice | 1 1/2 tsp. | 3 tsp. | 3 tsp. | 3 1/2 tsp. | 4 1/2 tsp. |
| Onion salt | 1/2 tsp. | 3/4 tsp. | 1 tsp. | 1 tsp. | 1 tsp. |
| Garlic salt | 1/2 tsp. | 1/2 tsp. | 1/2 tsp. | 1/2 tsp. | 1/2 tsp. |
| Beau Monde seasoning | 1 tsp. | 2 tsp. | 4 tsp. | 5 tsp. | 2 tbsp |

In a large bowl, stir sour cream and mayonnaise together. Add dill, Worcestershire, lemon juice, onion salt, garlic salt and Beau Monde seasoning; mix well. (You can use salad dressing instead of mayonnaise, but I prefer mayonnaise.)

# Gelatin Salads

Many caterers refer to gelatin as "colored water." Prepared without any additions, it is the least expensive salad to serve. No matter how young or how old, everyone likes flavored gelatin. The red gelatins, such as strawberry or cherry, are a favorite with children. Canned fruit cocktail is a popular addition. It is an inexpensive mix of fruits and only small amounts need to be added. Save the fruit juices when draining canned fruits for other recipes, or use the juice in place of some of the water called for when making gelatin.

Flavored gelatin mix can be purchased by the case. A case of twelve 24-ounce bags will contain an assortment of flavors. A citrus combination will consist of lemon, lime and orange flavors. The red case will have cherry, strawberry and raspberry gelatin. Cases of a single flavor will contain six 4-pound 8-ounce bags.

### Finger Gelatin
*Serves 70-80 — Yield: two 12 x 20-inch pans*
*(112 cubes per pan)*

1 bag (24 ounces) gelatin (4 cups dry)
2 quarts water
6 cups cold water

In large pan, bring 2 quarts water to a boil. Boil 2 minutes; remove from heat. Whisk in dry gelatin. When dissolved, stir in 6 cups cold water. (*Note:* Package instructions call for 8 cups cold water. Cutting back to 6 cups results in a firmer gelatin that holds up better when transporting.) Have ready two 12 x 20-inch disposable aluminum pans or two 2-inch-deep full-sized chafing inserts. Pour 7 cups of prepared gelatin into each pan. Chill until firm.

Cut 14 pieces down and 8 pieces across for a total of 112 pieces in each pan. Allow 3 pieces finger gelatin per adult and 2 per small child.

*Serves 200 — Yield: eight 12 x 20-inch pans*
*(28 squares per pan)*

1 bag (4 pounds 8 ounces) gelatin
6 quarts water
4 cups fruit juice (or cold water)
4 quarts plus 2 cups cold water

Bring 6 quarts of water to a boil in very large pan; boil 2 minutes. Turn off heat. Add bag of dry gelatin (12 1/2 cups). Whisk until dissolved. Stir in fruit juice and cold water. Ladle 6 cups into each of eight 12 x 20-inch pans.

*Note:* You can buy gelatin in 14-pound 8-ounce bags. Just measure out the amount needed for various sized molds or pans. Be sure to mark on the bag how much was taken out so the next worker knows how many cups remain.

### Fruit Cocktail Gelatin
*Serves 50-60 — Yield: two 12 x 20-inch pans*
*(28 squares per pan)*

1 bag (24 ounces) gelatin (4 cups dry)
2 quarts water
6 cups cold water
6 cups fruit cocktail, drained

In large pan, bring 2 quarts water to a boil. Boil 2 minutes; remove from heat. Whisk in dry gelatin. When dissolved, stir in 6 cups cold water. Have ready two 12 x 20-inch disposable aluminum pans or two 2-inch-deep full-sized chafing inserts. Pour 6 cups of prepared gelatin into each pan. Add 3 cups well-drained fruit cocktail and mix well. Chill for 4 hours. Cut across 4 and down 7 for total of 28 squares.

### Garnished Gelatin Squares
*Serves 50-60 — Yield: two 12 x 20-inch pans*
*(28 squares per pan)*

2 pans (12 x 20 inches each) prepared

*Continued on next page*

*Gelatin, continued*

gelatin squares
1 cup whipped non-dairy topping

Place 1 cup whipped topping in pastry bag fitted with a number 1 star tip. Pipe a small star on each cut square. Cut large Maraschino cherries into 12 pieces each. Stand 1 piece of cherry up in each star. This is a nice added touch and gives dimension to each square. Cover pan with aluminum cover and carry in insulated carriers to the picnic.

## FRUITED GELATIN

Fruits to avoid: Fresh or frozen pineapple, papaya, kiwi, ginger, figs or guava. These foods contain an enzyme that will prevent the gelling process.

| Gelatin flavor | Complementary Fruit |
|---|---|
| Lime | Canned pineapple or pears |
| Strawberry, cherry | Peaches |
| Black cherry | Black cherries |
| Raspberry | Canned pineapple, fruit cocktail |
| Orange | Mandarin oranges or crushed pineapple |
| Lemon | Crushed pineapple |

(I mainly use fruit cocktail or crushed pineapple.)

FRUIT COCKTAIL— See information in Fruit Cocktail Salad (page 59). Use 1/2 cup well-drained fruit cocktail for every 3-ounce package of gelatin.

CRUSHED PINEAPPLE—An 8-ounce can contains 4 ounces (1/2 cup) fruit and 4 ounces juice. A 1-pound 4-ounce can contains 14 ounces (2 cups) fruit and 6 ounces juice. A No. 10 can (6 pound 8 ounces) contains 4 pounds 4 ounces (8 1/3 cups) fruit and 2 pounds 4 ounces juice.

SUGAR-FREE GELATIN—This is readily available for people with special dietary needs. A favorite combination is any red gelatin with banana slices and chopped apples. Dip the banana slices and apple pieces into lemon juice to prevent browning. Drain the fruit well before adding to the gelatin.

## MOLDED GELATIN

One medium molded gelatin weighs 3 pounds and yields 20 slices. Add 1 cup fruit per medium mold. Let the gelatin thicken first (chill 1 1/2 hours) before adding fruit. That way, the fruit will not rise to the top and float in the mold. Chill 3 to 4 hours.

To unmold: Dip bottom and sides of pan in hot water. Twist the mold in circular motion to see if gelatin has loosened. Place lettuce leaves on top of mold; put a 12-inch tray over lettuce. Turn the whole thing over. The gelatin should slip out of the mold onto the lettuce-lined tray without cracking. Garnish with orange slices, 3 Maraschino cherries and 3 pieces of parsley. Cover mold with 12-inch dome cover and refrigerate.

I once needed to make 20 gelatin molds for a picnic. The molds were overfilled, so every time the worker carried one into the cooler, the floor and cooler were baptized with gelatin. To avoid this sticky situation, place large baking sheets on cooler racks. Fill the molds 3/4 full; carry to the cooler and place on baking sheets. Add the remainder of the gelatin to completely fill the mold.

TIP: Gelatin will melt quickly in the heat. At the picnic site, use a shallow 3-foot plastic container. Fill with ice packs and camouflage with lettuce, table covers and flowers. Place the trayed gelatin molds on the ice packs.

# Fruit Trays

Fruit is well received at a picnic especially during very hot weather. Use at least five varieties of fruit on each tray. Choose from cantaloupe, fresh pineapple, honeydew melon, strawberries and red or green grapes. Guests can pick and choose their favorites.

Using a variety of different colored fruits creates visual impact. Put bright red strawberries in the center of trays for an eye-catching effect. Position trays on different tiers for a multi-dimensional buffet table. Serve delicious dips to complement flavors of the fresh fruit. You can purchase pre-cut fruit for larger crowds to help save labor.

WATERMELON—Watermelon is a low-cost item to serve in the salad section of your picnic buffet line. It is very refreshing on a hot summer day. It is one of those simple foods that can be presented in a most impressive way, whether just cut into wedges and arranged attractively on a platter and garnished with parsley or cut into baskets, baby carriages, or whales to hold other foods. It can even be cut into vases to hold fresh flowers as a very unusual centerpiece. (See diagrams on pages 66-70.)

Wash the melon, and dry. One 23-pound melon will yield 128 pieces, 3 x 4 inches each. Use a 18-inch tray serve the wedges, 50 wedges per tray. Watermelon can also be cut and served in sixteen 8-inch-long sections.

CANTALOUPE—An average cantaloupe weighs 3 pounds. Peel cantaloupe. Cut in half, remove the seeds, and cut into wedges. There are 24 wedges to a 3-pound cantaloupe; each wedge is 4 to 6 inches in length. One cantaloupe serves 20 people.

HONEYDEW—Peel honeydew with a sharp knife. Cut in half, remove the seeds. Rinse off. Lay the honeydew half cut side down. Cut into wedges; cut wedges in half. There are 40-50 pieces per melon. One honeydew serves 40 people.

FRESH PINEAPPLE—The average fresh pineapple weighs 4 to 4 1/2 pounds and will yield 1 1/2 pounds of fruit. To cut a fresh pineapple: Cut off the leafy top. With pineapple upright, cut in half lengthwise. Cut each half in two lengthwise. Cut out the tough core. Lay the pineapple quarter skin side down on cutting board. Cutting close to skin, cut fruit from skin. Slice each quarter into 12 wedges, giving you a total of 48 wedges per pineapple. (See diagrams on pages 64-65.)

STRAWBERRIES—1 pint fresh strawberries contains 22 to 25 berries. One flat contains 12 pints. Wash berries just before using and pat dry, leaving hulls in place to keep berries fresh and firm.

GRAPES—Wash and pat dry. Serve all red grapes, all green grapes, or half of each.

## Fruit Tray Portions at a Glance

| Servings | 20 | 40 | 60 | 80 | 100 |
|---|---|---|---|---|---|
| Cantaloupe | 1 melon | 2 melons | 3 melons | 4 melons | 5 melons |
| Honeydew | 1/2 melon | 1 melon | 1 1/2 melons | 2 melons | 2 1/2 melons |
| Pineapple | 1 whole | 2 whole | 3 whole | 4 whole | 5 whole |
| Strawberries | 1 pint | 1 quart | 3 pints | 2 quarts | 5 pints |
| Grapes | 1 pound | 2 pounds | 3 pounds | 4 pounds | 5 pounds |
| Tray sizes | one 14" tray | one 18" tray | two 16" trays | two 16" trays | two 18" trays |

### Dressings

A wide variety of dressings add flavor to fruit salads. Many people are very conscious about watching fats. There are many lowfat and fat-free dressings available. Diabetics and other folks with special needs need to be considered. If you have a customer that alerts you of these special needs it is in your best interest to run that extra mile for that customer.

### Basic Amaretto Fruit Dip

| Servings | 20 | 40 | 60 | 80 | 100 |
|---|---|---|---|---|---|
| Sour cream | 1 pint | 2 pints | 3 pints | 4 pints | 5 pints |
| Powdered sugar | 1/2 cup | 1 cup | 1 1/4 cups | 1 1/2 cups | 2 cups |
| Red food coloring | 1 drop | 2 drops | 2 drops | 3 drops | 3 drops |
| Almond extract | 1 tsp. | 2 tsp. | 3 tsp. | 3 1/2 tsp. | 4 tsp. |
| Maraschino cherry juice | 1 tsp. | 2 tsp. | 2 1/2 tsp. | 2 3/4 tsp. | 3 tsp. |

In a large bowl(s), mix sour cream, sugar, food coloring, extract and cherry juice until well blended. Refrigerate. Serve with fruit tray(s).

*Variation:* You can substitute amaretto liqueur, in same amounts, for almond extract and Maraschino cherry juice.

## A Fruit Tray Story

When I first began catering I served fruit on big trays only because I only owned very large and very small trays. I would bag the trays and put ice pack on top of the fruit. As my business grew I got boxes to carry fruit trays and bought trays of every size. Once as we were riding to the party one of the workers put the bagged fruit tray on top of a hot box. The tray slid off the box and fell upside down. The fruit fell into the bag. As I was reassembling the tray in the truck a guest came by and peered in.

She said, "I heard you always run that extra mile for your customers. This is something how you arrange your fresh fruit at the party." I told her she was special and I cared about her. She told everyone at the party how fresh the fruit was. One more time my you-know-what was covered and the party went very well.

# Peach Dream Salad

| Servings | 12 | 20 | 50 | 100 |
|---|---|---|---|---|
| Pounds of salad | 3 | 5 | 12 | 25 |
| Peaches, sliced | 2 lbs. 4 oz. | 4 lbs. 8 oz. | 10 lbs. | 20 lbs. |
| Marshmallows | 1 c. | 2 c. | 1 lb. | 2 lb. |
| Whipped topping | 1 c. | 2 c. | 1 lb. | 2 lb. |
| Almond extract | 1/2 tsp. | 1 tsp. | 1 1/2 tsp. | 2 tsp. |
| Sliced almonds | 1/4 c. | 1/2 c. | 2 1/2 c. | 3 1/2 c. |
| Kiwi | 1 | 2 | 2 | 3 |
| Strawberries | 16 | 12 | 12 | 22-24 (1 pt.) |
| Parsley for garnish | | | | |

Drain peaches on a paper towel. (Save the peach juice for making gelatin.) Place peaches in bowl; stir in marshmallows, whipped topping and almond extract.

Spread peach salad into pan(s). Sprinkle sliced almonds over the peaches.

For 12 servings use a 9x13-inch pan. For 20 servings, spread 5 pounds peach salad into an aluminum full-size 2-inch-deep pan. Garnish with 12 slices of kiwi and 12 strawberries with hull. (Each kiwi yields 6 slices.) Alternate the strawberries with the kiwi.

For 50 servings use two 4-inch-deep aluminum half-pans, 6 pounds of peach salad in each. Garnish each pan with one sliced kiwi, and 6 strawberries with hull.

Divide 100 servings into 3 containers. Use 1/2 cup sliced almonds to garnish each container. You can place the peach salad on a 16-inch or a 18-inch lettuce-lined tray. After tasting this salad you will know that it is a peach dream come true.

CANNED PEACHES—A 15 1/4-ounce can of peach slices contains 7 ounces juice and 8 ounces peaches (12 to 13 peach slices). A 1-pound 13-ounce can contains 7 ounces juice and 1 pound 6 ounces peaches. (40 to 42 peach slices). There is the same amount of juice in a 15 1/4-ounce can as in a 1-pound 13-ounce can. The fruit yield is almost three times higher in the larger can.

A No. 10 can (6 pounds 10 ounces)of peach slices has 2 pounds 4 ounces juice and 4 pounds 6 ounces peaches (60 to 80 slices). The premium sliced peaches have thicker slices. However, a No. 10 can of premium peaches contains about 60 slices, while a No. 10 can of standard peaches contains about 80 (thinner) slices. The premium and standard cans have equal amounts of juice.

# Mandarin Orange Layered Salad

This easily assembled and colorful fruit salad has something for everyone: mandarin oranges, pineapple, bananas and Maraschino cherries. Garnish with fresh strawberries when in season.

MANDARIN ORANGES—A 15-ounce can of mandarin orange sections contains 7 ounces of juice, and 8 ounces of orange sections (45 to 55 sections). One cup of fruit contains 55 to 60 orange sections. Six 15-ounce cans of mandarin oranges drained contains 3 pounds of fruit. A No. 10 can weighs 6 pounds 11 ounces and contains 2 pounds 6 ounces of juice and 4 pounds 5 ounces, or 9 cups, of fruit(approximately 500 orange sections). There are 6 No. 10 cans to a case (approximately 3000 orange sections).

CANNED PINEAPPLE—A 1-pound 4-ounce can of pineapple chunks contains 14 ounces (2 cups) of fruit and 6 ounces of juice (approximately 48 pineapple chunks). A No. 10 can (6 pounds 12 ounces) contains 2 pounds 6 ounces of juice and 4 pounds 6 ounces of fruit (approximately 275 pineapple chunks). There are 6 No. 10 cans to a case (approximately 1,650 pineapple chunks).

BANANAS—A medium peeled banana weighs 4 to 6 ounces. An 8-ounce banana, peeled, weighs 6 ounces and yields forty-six 1/8-inch slices. A 6-ounce banana, peeled, weighs 3 to 4 ounces and yields forty-four 1/8-inch slices. A 4-ounce banana, peeled, weighs 2 ounces and yields twenty-five 1/8-inch slices. Two ounces of sliced banana yields approximately 3/4 cup. Dip sliced bananas in undiluted lemon juice to keep them from turning brown.

COCONUT—A 1-pound package contains 5 1/3 cups. One cup contains 3.5 ounces of flaked coconut.

ROMAINE LETTUCE—One head weighs 1 pound. The core weighs approximate 2 ounces. There are 8 big leaves, 8 medium leaves and 12 small leaves to each trimmed head (14 ounces).

LEAF LETTUCE—A head of leaf lettuce weighs 3/4 to 1 pound. The core is approximately 2 ounces. There are 20 leaves per head.

PARSLEY—A bunch of parsley weighs 1 to 2 ounces. There are 30 to 35 sprigs per bunch. There are 5 to 6 pieces of parsley per sprig.

MARASCHINO CHERRIES—10 ounces of Maraschino cherries yield 30-35 cherries. A half-gallon of cherries weighs 4 pounds 8 ounces (155 to 185 cherries). A gallon weighs 9 pounds 6 ounces. There are 510-560 large cherries per gallon. There are 4 gallons per case, or 6 half-gallons per case.

## Mandarin Orange Layered Salad

| Servings | 25 | 40 | 70 | 150 |
|---|---|---|---|---|
| Pounds of salad | 4 lbs. | 6-7 lbs. | 13 lbs. | 25 lbs. |
| Lettuce leaves per tray | 6 | 7 | 7 | 7 |
| Pineapple chunks | 2 lbs. 3 oz. | 4 lbs. 6 oz. | 4 lbs. 6 oz. | 8 lbs. 12 oz. |
| Bananas | 12 oz. | 1 lb. 8 oz. | 1 lbs. 8 oz. | 3 lbs. 4 oz |
| Mandarin orange sections | 1 lbs. 8 oz. | 3 lbs. | 7 lbs. | 14 lbs. |
| Coconut | 1/2 c. | 1 c. | 2c. | 3c. |
| Maraschino cherries | 6 | 6 | 12 | 24 |
| Parsley pieces | 6 | 6 | 12 | 24 |
| Serving tray(s) | one 12" | one 16" | two 16" | four 16" or three 18" |

Line serving tray(s) with romaine or leaf lettuce. Dip banana slices in undiluted lemon juice to prevent them from turning color. Drain mandarin orange sections and pineapple chunks; pat dry. On serving tray(s), layer pineapple, bananas and mandarin orange segments. Sprinkle coconut over top. Garnish each tray with 5 Maraschino cherries, placing 2 pieces of parsley next to each cherry. Cover with plastic wrap or domed cover. Transport to picnic in a cambro carrier.

# Old Glory Fruit Salad

This fresh fruit salad is used in the Red, White and Blue picnic. The fruits used are watermelon, pineapple, strawberries, blueberries and raspberries. Generally you can fit up to 50 servings on one oblong tray. The color combination gets the guests to ooh and ah. It can be a centerpiece.

| Servings | 20 | 40 | 50 | 100 |
|---|---|---|---|---|
| Watermelon wedges | 20 | 40 | 50 | 100 |
| Fresh pineapple | 1 whole | 2 whole | 2 1/2 whole | 5 whole |
| Blueberries | 1/2 pints | 1/2 pint | 1/2 pint | 1 pint |
| Strawberries | 1 pint | 2 pints | 2 1/2 pints | 5 pints |
| Raspberries | 1 pint | 1 pint | 1 pint | 2 pints |
| Parsley | | | | |

Use raspberries and blueberries very sparingly because they are expensive. It is the color you are looking for on each tray. For 100 servings, use two 12 x 18-inch trays. For 20 servings use a 16-inch round platter. For 40 servings use an 18-inch round tray.

Place watermelon wedges around the outside of the platter. Place pineapple wedges in the middle of the platter. Layer strawberries on top of the pineapple wedges. Sprinkle the blueberries and raspberries over the entire salad. Garnish with parsley.

*Note*: There are 40 raspberries in 1/2 pint. There are 130 blueberries in 1/2 pint.

58

# Summer Dream Salad

*Serves 18-20*

2 cans (1 pound 4 ounces each) pineapple tidbits
2 cans (15 ounces each) mandarin oranges
4 medium bananas
2 tablespoons lemon juice
1 pint fresh strawberries, sliced
1 box (3.4 ounces) instant lemon pudding mix
8 romaine leaves
2 kiwi, peeled and sliced, for garnish
10 strawberries, halved, for garnish
3 sprigs parsley, for garnish

Drain pineapple and oranges and mix the juices together; reserve 1½ cups juice. In a large bowl, blend reserved juice with pudding mix; beat until thickened.

Peel and slice bananas; dip slices into lemon juice to prevent discoloration. Pat dry with paper towels. Fold bananas, sliced strawberries, and pineapple into pudding.

Line a footed glass bowl with romaine leaves. Pour fruit salad into bowl. Garnish with kiwi slices, strawberry halves and parsley.

◆◆◆

# Fruit Cocktail Salad

FRUIT COCKTAIL—A No. 10 can (6 pounds 9 ounces) contains 5 pounds (10½ cups) fruit and 1 pound 9 ounces unsweetened pear juice from concentrate. These cans may be purchased by the case, 6 cans to a case. One case, drained, will yield 30 pounds of fruit cocktail. A 1-pound can of fruit cocktail contains 6 ounces of juice and 10 ounces of fruit. A No. 303 can (1 pound 14 ounces) of fruit cocktail contains 8 ounces of juice and 1 pound 6 ounces of fruit. 2 cups of fruit cocktail, drained, weighs 1 pound. One case of fruit cocktail mixed with 20 pounds of other ingredients would serve 200 people at 4 servings to a pound. 15 pounds of fruit cocktail (3 No. 10 cans, drained) mixed with 10 pounds of other ingredients would serve 100 people.

MINIATURE MARSHMALLOWS—1 cup (2 ounces) of miniature marshmallows contains 100 marshmallows. Approximately 800 miniature marshmallows come in a 1-pound bag. You can buy miniature marshmallows in multi-colors. I prefer using the plain white marshmallows. It seems more natural. Buy marshmallows in smaller amounts because they lose their freshness quickly once the bag is opened.

DELICIOUS APPLES—each medium-large apple weighs about 1/2 pound. Without the core the apple weighs 6 ounces and without the core and peel it weighs 1/4 pound. Sometimes I leave the apple peel on for the color. If you are serving a lot of senior citizens it is best to peel the apples because the peel can be difficult to chew.

NON-DAIRY WHIPPED TOPPING—A 1-pound container contains 6 cups; a 12-ounce container contains 5 cups (2½ ounces per cup). You have more volume in larger amounts of whipped topping because there is more air in it.

You can purchase frozen commercial non-dairy whipped topping, which is more stable. It comes in a dozen 2-pound (4-cup)containers to a case. Thaw in the refrigerator. Whip in a chilled bowl one pound at a time in a small mixer, or up to 4 pounds at a time in a commercial mixer. The topping will not whip if the bowl or the whipped topping is not cold. Two cups topping (1 pound) before whipping equals 5 cups whipped. You can cut a chunk at a time of frozen whipped topping and whip in needed amounts. The non-dairy topping is good for guests who cannot eat dairy products.

SOUR CREAM—2 cups weigh 1 pound. Buy sour cream in a 5-pound carton to save money.

## Fruit Cocktail Salad

| Guests | 12 | 25 | 50 | 100 |
|---|---|---|---|---|
| Fruit cocktail | 2 1/2 lbs. | 5 lbs. | 10 lbs. | 15 lbs. |
| Apples | 1/2 lb. (2 apples) | 1 lbs.(4 apples) | 2 lbs.(8 apples) | 4 lbs.(16 apples) |
| Bananas | 1/2 lb. (2 bananas) | 1 lbs.(4 bananas) | 2 lbs.(8 bananas) | 4 lbs. (16 bananas) |
| Coconut | 1 cup | 2 cups | 4 cups | 8 cups |
| Marshmallows | 1 cup | 2 cups. | 4 cups | 8 cups |
| Sour cream | 1/2 cup | 1 cups | 2 cups | 4 cups. |
| Whipped topping | 1 cup | 2 cups. | 4 cups | 8 cups |
| Almond extract | 1/2 tsp. | 1 tsp. | 2 tsp. | 3 tsp. |

Maraschino cherries, for garnish
Parsley, for garnish

Drain the fruit cocktail and place fruit in a large bowl. (Save the juice for another recipe.) Peel and core apples. Peel and slice bananas. Add bananas, apples, coconut, and marshmallows to the drained fruit cocktail. In a separate bowl, combine sour cream, whipped topping, and almond extract together. Fold into the fruit cocktail mixture. Place into serving bowls and garnish with Maraschino cherries and parsley.

## Variation on Fruit Cocktail Salad

| Guests | 12 | 25 | 50 | 100 |
|---|---|---|---|---|
| Maraschino cherry juice | 2 tsp. | 4 tsp. | 6 tsp. | 8 tsp. |
| Red food coloring | 1 drop | 1 drop | 2 drops | 2 drops |
| Powdered sugar | 2 tbsp. | 1/4 cup | 1/3 cup | 2/3 cup |

Add the above ingredients to the sour cream and whipped topping. The Maraschino cherry juice and almond are a great substitute for amaretto liqueur.

You can use all sour cream or all whipped topping if you so desire. All whipped topping makes the fruit cocktail salad sweeter. However, if you want to make the variation recipe you should use the sour cream and whip cream combination.

TIP: You can also substitute fat-free sour cream for regular sour cream and fruit cocktail packed in water to make a diabetic and fat-free fruit cocktail salad. Use diabetic sweetener sparingly to sweeten the salad. Just remember a little sweetener goes a long way.

# Pistachio Salad

This is very colorful and easy to make. It is a medium cost salad and is very popular especially with senior citizens because of its soft texture. It looks particularly attractive presented in clear glass bowls glass bowls lined with lettuce.

COTTAGE CHEESE—A 1-pound container equals 2 cups. Cottage cheese also comes in 5-pound containers (10 cups). If planning to do large quantities, buy it from your wholesaler in even larger containers. Regular cottage cheese has 4 percent milkfat. Look for 1 or 2 percent cottage cheese to reduce the fat content. Cottage cheese does add protein to the salad.

Other ingredients include canned pineapple (see page 57 for details), whipped topping and miniature marshmallows (see page 59 for details). One ingredient to pay particular attention to is the pineapple juice in the 50 and 100 servings recipes. Accurately weigh out those quantities to ensure the correct consistency of the salad. If the salad is too runny, add more pudding mix.

### Serves 10 —Yield: 2½ pounds
8 ounces cottage cheese
1 can (1 pound 4 ounces) pineapple chunks in juice, undrained
1 box (3.4 ounces) instant pistachio pudding mix
1 cup prepared whipped topping
1 cup miniature marshmallows

### Serves 20 —Yield: 5 pounds
1¼ pounds cottage cheese
2 cans (1 pound 4 ounces each) pineapple chunks in juice, undrained
2 boxes (3.4 ounces each) instant pistachio pudding mix
2 cups prepared whipped topping
2 cups miniature marshmallows

### Serves 50 —Yield: 10¾ pounds
2½ pounds cottage cheese
1 No. 10 can (6 pounds 12 ounces) pineapple chunks in juice, drained (reserve juice)
24 ounces (by weight) juice from drained pineapple (above)
4 boxes (3.4 ounces each) instant pistachio pudding mix
8 ounces (by weight) prepared whipped topping
1 pound miniature marshmallows

### Serves 100 —Yield: 20 pounds
3 pounds cottage cheese
2 No. 10 cans (6 pounds 12 ounces each) pineapple chunks in juice, drained (reserve juice)
3 pounds (by weight) juice from drained pineapple (above)
8 boxes (3.4 ounces each) instant pistachio pudding mix
1¼ pounds prepared whipped topping
2 pounds miniature marshmallows

*Garnish*
Red leaf lettuce
Maraschino cherries or strawberries
Parsley

Combine cottage cheese, pineapple chunks, pineapple juice and pudding mix. Fold in whipped topping; stir in marshmallows. Line glass bowl(s) with lettuce leaves. Turn salad into serving bowl(s). Garnish with Maraschino cherries or strawberries and parsley.

*Note:* One large glass or shell-shaped bowl will hold 8 pounds of salad.

# Peach Tower Salad

This eye-catching salad of fruit kabobs is served on romaine lettuce-lined trays. Each strawberry-parsley-pineapple kabob is stacked on a frilled toothpick and anchored in a peach half base. Plan on one Peach Tower per person. If there is an abundance of food on the buffet table, reduce the number of Peach Towers by 10 percent. For example, if you are serving 100 guests, only make up 90 Peach Towers. While this dish is time-consuming to assemble, it is worth the effort for its visual impact. Do not garnish as these trays of simple fruit combinations are pictures in themselves.

PEACHES—Use No. 10 cans of peach halves. Each can contains 28 to 29 peach halves (4 pounds 4 ounces of fruit) and 2 pounds 4 ounces of juice. There are six No. 10 cans to a case; each case contains 168 to 174 peach halves.

FRESH PINEAPPLE—See page 54.
STRAWBERRIES—See page 54.

*Serve 1 tower per person*

| Servings | 25 | 50 | 100 |
|---|---|---|---|
| No. 10 cans peach halves, drained | 1 can | 2 cans | 4 cans |
| Romaine lettuce | 8 leaves | 9 leaves | 18 leaves |
| Fresh parsley | 5 sprigs | 10 sprigs | 20 sprigs |
| Fresh whole pineapple | 1/2 | 1 | 2 |
| Fresh strawberries | 1 pint | 2 pints | 4 pints |

Drain peach halves and place on paper towel to dry. Wash and dry romaine. Separate into leaves. Line trays with outer leaves, letting them overhang edge of tray. Wash and dry parsley and separate sprigs into pieces. Arrange peach halves, cut side down, on tray.

Using a 4-inch frilled toothpick, slide 1 strawberry onto pick to just below frill. Slide 1 parsley piece onto pick, touching bottom of strawberry. Slide pineapple wedge onto pick below parsley piece. Anchor filled pick into peach half. Each pick, from frilled end down, will have a strawberry, parsley piece and pineapple wedge.

Use appropriate sized plastic dome cover to cover each tray. Carry covered trays to picnic in an insulated box on wheels.

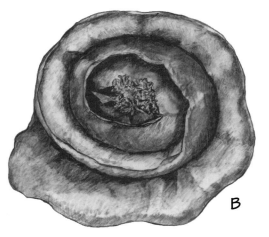

How to make a Tomato Rose (page 48)

How to make a green onion garnish
(see page 5)

Trim root end of green onion. With a sharp paring knife, slice green portion of onion into vertical strips, starting just above the white and leaving white section intact.

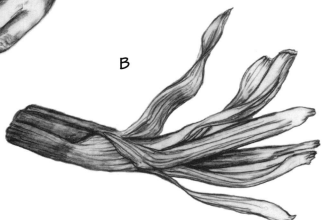

A

How to cut a pineapple into serving Pieces (page 54)

B

C

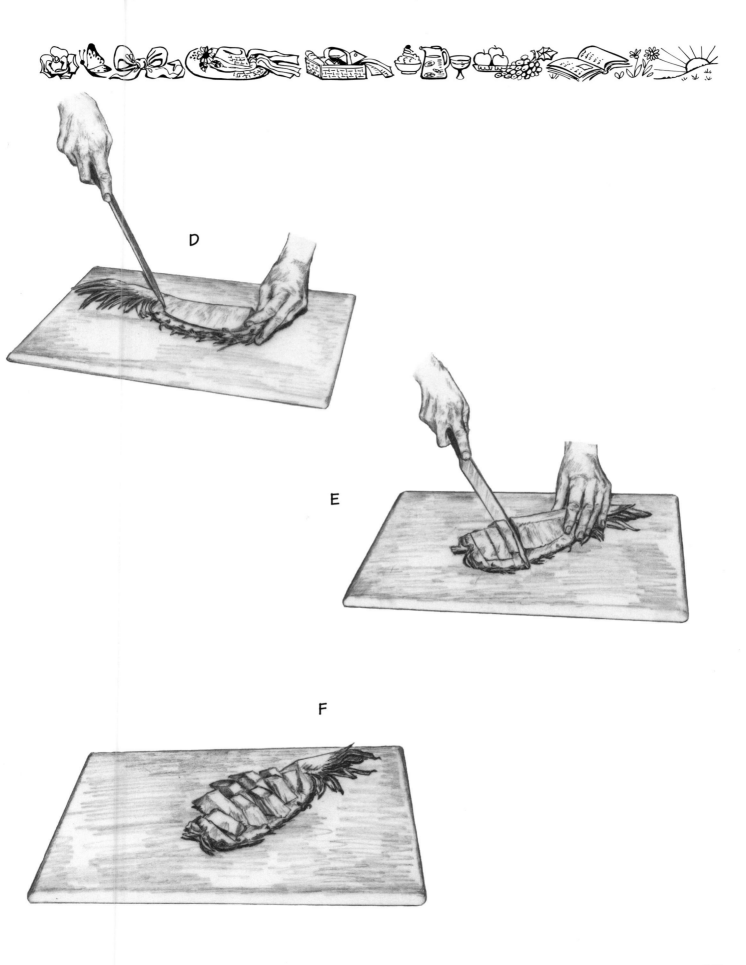

D

E

F

65

How to cut a watermelon into serving pieces (page 54)

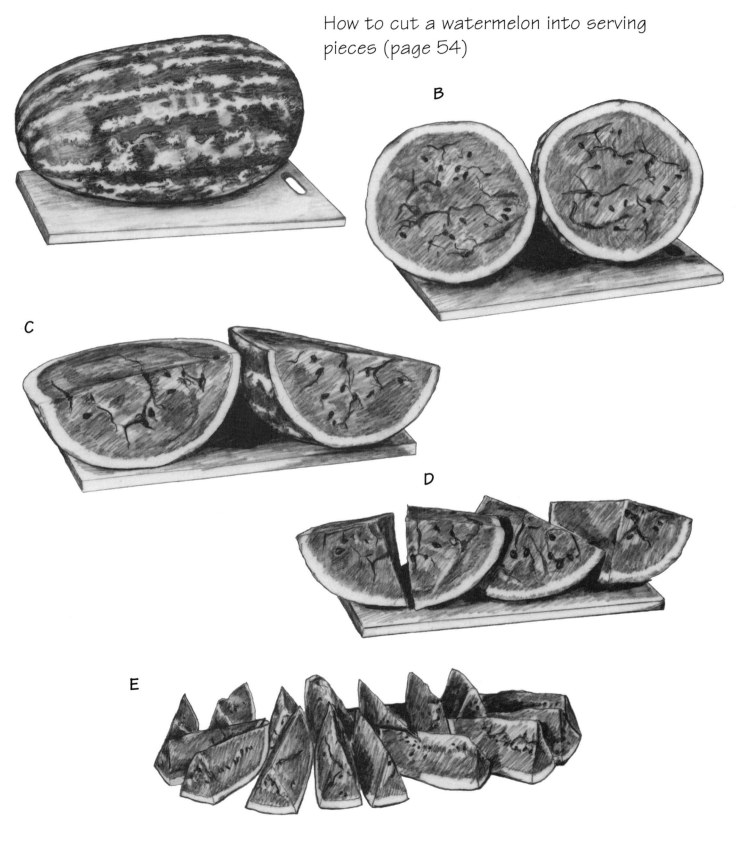

B

C

D

E

A

## How to make a vertical watermelon basket

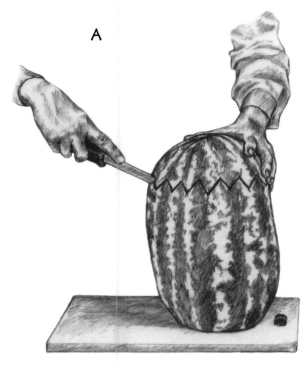

B

C

Cut a thin slice off the bottom of the watermelon to enable it to stand upright. Draw the shape of the desired handle and basket on the watermelon. Cut watermelon following your drawing. Scoop out watermelon flesh and set aside; leave shell at least 1 inch thick. Drain any excess liquid from basket. Cut V-shaped notches around basket handle and edges for a fancier look, if desired. Cut watermelon flesh into cubes and return to basket. Garnish handle with a sprig of parsley and a strawberry.

How to make a watermelon
basket

A

B

C

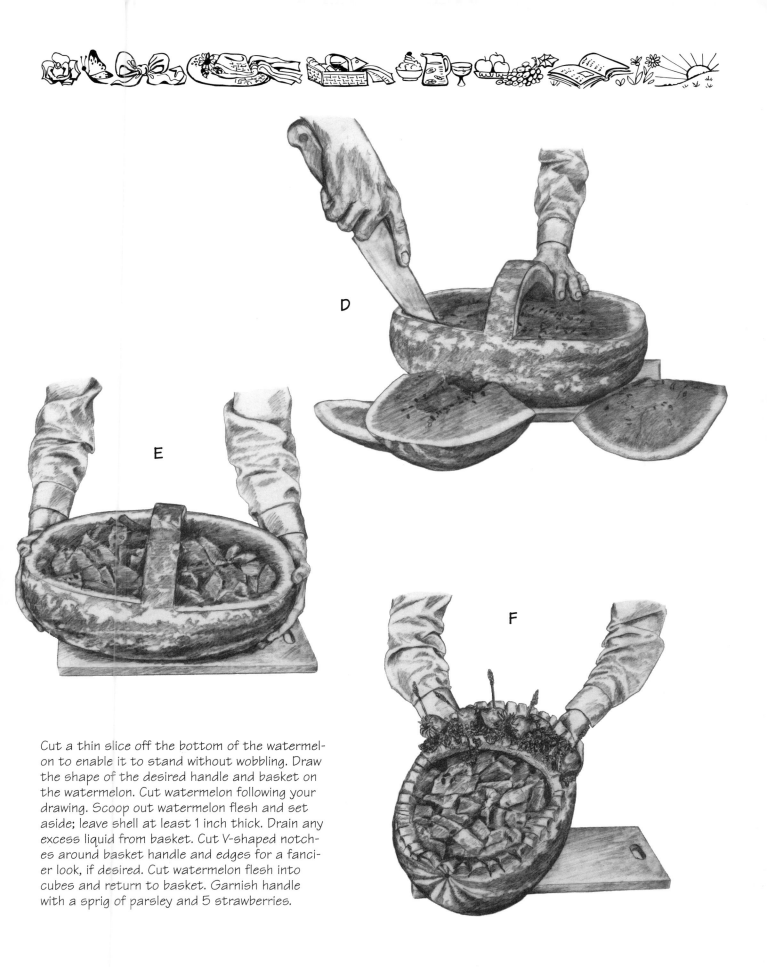

D

E

F

Cut a thin slice off the bottom of the watermelon to enable it to stand without wobbling. Draw the shape of the desired handle and basket on the watermelon. Cut watermelon following your drawing. Scoop out watermelon flesh and set aside; leave shell at least 1 inch thick. Drain any excess liquid from basket. Cut V-shaped notches around basket handle and edges for a fancier look, if desired. Cut watermelon flesh into cubes and return to basket. Garnish handle with a sprig of parsley and 5 strawberries.

## How to make a watermelon buggy

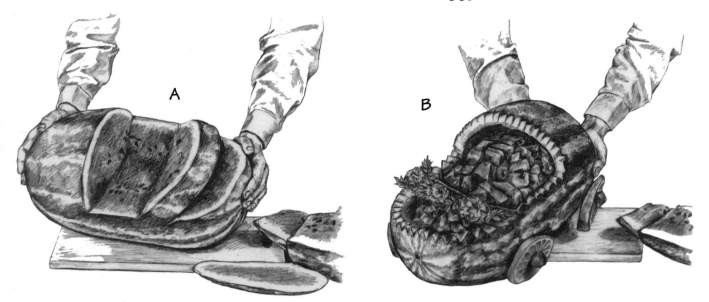

Draw the shape of the desired handle and back of the buggy on the watermelon. Cut watermelon following your drawing. Scoop out watermelon flesh and set aside; leave shell at least 1 inch thick. Drain any excess liquid from basket. Cut V-shaped notches around handle and edges for a fancier look, if desired. Cut watermelon flesh into cubes and return to basket. For wheels, cut 4 thick slices of grapefruit; attach to sides of watermelon with tooth-picks and garnish with cherries. Garnish handle with ferns and fresh flowers.

## How to make a watermelon whale

Draw the shape of the whale's tail on the watermelon. Cut watermelon following your drawing. Scoop out watermelon flesh and set aside; leave shell at least 1 inch thick. Drain any excess liquid from opening. Cut a thin slice of rind out of front of melon for the smile, and smaller slices for eyebrows. For the eyes and nose, attach cherries with toothpicks. Cut watermelon flesh into cubes and return to basket. Make a small hole at the top of the whale; insert a bamboo spiral for the spout (available at florists). Add a piece of parsley at the base of the spout. Garnish side of whale with grapes.

# 4 • Meats on the Grill

# Meats on the Grill

◆◆◆

### FUN AT THE STADIUM: THINKING ON YOUR FEET EVEN WHEN FORGETTING YOUR LEGS

It is 10:00 a.m. We have just arrived to cater a party at the Milwaukee County Stadium, home of the Milwaukee Brewers, only to discover that we do not have grill legs for the grill. There is no time to go back to the shop, and I am short-handed. So I take two galvanized barrels that we brought to dump the hot coals in after grilling, and place one under each end of the grill. The president of the company we are serving approaches me, asks how things are going, and scrutinizes the work area. "Boy," he said, "you have an interesting setup. How come you have those barrels on each end of your grill?"

"Well, sir, you are having corn on the cob today. The ball park wants everything to be neat and tidy. I always want to please the boss at County Stadium. You know how that goes."

"Yeah, right! That is a very interesting concept," the president said.

"I think so," I replied. "It really works slick."

As the party gets going, the president returns to the grill. "You really are throwing the corn shucks into the barrels," he said. "Gee, that is a great idea! I'll have to try that the next time myself." "Thanks," I said as I smiled. "I'm glad you like my great idea."

### "GRILLIN' IN THE RAIN"

Once at an event we were caught in the rain unexpectedly and needed to make a cover for the grill. We took two 8-foot banquet tables and stacked one on top of the other. We used duct tape to tape two linen tablecloths across the top edge of the step van and taped the other end of the tablecloths to the 8-foot table. We managed to get the grilling done before it rained too hard. From then on I carried tarps when the weather threatened rain.

### TIP

You need to be prepared to adapt to any circumstance when you are catering off-premises. When I get a contract to do an off-site party I always find out where the closest grocery store is to the party location, so I can grab any last-minute ingredients if I run short.

### THE SHOW MUST GO ON

Another time, I drove from Milwaukee to Chicago to do a party. The packer had assured me that I had everything. Being the trusting type, I believed him. When I arrived, I discovered I had no grill top. The food had been brought to the party location and was to be cooked on-site. I took a quick inventory: I had large baking sheets, cooling racks and chafing dish bottoms that were solid. I used the baking sheets and cooling racks to cook on, then wrapped the bottoms of the chafing dish inserts with foil and placed them directly into the fire. With a little ingenuity, I managed to cook the food to perfection.

As a good caterer, you need to think on your feet and improvise if necessary. Stay cool and tell the hostess everything is wonderful. Just keep smiling because you have pulled off another successful party!

### PREPARING THE GRILL

The first thing to do is line the grill with three sheets of foil—one sheet of foil on each side and one piece down the center. Lining the grill preserves it and helps keep the grill bottom clean. Spread 30 pounds of charcoal on top of the foil in the grill. Douse the coals with charcoal lighter and light them. It takes about 30 minutes for the

coals to turn gray and get to cooking temperature.

When you're done cooking, pour water over the coals to extinguish the fire. Wrap the foil around the coals to meet in the center. Begin to roll up into a thick log. After the coals are rolled up, place the foil package into a metal container to carry back to your shop. (See diagram on page 83.) Make sure the can is not placed on fabric or carpet; the can will burn it.

# Grilling Various Meats

### BONE-IN CHICKEN

Cut whole chickens into quarters and bake skin side up, uncovered, at 350 degrees for 40 minutes. (Cooking chicken covered will steam it.) Line a hot box with foil and place baked chicken into it (40 pieces per hot box), cover with foil, and put on the lid. The precooked chicken is then grilled 12 to 15 minutes for showmanship and for the barbecued flavor. The larger the chicken, the longer it will take to cook.

Many guests do not want a big piece of chicken nor do they want to deal with bones, so it is a good idea to disjoint the thigh from the leg, making 6 pieces per chicken. A 5-ounce boneless breast can be made into a sandwich. I usually do half the chicken with barbecue sauce and half with seasoning salt. Picnickers like choices.

### PORK CHOPS

To prevent burning pork chops when grilling, raise the grill top or wait until coals are less hot.

### WHOLE BEEF TENDERLOIN

Three- to four-pound whole beef tenderloins should be grilled for 20-25 minutes. Place a thermometer in the center of the tenderloin. Cook to 120 degrees for rare, 140 degrees for medium and 160 degrees for well-done. When tenderloins are cooked in advance, they continue to cook in a hot box. It is best to cook to an internal temperature of 120 to 130 degrees. If you are going to precook the tenderloins I suggest that you do it at the party site for best results, as they taste better if cooked at the party.

### FRESH ITALIAN SAUSAGES

Thaw sausages if frozen and boil them in water for 20-30 minutes (the more you have in the pot, the longer it takes). Drain. Cool. Store in 4-inch deep full-size hotel pans. Finish sausages on the grill the day of the party and serve with Chef's Romantic Sauce for Italian Sausages (page 79).

### HOT DOGS

Inexpensive hot dogs sometimes blister. A 6-per-pound all-beef hot dog is my recommendation for taste and visual appeal.

### FRESH BRATWURST

One day before the party, place brats into hot water with 1 can of beer and 1 cup dehydrated onions per 60 brats. Boil for 20 minutes. Drain and refrigerate brats in a 4-inch deep half-size hotel pan. Grill the bratwurst at the party site. Place the cooked brats into a hotel pan with 2 inches of water and 1 can of beer. Lace brats with sauerkraut and serve hot.

(See illustration on page 84) Precooked bratwurst are just heated up on the grill at the party. Many customers request fresh bratwurst. It is to your advantage to serve a good brat, especially in Wisconsin.

## HAM STEAK

Place ham slices on the grill and cook on each side for about 5 minutes or until ham is heated through. Make sure the fire is not too hot. Ham can be cut ahead of time into half-pound portions; you can expect it to shrink somewhat on the grill. Slice meat 3/4 inch to 1 inch thick. If it's sliced too thinly, it will curl while it cooks.

## COUNTRY RIBS

Prepare ribs in the kitchen the day before and finish them on the grill at the party. Spread liquid smoke onto each rib. Place ribs onto a 4-inch deep hotel pan and add enough water to cover. Cover with foil and cook in the convection oven at 275 to 300 degrees for 2 to 3 hours or until tender. Forty to forty-five ribs will fit into a 4-inch deep full-size hotel pan. When ribs are tender and cooked through, drain off the liquid and refrigerate the ribs. After they are thoroughly cooled, pour barbecue sauce over them and marinate overnight. You can buy your favorite bottled barbecue sauce by the gallon at your local wholesale vendor or a warehouse foods company. One gallon will cover 60 quarter-pound country ribs. Heat up extra barbecue sauce at your shop or at the grill to take along to the picnic. When you are ready to grill, dip the ribs into the sauce and grill them for 8 to 10 minutes. Be sure to turn the ribs over 2 to 4 times (depending on the thickness of the ribs) so they cook evenly on both sides, and watch them carefully so they don't burn. Serve ribs with extra barbecue sauce on the side. Some of the guests will ask for extra sauce if they do not see it on the buffet line. You will need extra sauce for only half of the crowd. If time permits, make your own special sauce.

## BARBECUED PORK

Place a 10-pound pork loin on a roasting rack with the fat side up. Add 1 inch of water to the bottom of the pan. Pour 1 can of beer over the pork. Insert a meat thermometer and bake at 325 degrees until the thermometer registers 160 to 165 degrees (20 minutes per pound). Pork normally should be cooked to an internal temperature of 170 to 180 degrees; this pork loin is undercooked so that reheating won't dry it out. Refrigerate overnight. Slice the meat medium thinly. Place in a 4-inch deep full-size hotel pan. Cover the meat with barbecue sauce. On the day of the party, cover the meat with foil and bake at 350 degrees for about 1 hour or until meat is heated through and the barbecue sauce is piping hot and bubbly. A 4-inch deep half-size hotel pan holds 6 to 8 pounds of meat; a 4-inch deep full-size hotel pan holds 9 to 15 pounds.

## SHISH KABOBS

**VARIOUS MEATS AND VEGETABLES:** Using 2-ounce portions of venison, chicken breast or veal, assemble shish kabobs on metal skewers, alternating meat with chunks of onion, whole mushrooms and slices of green pepper, beginning and ending with meat. Grill the kabobs for 12 to 16 minutes or until the meat is completely cooked through. Brush with caramel coloring, then sprinkle with garlic salt or onion salt. To add color, place a cherry tomato at the end of each shish kabob after cooking. If the cherry tomato overcooks it may shrivel up and burst. Make sure chicken breast pieces are well done.

**ALL-MEAT BEEF TENDERLOIN SHISH KABOBS:** Place 4 to 5 cubes of beef tenderloin on each metal skewer. Brush with caramel coloring and sprinkle with onion salt or garlic salt. Marinate overnight. Cook on the grill for 10 to 18 minutes depending on how well done you want the meat.

**ALL-MEAT CHICKEN TENDER KABOBS:** Place four to five 2-ounce chicken tenders on each metal skewer. Brush with lime juice, then with soy sauce or teriyaki sauce. Roll each kabob in sesame seeds and marinate overnight. Grill for 15 to 20 minutes or until chicken pieces are thoroughly cooked.

## GRILLED STUFFED TROUT

I make these trout for small parties only; they are time-consuming but worth the effort. Use grill baskets if you have them so the trout will not fall apart. You can remove the heads before serving if your guests are squeamish.

>   3   whole trout (1 pound each)
> 1/2   cup plus 1 teaspoon lemon juice, divided
>  14   tablespoons butter, divided
> 11/4  teaspoons Old Bay seasoning, divided
> 1/2   teaspoon cracked pepper
> 1/8   teaspoon garlic seasoning
>   2   ounces sliced almonds
> 3/4   pound imitation crab, chopped
> 11/2  teaspoons crushed garlic
> 1/2   cup plain bread crumbs
> 3/4   teaspoon pasta seasoning
>   1   tablespoon prepared horseradish

Remove spine from each trout starting at the head. Remove as many of the small bones as possible. Rinse trout with 1/2 cup lemon juice mixed with 1/4 cup water; dry outsides only. In microwave, melt 6 tablespoons butter with 3/4 teaspoon Old Bay, pepper and garlic seasoning; spread inside each trout. Melt 1/4 cup butter in a skillet; saute almonds. Add crab, crushed garlic, bread crumbs, pasta seasoning and horseradish. Mix well and stuff each trout with mixture. Melt remaining 1/4 cup butter and add remaining 1 teaspoon lemon juice and 1/2 teaspoon Old Bay. Grill trout 4-6 inches from coals 20-30 minutes or until fish is cooked through, turning every 5-10 minutes and basting with lemon butter. Serve with extra lemon butter.

# Pig Roasts

Roasting a pig is very labor-intensive, but it makes a great display for a picnic and people seem to enjoy the novelty of seeing the pig on the spit.

There are many methods used for roasting a pig. When I first roasted one, I used a rotisserie with a stainless steel spit and cooked with charcoal. The meat turned on the rotisserie, but with the charcoal, it was a hard assignment to control the heat.

We searched for other alternatives and located someone with a gas cooker. He specialized in roasting pigs, and we knew we could trust him to be on time at the party with the roasted pig. He displayed the pig for the picnickers. People get very excited when they see this pig on a spit in this big piece of equipment. The gentleman made a cradle for the pig with nuts, bolts, and rods so when it traveled the rod cradle system would hold the pig inside the cradle and it would not fall apart. One rod went through the middle of the pig's entire body and connect from the end of the spoke to the other end. So there were two spokes, one coming through the mouth and one through the bottom of the pig. Four other rods connected on the outside of the pig to act as a cradle. The rod or the spit turns the pig while it is cooking.

The secret of a tender, tasty pig is slow cooking with gas. Be sure the grill hood is closed while cooking the pig. Gas is a cleaner and hotter heat than charcoal and cooks the pig more evenly. The pig roaster is portable and pulled on a trailer. These roasters can be rented.

Slide the pig onto the stainless steel rod and connect it to the rotisserie. Common seasonings are garlic salt, onion salt, celery salt, mesquite seasoning, pepper and salt. Have a spice company blend your favorite spices for you. Rub spices inside the cavity, poke the skin, and rub spices on the outside, or insert garlic cloves in slits in the skin. Prepare the pig on the spit. If you stuff the pig, sauerkraut and precooked brats are tasty. Do not stuff a pig with chickens; they won't brown, and they'll come out tasting more like pork than chicken.

IMPORTANT: Shut off the gas for the roaster as the pig travels. Arrive at least an hour before the party. Finish cooking the pig at the party site. For crispy skin, wet the skin with water during the last half hour of cooking. Put a thermometer into the pig in the front shoulder or ham part in the back. Make sure the thermometer in the meaty part of the pig, not touching a bone, to reach a correct temperature; it should be at least 170 degrees. If the pig is overcooked, just add water after carving it to moisten the meat; it will still be tasty.

## CARVING THE PIG

Season the pig with onion salt or salt and pepper as it is being cut. Take the skin off one side at a time. Next take the ribs out because this opens the cavity and cools down the pig somewhat. Cut the front first. The ham has more white meat. Put meat from the front and back in the same chafing dish. You can leave meat on the ribs or take it off depending on the customer's request. If you have an electric roaster make sure your picnic site has electricity. If you use a chafing dish use two sternos per chafing unit.

Another way to roast a pig is to cook it in a pit in the ground, but it takes longer to cook and someone has to attend to it constantly while it cooks. I had the opportunity to attend an elegant luau on the big island in Hawaii, where I witnessed the pig roasting in a pit. In

Hawaii they do pigs over hot coals and cover it with palm leaves.

There is a lot of waste on a pig. A 50-pound pig, for example, yields only 8 to 10 pounds of meat. Cooking a 150-pound pig is more cost-effective than cooking three 50-pound pigs. The larger the pig the more meat it yields.

One 4-inch deep full-size hotel pan will hold all the cooked meat from a 50-pound pig, about 10 pounds.

**Packing list for a pig roast:** Apron, gloves, warm water, soap, cutting board (NSF approved), sharp butcher knife, extra seasoning, and an electric roaster or chafing dishes.

## COOKING TIME CHART FOR PIG ROASTING

| Size | Gas Cooker Method | In-Ground Method | Yield of Meat | Servings |
|---|---|---|---|---|
| 50 lbs. | 4 1/2-5 hours | 6 hours | 20% (8-10 lbs.) | 25-30 |
| 100 lbs. | 6 1/2-7 hours | 10 hours | 45% (45 lbs.) | 90 |
| 150 lbs. | 8 1/2-9 hours | 12-13 hours | 45% (67 lbs.) | 130 |
| 200 lbs. | 12-13 hours | 15-18 hours | 45% (90 lbs.) | 180 |
| 250 lbs. | 15 hours | 22-24 hours | 45% (112 lbs.) | 220 |

# Grilling Other Meats on a Spit

ROUND OF BEEF: Inside round can be 18-23 pounds. Boneless inside rounds takes 3 1/2-4 hours. Figure 1/2 pound per person. Rub the meat with caramel coloring and onion salt. Spear the rod through the center. Hold down with three rods because it is easier to handle. A 40- to 50-pound steamship round cooks for 7 hours to a temperature of 140 degrees with the spoke gas method.

CHICKEN: 10-12 chickens at 3 pounds each can go on each spit. Season chickens with paprika and seasoned salt. The gas cooker will cook 100 chickens at a time. Each chicken will yield 6 pieces. Figure 1-1 1/2 hours to complete the chickens.

LAMB: Figure 1/2 pound of lamb per person. Two 50-pound lambs will serve 100 people. It takes 6 hours to cook one 50-pound lamb. Rub garlic and onion salt over the body of the lamb. Cook until interior temperature reaches 170 degrees. Remove the thin skin. Cut the front shoulder first and then the hind. The hind has more meat. Serve with mint jelly, dill sauce, or creamy cucumber sauce. You can purchase mint jelly in 4-pound jars. Place 1-ounce souffle cups with mint jelly on a tray and serve on the side next to the lamb on the buffet line.

# Sauces and Condiments

### Homemade Barbecue Sauce
*Yield: 12 servings*
*Cooking time: 30 minutes*

1  bottle (1 pound 12 ounces) catsup
1/4  teaspoon black pepper
1  onion, finely diced
1/2  cup finely diced green bell pepper
1  cup water
1/3  cup lemon juice
1/3  cup brown sugar
1  teaspoon Worcestershire sauce

*Yield: 1 gallon*
*Cooking time: 1 hour*

1  gallon catsup
1/2  teaspoon black pepper
2  onions, finely diced
1  green bell pepper, finely diced
3  cups water
2/3  cup lemon juice
2/3  cup brown sugar
1  tablespoon Worcestershire sauce

In a large stockpot pour catsup; add black pepper, onions, green pepper, water, lemon juice, brown sugar and Worcestershire sauce. Cook over low heat for length of time indicated, stirring occasionally. If you want a thicker barbecue sauce, reduce water. One gallon serves 50 people if used on the side.

### Chef's Romantic Sauce for Italian Sausages
*Yield: 35-40 servings*

1  No. 10 can (6 pounds 8 ounces) tomato sauce
1  tablespoon Italian seasoning
1  teaspoon garlic powder
1  teaspoon onion powder
2  medium onions, sliced
2  green bell peppers (1 pound each), cut into strips

Mix tomato sauce with Italian seasoning, garlic powder, onion powder, onions, and green pepper. Cook over low heat for 1 hour; cool. Pour sauce over cooked, cooled Italian sausages. To save time use a No. 10 can of seasoned pizza sauce (6 pounds 8 ounces) and add just the green peppers and onions (no seasonings).

### Creamy Dill Sauce
*Yield: 3/4 cup — 6-8 servings*

1/4  cup mayonnaise
1/2  cup sour cream
1/2  teaspoon dried dill
1/2  teaspoon Worcestershire sauce
1  teaspoon lemon juice
1/2  teaspoon garlic powder

Mix together mayonnaise, sour cream, dill, Worcestershire sauce, lemon juice, and garlic powder. Make one day in advance for the flavors to blend.

### Creamy Cucumber Sauce

*Yield: 4 1/2 cups (eighteen 2-ounce servings)*

- 2 medium cucumbers, peeled, seeded, and diced
- 4 cups sour cream
- 1/2 teaspoon black pepper
- 1 teaspoon Worcestershire sauce
- 1/2 teaspoon onion powder
- 1/2 teaspoon garlic powder

Place the cucumbers into a kitchen towel, squeeze out any excess moisture, and place in a bowl. Add sour cream, pepper, Worcestershire, onion powder and garlic powder and mix well. Make one day ahead to blend flavors. Serve with lamb, or with raw vegetables or whole-grain crackers. You may use nonfat sour cream instead of regular sour cream.

You can purchase pre-made cucumber sauce in your grocery store; however, I like the homemade sauce better.

# Condiments

Fixings are an important part of making a scrumptious sandwich at a picnic. The following items are usually carried to any picnic: Catsup, yellow mustard, brown mustard, gourmet mustard (optional), mayonnaise, diced onions, sliced tomatoes, sliced lettuce, sweet pickle relish, dill pickle relish, dill pickle slices, and margarine or butter. A basic condiment setup is catsup, yellow mustard, and mayonnaise. Catsup is the number one condiment in the Midwest with hamburgers, bratwurst, or hot dogs. Bring at least two if not three catsup packets per person. While there are numerous styles of mustards, yellow mustard is the most widely used at a picnic. Use packets to insure good sanitation.

For large parties purchase diced and sliced onions prepared for use in 5-pound bags; one bag will serve 100 people. Not every person will take onions.

Buy cheese slices in 5-pound packages. The package has markings to show where to cut the cheese slice. If you run short of cheese cut the cheese slices in half diagonally. Put the cheese on the hamburgers and melt. Or arrange cheese slices on a tray and place on the buffet line. You will save cheese by putting the cheese on the hamburger at the guest's request. However you will not save time and it isn't feasible when serving a very large party.

Slice lettuce on the meat slicer. One head of lettuce will serve 20 people, for not every guest will take lettuce. Dip lettuce in whitener before slicing. If you slice lettuce the day of the party you may be able to get by without the whitener.

For tomatoes allow 1 slice per customer. Use 1/2-pound tomatoes, 8 slices per tomato. The problem of buying pre-sliced tomatoes is that they may not be fresh; you would be taking a chance. I always prefer slicing my own tomatoes. The meat slicer will make the job go quickly and will guarantee neat, even slices.

About 20 out of 100 people take mayonnaise at a picnic. Since more publicity is given to eating less fat many people will not choose mayonnaise for their sandwiches.

# Miscellaneous Grill Information

## CONDIMENTS IN INDIVIDUAL PACKETS

Catsup — 1000 per case

Mayonnaise — 200 per case

Yellow mustard — 500 per case

Brown mustard — 200 per case

Pickle relish — 200 per case

Margarine — 900 individual serving cups
   per case

Butter — 500 individual pats per case

## NUMBER OF PIECES OF MEAT PER BOX

Hamburgers — 40 quarter-pounders to a
   10-pound box

Hot dogs — 60 to a 10-pound box

1/4-pound hot dogs — 40 to a 10-pound box

Italian sausages and brats — 38-40 to a
   10-pound box

5-ounce chicken breasts — about 30 to a
   10-pound box

Cut-up chickens — 40-50 pounds per box
(Order as many chicken as you need and have
the meat vendor cut them into quarters or
according to your specifications.)

## WHAT WILL FIT IN A 4-INCH-DEEP FULL-SIZE HOTEL PAN

Hamburgers (1/4 lb.) — 60

Italian sausages (1/4 lb.) — 80

New York strip steaks (1/2 lb.) — 35-40

Porterhouse steaks (1 lb.) — 24-30

Pork chops (1/4 lb.) — 45-50

Chicken breasts (1/4 lb.) — 60-70

Tenderloin steaks (1/4 lb.) — 60-70

Quartered chickens, bone-in — 40-50 quarters

## COOKING TIME ON THE GRILL

Hamburgers — 12-15 minutes

Hot dogs (1/4 lb.) — 4-6 minutes

Hot dogs (2 oz.) — 2-3 minutes

Fresh Italian sausages, pre-boiled — 15 minutes

Fresh bratwurst, pre-boiled — 15 minutes

Precooked brats — 6-8 minutes

New York strips (1/2 lb.)— 12-15 minutes
   (medium-rare)

New York strips (1/2 lb.) — 18-20 minutes
   (well-done)

Chicken breasts (1/4 lb.) — 15-20 minutes

Cooking time on the grill will vary depending
on how hot the coals are and where the food is
positioned on the grill.

## HOW MUCH FITS ON A 2 X 5-FOOT COMMERCIAL GRILL

40 hamburgers (1/4 lb. each)

60 all-beef hot dogs (6 per lb.)

50-55 brats (1/4 lb. each)

50-55 Italian sausages (1/4 lb. each)

20 porterhouse steaks (1 lb. each)

40 pork chops (1/4 lb. each)

40 boneless chicken breasts (1/4 lb. each)

### TIP

Be sure to carry containers of water to your
outdoor party. You cannot rely on getting
water at a park or zoo or in an open field. Be
prepared with your own water.

# A Grill Packing List

NAME OF CLIENT _____

NUMBER TO BE SERVED _____ DATE OF PARTY _____

DEPARTURE TIME_____ CHINA _____ or PAPER PRODUCTS _____

_____ MATCHES (1 BOX)

_____ GRILL FIREBOX AND GRID

_____ EXTRA HOT BOX

_____ GRILL TOP AND LEGS

_____ CHARCOAL (30 POUNDS PER GRILL)

_____ CHARCOAL LIGHTER

_____ METAL TRASH CAN (1 SMALL PER GRILL)

_____ SHOVEL FOR COALS

_____ LEATHER (WELDING) GLOVES

_____ TONGS, SPATULA, FORK USED ON THE GRILL (1-2 SETS PER GRILL)

_____ HOT PADS (MITTENS)

_____ FOIL (18" HEAVY DUTY)

_____ FULL SIZE HOTEL PANS 4" DEEP AND LIDS (PER GRILL)

_____ HALF-SIZE HOTEL PANS AND LIDS

_____ QUARTER-SIZE PANS (FOR SEASONING HAMBURGERS)
OR BAIN MARIE WITH INSERT (FOR BUTTER FOR CORN ROAST)

_____ PASTRY BRUSH

_____ A.1 STEAK SAUCE

_____ PORTION CUPS (BARBECUE SAUCE)

_____ EXTRA PAN FOR BARBECUE SAUCE

_____ BARBECUE SAUCE

_____ EXTRA KETCHUP, MUSTARD AND RELISH

_____ SOY SAUCE

_____ METAL SALT AND PEPPER (FOR BACKUP ONLY) SHAKERS (2 SETS)

_____ ONION OR GARLIC SALT

_____ 1-POUND BLOCKS OF BUTTER (FOR CORN ROAST)

_____ PAPER TOWELS

_____ MOIST TOWELETTES (DOZEN)

_____ WASH CLOTH

_____ GARBAGE BAGS (2-6)

_____ JAR AND LID FOR SPRINKLING WATER ON FLAMES (1 PER GRILL)

_____ SQUARE TABLE AND PLASTIC TABLE COVER

_____ WATER JUG WITH ICE WATER (1 PER GRILLING TABLE, FOR WORKERS)

_____ BROCHURES (6-12 IN AN ENVELOPE; USE FOR ADVERTISING)

Use this list to help you prepare for packing for a catered picnic with grilled food. This list will help you remember every item necessary for your picnic.

How to clean up the grill (page 74)

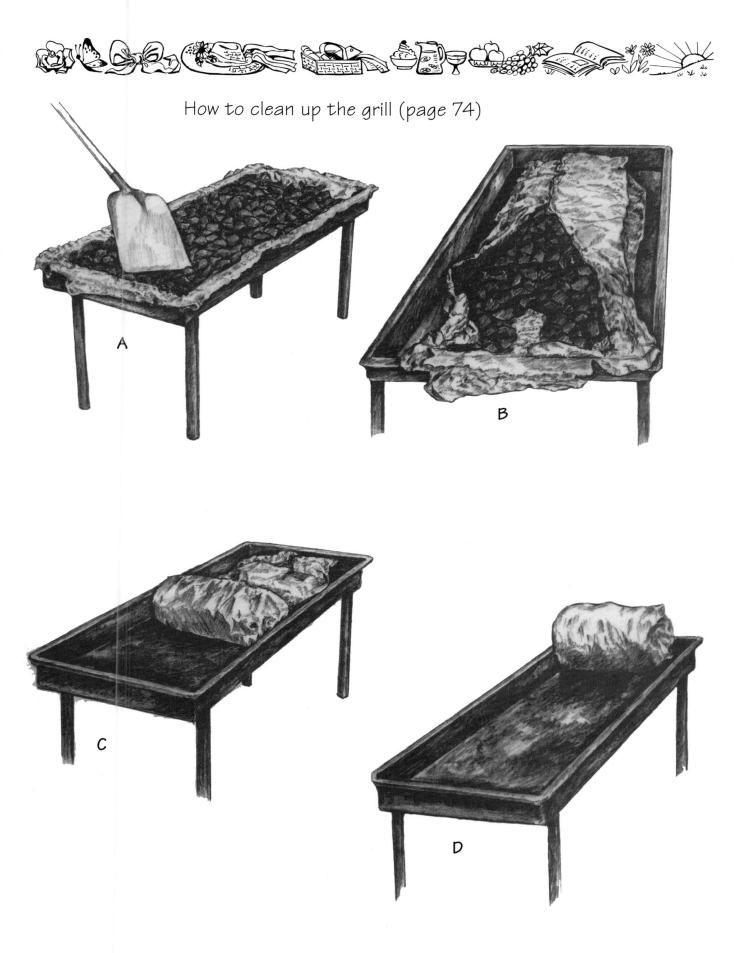

A

B

C

D

How to serve bratwurst and
sauerkraut (page 75)

# 5 ◆ Hot Vegetables

# Hot Vegetables

## POPULAR, VERSATILE AND INEXPENSIVE

Baked beans are served at picnics throughout the United States. It's been my observation that some guests will really load up their plates while other guests will say, "Hold the beans, please." When I was a youngster Mom made baked beans so frequently that it took me a long time to decide to eat them again as an adult. Baked beans are served at most casual picnics.

Each region has a different version of how baked beans should be prepared. In the South, people tend to like baked beans to be drier, while Northerners like more sauce. When catering a party it is fun to try various styles of baked beans. The most common baked bean recipe is called Old-Fashioned Baked Beans.

You can purchase baked beans with brown sugar or onion, and also heat-and-serve baked beans. Heat-and-serve baked beans, with bacon and brown sugar already included, are the least expensive to prepare. Plain canned baked beans are relatively inexpensive and can taste homemade when extra seasonings are added. Many caterers will take a plain can of baked beans and add their own personal touch. So be creative when making baked beans.

Suggest different baked bean recipes to your customers for various theme parties—calico beans for a Red, White and Blue picnic, for example. Many young children do not like baked beans; they are more popular with adults. Baked beans go a long way—remember, 1 pound serves 5 people.

Keep in mind that extra ingredients, such as bacon, hamburger, sausage, hot dogs and fresh vegetables, add to the cost. If you are catering a picnic where you need to keep costs low, use only the heat-and-serve baked beans. Other types, such as calico beans, are more expensive

### ◆◆◆
### TIPS

◆ Baked beans do not have do be measured exactly.

◆ Buy high quality canned baked beans and "doctor them up." They will taste better than with less expensive canned baked beans.

◆ If baked beans are cooked at too high a temperature they will burn or turn to mush. Do not freeze baked beans in quantity, as this also will cause the beans to turn to mush.

◆ To make baked beans in quantity in an assembly line: Line up pans and put 2 No. 10 cans into each 4-inch deep full-size hotel pan. After all the beans are in the pans go from pan to pan and add the seasonings. Mix all the ingredients well.

to prepare.

The Swedish baked bean dish is unusual. Because it is so different many people have to be coaxed to try this dish; it's best served with a regional picnic theme. Many people just like good down-to-earth wholesome and simple picnic food and plenty of it.

A 4-inch deep half-size hotel pan will hold 7-10 pounds of baked beans. A 4-inch deep full-size pan will hold 14-21 pounds of baked beans (up to 3 No. 10 cans). A disposable full-size aluminum pan will hold up to 10 pounds of baked beans. A disposable half-size aluminum pan will hold up to 7 pounds of baked beans.

# Barbecued Baked Beans

*Yield: 15 servings — one 9x13x2-inch pan*
*Cooking time: 20-30 minutes*

1 can (3 pounds 5 ounces) baked beans
1/2 cup diced onions
1/4 cup diced green bell pepper
1/4 cup diced celery
2 tablespoons brown sugar
1/4 cup spicy barbecue sauce
3/4 pound hot dogs, sliced
1 tablespoon yellow mustard

*Yield: 30 servings — 4-inch deep half-size pan*
*Cooking time: 45 minutes*

1 No. 10 can (7 pounds 3 ounces)
   baked beans
1/4 cup diced onions
1/2 cup diced green bell pepper
1/2 cup diced celery
1/4 cup brown sugar
1/2 cup spicy barbecue sauce
1 pound hot dogs, sliced
2 tablespoons yellow mustard

*Yield: 70 servings — 4-inch deep full-size pan*
*Cooking time: 55 minutes*

2 No. 10 cans (7 pounds 3 ounces each)
   baked beans
1 cup diced onions
1 cup diced green bell pepper
3/4 cup diced celery
1/3 cup brown sugar
1 1/2 cups spicy barbecue sauce
1 1/2 pounds hot dogs, sliced
3 tablespoons yellow mustard

*Yield: 100 servings — 4-inch deep full-size pan*
*Cooking time: 66 minutes*

3 No. 10 cans (7 pounds 3 ounces each)
   baked beans
1 1/2 cups diced onions
1 cup diced green bell pepper
1 cup diced celery
2/3 cup brown sugar
2 cups spicy barbecue sauce
2 pounds hot dogs, sliced
1/4 cup yellow mustard

Preheat oven to 350 degrees. Combine baked beans with onions, green pepper, celery, brown sugar, barbecue sauce, hot dogs, and mustard. (Skip the brown sugar if canned baked beans contain it already.) Cover with foil and bake for length of time indicated until bubbly.

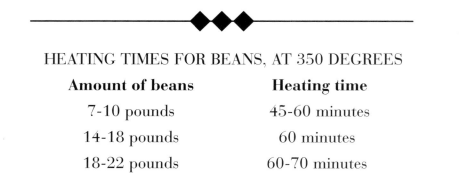

## HEATING TIMES FOR BEANS, AT 350 DEGREES

| Amount of beans | Heating time |
| --- | --- |
| 7-10 pounds | 45-60 minutes |
| 14-18 pounds | 60 minutes |
| 18-22 pounds | 60-70 minutes |

# Calico Baked Beans

*Yield: 25 servings*
*Cooking time: 30-35 minutes*

1 can (15.8 ounces) great Northern beans, drained and rinsed
1 can (15 ounces) lima beans, drained and rinsed
1 can (15 ounces) pinto beans, drained and rinsed
1 can (28 ounces) baked beans
1 pound ground beef
1/2 pound bacon
1/3 cup diced onions
1/4 cup brown sugar
1/2 cup catsup
1 tablespoon vinegar
1 tablespoon yellow mustard

*Yield: 50 servings*
*Cooking time: 30-35 minutes*

2 cans (15.8 ounces each) great Northern beans, drained and rinsed
2 cans (15 ounces each) lima beans, drained and rinsed
2 cans (15 ounces each) pinto beans, drained and rinsed
1 can (3 pounds 5 ounces) baked beans
2 pounds ground beef
1 pound bacon
3/4 cup diced onions
1/2 cup brown sugar
1 cup catsup
2 tablespoons vinegar
2 tablespoons yellow mustard

*Yield: 90 servings*
*Cooking time: 55-60 minutes*

3 cans (15.8 ounces each) great Northern beans, drained and rinsed
3 cans (15 ounces each) lima beans, drained and rinsed
3 cans (15 ounces each) pinto beans, drained and rinsed
1 No. 10 can (7 pounds 3 ounces) baked beans
3 pounds ground beef
1 1/2 pounds bacon
2 cups diced onions
3/4 cup brown sugar
1 3/4 cups catsup
3 tablespoons vinegar
3 tablespoons yellow mustard

*Yield: 150 servings*
*Cooking time: 55-60 minutes*

4 cans (15.8 ounces each) great Northern beans, drained and rinsed
4 cans (15 ounces each) lima beans, drained and rinsed
4 cans (15 ounces each) pinto beans, drained and rinsed
2 No. 10 cans (7 pounds 3 ounces each) baked beans
4 pounds ground beef
2 pounds bacon
3 cups diced onions
1 cup brown sugar
2 1/2 cups catsup
1/4 cup vinegar
1/4 cup yellow mustard

Preheat oven to 350 degrees. Combine Northern, lima, pinto, and baked beans. In a skillet brown ground beef; drain and set aside. In the same skillet, cook bacon until crisp. Drain bacon and crumble; set aside. Preheat oven to 350 degrees. Cook onions in bacon drippings in skillet. Drain. Add beef, bacon, onions, brown sugar, catsup, vinegar and mustard to beans. Place beans in baking pans and cover with foil. Bake for length of time indicated or until bubbly.

# Boston Baked Beans

*Yield: 15 servings*
*Cooking time: 25-35 minutes covered,*
*then 15 minutes uncovered*

| | |
|---|---|
| 1 | teaspoon dry mustard |
| 2 | tablespoons catsup |
| 2 | tablespoons barbecue sauce |
| 2 | tablespoons brown sugar |
| 1/4 | cup diced onions |
| 1 | can (3 pounds 5 ounces) baked beans |
| 6 | slices bacon |

*Yield: 30 servings*
*Cooking time: 45-50 minutes covered,*
*then 15 minutes uncovered*

| | |
|---|---|
| 2 | teaspoons dry mustard |
| 1/4 | cup catsup |
| 1/4 | cup barbecue sauce |
| 1/4 | cup brown sugar |
| 1/2 | cup diced onions |
| 1 | No. 10 can (7 pounds 3 ounces) baked beans |
| 6 | slices bacon |

*Yield: 70 servings*
*Cooking time: 40-45 minutes covered,*
*then 15 minutes uncovered*

| | |
|---|---|
| 2 1/2 | teaspoons dry mustard |
| 1/2 | cup catsup |
| 1/2 | cup barbecue sauce |
| 1/2 | cup brown sugar |
| 1/2 | cup diced onions |
| 2 | No. 10 cans (7 pounds 3 ounces each) baked beans |
| 10 | slices bacon |

*Yield: 100 servings*
*Cooking time: 55-60 minutes covered,*
*then 15 minutes uncovered*

| | |
|---|---|
| 1 | tablespoon dry mustard |
| 3/4 | cup catsup |
| 3/4 | cup barbecue sauce |
| 3/4 | cup brown sugar |
| 1 | cup diced onions |
| 3 | No. 10 cans (7 pounds 3 ounces each) baked beans |
| 12 | slices bacon |

Preheat oven to 350 degrees. Combine mustard, catsup, barbecue sauce, brown sugar and onions with baked beans. Place into baking pan(s) and arrange bacon strips across the top. Cover with foil and bake for the length of time indicated. Remove foil and continue baking as indicated until bacon is crisp.

◆ ◆ ◆

## BAKED BEAN TIPS

◆ A pound of beans serves 5. So the number of pounds of beans used in each recipe multiplied by 5 will give you the approximate number of servings.

◆ Make beans on the day of the party if time permits.

◆ It will take 10 to 15 minutes longer to heat the baked beans at 300 degrees than at 350 degrees.

◆ Start beans at room temperature to expedite heating time.

# Cattle Ranch Beans

*Yield: 15 servings*
*Cooking time: 30-35 minutes*
1 can (53 ounces) baked beans
1 tablespoon yellow mustard
1/2 cup hickory-smoked barbecue sauce
2 tablespoons brown sugar
1 teaspoon Worcestershire sauce
2 tablespoons diced onion

*Yield: 30 servings*
*Cooking time: 35-40 minutes*
1 No. 10 can (7 pounds 3 ounces) baked beans
2 tablespoons yellow mustard
1 cup hickory-smoked barbecue sauce
1/4 cup brown sugar
2 teaspoons Worcestershire sauce
1/4 cup diced onions

*Yield: 70 servings*
*Cooking time: 45-55 minutes*
2 No. 10 cans (7 pounds 3 ounces each) baked beans
1/3 cup yellow mustard
2 cups hickory-smoked barbecue sauce
1/2 cup brown sugar
1 tablespoon Worcestershire sauce
1/2 cup diced onions

*Yield: 100 servings*
*Cooking time: 65-75 minutes*
3 No. 10 cans (7 pounds 3 ounces each) baked beans
1/2 cup yellow mustard
3 cups hickory-smoked barbecue sauce
1/2 cup brown sugar
4 teaspoons Worcestershire sauce
2 small onions, diced

Preheat oven to 350 degrees. Combine baked beans, mustard, barbecue sauce, brown sugar, Worcestershire sauce and onions. Pour into baking pan and cover with foil. Bake for length of time indicated or until bubbly.

# Five-Bean Casserole

*Yield: 30 servings*
*Cooking time: 25-35 minutes*
1 can (31 ounces) baked beans
1 can (15 ounces) lima beans, drained and rinsed
1 can (15 ounces) garbanzo beans, drained and rinsed
1 can (15.8 ounces) great Northern beans, drained and rinsed
1 can (15 1/2 ounces) butter beans with molasses and bacon, undrained
1 tablespoon yellow mustard
1/4 cup catsup
1 teaspoon Worcestershire sauce
2 tablespoons molasses
1/4 teaspoon onion powder
1/4 teaspoon garlic powder
8 slices bacon
1 medium onion, sliced
5 tablespoons brown sugar
1/3 cup vinegar
1 tablespoon flour

*Continued on next page*

*Five-Bean Casserole, continued*

### Yield: 50 servings
### Cooking time: 30-40 minutes

2 cans (31 ounces each) baked beans
2 cans (15 ounces each) lima beans, drained and rinsed
2 cans (15 ounces each) garbanzo beans, drained and rinsed
2 cans (15.8 ounces each) great Northern beans, drained and rinsed
2 cans (15 1/2 ounces each) butter beans with molasses and bacon, undrained
2 tablespoons yellow mustard
1/2 cup catsup
2 teaspoons Worcestershire sauce
1/4 cup molasses
1/2 teaspoon onion powder
1/2 teaspoon garlic powder
1 pound bacon
3 small onions, sliced
2/3 cup brown sugar
2/3 cup vinegar
2 tablespoons flour

### Yield: 90 servings
### Cooking time: 45-50 minutes

1 can (3 pounds 7 ounces) baked beans
1 can (1 pound 4 ounces) baked beans
3 cans (15 ounces each) lima beans, drained and rinsed
3 cans (16 ounces each) garbanzo beans, drained and rinsed
3 cans (15.8 ounces each) great Northern beans, drained and rinsed
3 cans (15 1/2 ounces each) butter beans with molasses and bacon, undrained
3 tablespoons yellow mustard
3/4 cup catsup
1 tablespoon Worcestershire sauce
6 tablespoons molasses
3/4 teaspoon onion powder
3/4 teaspoon garlic powder
1 1/2 pounds bacon
3 1/2 small onions, sliced
1 cup brown sugar
1 cup vinegar
3 tablespoons flour

### Yield: 120 servings
### Cooking time: 55-60 minutes

1 can (3 pound 5 ounces) baked beans
1 can (1 pound 15 ounces) baked beans
4 cans (15 ounces each) lima beans, drained and rinsed
4 cans (16 ounces each) kidney beans, drained and rinsed
4 cans (15.8 ounces each) great Northern beans, drained and rinsed
4 cans (15 1/2 ounces each) butter beans with molasses and bacon, undrained
1/4 cup yellow mustard
1 cup catsup
4 teaspoons Worcestershire sauce
1/2 cup molasses
1 teaspoon onion powder
1 teaspoon garlic powder
2 pounds bacon
4 small onions, sliced
1 1/3 cups brown sugar
1 1/3 cups vinegar
1/4 cup flour

Preheat oven to 350 degrees. Combine baked, lima, garbanzo, great Northern and butter beans, mustard, catsup, Worcestershire, molasses, onion powder and garlic powder. In a skillet, cook bacon until crisp; drain and crumble. Cook onions in bacon grease until transparent; set aside. Add sugar, vinegar and flour to fat in skillet. Whisk over medium heat or until sauce is smooth and creamy, 5-6 minutes. Stir sauce into beans; add bacon and onions. Pour into baking pan(s) and cover with foil. Bake for length of time indicated.

# Hearty Pork 'n' Beans

*Yield: 15 servings*
*Cooking time: 35-45 minutes*

1/2 pound hot dogs
3/4 pound ground beef
5 slices bacon, diced
1 can (53 ounces) pork & beans
1/4 cup diced onion
1/4 cup barbecue sauce
1/4 cup catsup
1 tablespoons yellow mustard
2 tablespoons brown sugar
1 teaspoon Worcestershire sauce

*Yield: 50 servings*
*Cooking time:  35-45 minutes*

1 pound hot dogs
1 pound ground beef
3/4 pound bacon, diced
1 No. 10 can (7 pounds 3 ounces) pork & beans
1/2 cup diced onions
1/2 cup barbecue sauce
1/2 cup catsup
2 tablespoons yellow mustard
1/3 cup brown sugar
2 teaspoons Worcestershire sauce

*Yield: 80 servings*
*Cooking time: 45-50 minutes*

11/2 pounds hot dogs
13/4 pounds ground beef
1 pound bacon, diced
2 No. 10 cans (7 pounds 3 ounces each) pork & beans
3/4 cup diced onions
3/4 cup barbecue sauce
3/4 cup catsup
3 tablespoons yellow mustard
1/2 cup brown sugar
1 tablespoon Worcestershire sauce

*Yield: 120 servings*
*Cooking time: 55-65 minutes*

2 pounds hot dogs
21/4 pounds ground beef
11/2 pounds bacon, diced
3 No. 10 cans (7 pounds 3 ounces each) pork & beans
1 cup diced onions
11/4 cups barbecue sauce
11/4 cups catsup
1/4 cup yellow mustard
3/4 cup brown sugar
4 teaspoons Worcestershire sauce

Preheat oven to 350 degrees. Slice hot dogs 1/4-inch thick. Brown ground beef in a skillet until cooked through; drain. In the same skillet, cook bacon until crisp. Drain. Combine pork & beans with hot dogs, ground beef, and bacon. Stir in onions, barbecue sauce, catsup, mustard, brown sugar, and Worcestershire. Place mixture into baking pan(s). Cover with foil and bake for length of time indicated or until bubbly.

# Grandma's Salt Pork Baked Beans

*Yield: 8 servings*

1 pound dried navy beans
1 1/2 quarts cold water
1 teaspoon salt
1/3 cup brown sugar

1/4 cup molasses
1 cup catsup
1 tablespoon yellow mustard
1/4 pound salt pork
1 medium onion, sliced

Rinse beans. Add to cold water in stockpot. Bring to a boil; reduce heat and simmer 2 minutes. Remove from heat, cover, and let stand 1 hour. (Or add beans to cold water and let soak overnight).

Add salt to beans and soaking water; cover, and simmer about 1 hour. Drain beans, reserving cooking liquid. Add water, if necessary, to make 1 3/4 cups. Preheat oven to 300 degrees. Combine reserved liquid with brown sugar, molasses, catsup and mustard. Cut salt pork in half. Score one half of salt pork and slice remainder thinly. In a 2-quart bean pot or casserole, alternate layers of beans, onions and sliced salt pork. Top with scored piece of salt pork. Pour reserved liquid over beans and pork. Cover; bake for 5 to 7 hours. Add more liquid partway through cooking if beans appear dry.

◆◆◆

# Southwestern Baked Beans

◆◆◆

### TIP

◆ If brown sugar has already been added to the canned baked beans, omit it from the Southwestern recipe.

*Yield: 30 servings*
*Cooking time: 45-50 minutes*

1 can (31 ounces) baked beans
1 can (15 1/2 ounces) butter beans with molasses and bacon, undrained
1 can (15 ounces) lima beans, drained and rinsed
1 can (16 ounces) dark red kidney beans, drained and rinsed
1 can (15.8 ounces) great Northern beans, drained and rinsed
1 teaspoon Worcestershire sauce

2 tablespoons brown sugar
1/2 pound bacon
1 medium onion, sliced
1/2 cup catsup
1 tablespoons molasses
1/2 teaspoon onion powder
1/4 teaspoon garlic powder
1 tablespoon yellow mustard
1 teaspoon Southwestern spice
1 teaspoon cumin

*Continued on next page*

*Southwestern Beans, continued*

### Yield: 50-55 servings
### Cooking time: 45-50 minutes

1 can (53 ounces) baked beans
2 cans (15½ ounces each) butter beans with molasses and bacon, undrained
2 cans (15 ounces each) lima beans, drained and rinsed
2 cans (16 ounces each) dark red kidney beans, drained and rinsed
2 cans (15.8 ounces each) great Northern beans, drained and rinsed
1½ teaspoons Worcestershire sauce
¼ cup brown sugar
1 pound bacon
2 medium onions, sliced
1 cup catsup
2 tablespoons molasses
1 teaspoon onion powder
½ teaspoon garlic powder
2 tablespoons yellow mustard
2 teaspoons Southwestern spice
2 teaspoons cumin

### Yield: 90 servings
### Cooking time: 50-55 minutes

1 No. 10 can (7 pounds 3 ounces) baked beans
3 cans (15½ ounces each) butter beans with molasses and bacon, undrained
3 cans (15 ounces each) lima beans, drained and rinsed
3 cans (16 ounces each) dark red kidney beans, drained and rinsed
3 cans (15.8 ounces each) great Northern beans, drained and rinsed

2 teaspoons Worcestershire sauce
6 tablespoons brown sugar
2½ pounds bacon
3 small onions, sliced
1½ cups catsup
¼ cup molasses
1½ teaspoons onion powder
1 teaspoon garlic powder
3 tablespoons yellow mustard
1 tablespoon Southwestern spice
1 tablespoon cumin

### Yield: 150 servings
### Cooking time: 45-50 minutes

2 No. 10 cans (7 pound 3 ounces each) baked beans
4 cans (15½ ounces each) butter beans with molasses and bacon, undrained
4 cans (15 ounces each) lima beans, drained and rinsed
4 cans (16 ounces each) dark red kidney beans, drained and rinsed
4 cans (15.8 ounces each) great Northern beans, drained and rinsed
2 tablespoons Worcestershire sauce
⅔ cup brown sugar
3 pounds bacon
4 small onions, sliced
2½ cups catsup
6 tablespoons molasses
2 teaspoons onion powder
1½ teaspoons garlic powder
5 tablespoons yellow mustard
4 teaspoons Southwestern spice
4 teaspoons cumin

Preheat oven to 350 degrees. Combine baked, butter, lima, kidney and great Northern beans, Worcestershire and brown sugar. Dice bacon and cook in skillet until crisp. Remove bacon and drain. Cook onions in bacon grease until transparent; drain. Add bacon, onions, catsup, molasses, onion powder, garlic powder, mustard, Southwestern spice and cumin to beans. Pour into baking pan (use 2 pans for 150 servings) and cover with foil. Bake for length of time indicated or until bubbly.

# Old-Fashioned Baked Beans

### Yield: 15 servings
### Cooking time: 25-30 minutes

1 can (53 ounces) baked beans
1 tablespoon yellow mustard
1/2 cup catsup
2 tablespoons molasses
2 tablespoons brown sugar
3 tablespoons diced onion
1 teaspoon Worcestershire sauce, optional

### Yield: 30 servings
### Cooking time: 35 minutes

1 No. 10 can (7 pounds 3 ounces) baked beans
2 tablespoons yellow mustard
3/4 cup catsup
3 tablespoons molasses
1/4 cup brown sugar
1/4 cup diced onions
2 teaspoons Worcestershire sauce, optional

### Yield: 70 servings
### Cooking time: 35-45 minutes

2 No. 10 cans (7 pounds 3 ounces each) baked beans
3 tablespoons yellow mustard
1 1/2 cups catsup
1/4 cup molasses
1/3 cup brown sugar
1/3 cup diced onions
3 teaspoons Worcestershire sauce, optional

### Yield: 100 servings
### Cooking time: 55-60 minutes

3 No. 10 cans (7 pounds 3 ounces each) baked beans
1/4 cup yellow mustard
2 cups catsup
1/3 cup molasses
1/2 cup brown sugar
1/2 cup diced onions
4 teaspoons Worcestershire sauce, optional

Combine beans with mustard, catsup, molasses, brown sugar, onions and Worcestershire. Place beans into baking pans; cover with foil. Bake for length of time indicated or until bubbly.

# Stovetop Franks 'n' Beans

### Yield: 15 servings

1 can (53 ounces) baked beans
1/2 pound hot dogs
1/4 cup diced onions
1/4 cup catsup
2 tablespoons brown sugar
1 tablespoon yellow mustard
1/2 teaspoon Worcestershire sauce

### Yield: 30-35 servings

1 No. 10 can (7 pounds 3 ounces) baked beans
1 pound hot dogs
1/2 cup diced onions
1/2 cup catsup
1/4 cup brown sugar
2 tablespoons yellow mustard
1 teaspoon Worcestershire sauce

*Continued on next page*

*Franks 'n' Beans, continued*

### Yield: 70 servings

2 No. 10 cans (7 pounds 3 ounces each) baked beans
1 1/2 pounds hot dogs
1 cup diced onions
1 cup catsup
1/2 cup brown sugar
1/4 cup yellow mustard
1 1/2 teaspoons Worcestershire sauce

### Yield: 100 servings

2 pounds hot dogs
3 No. 10 cans (7 pounds 3 ounces each) baked beans
1 1/2 cups diced onion
1 1/2 cups catsup
3/4 cup brown sugar
1/4 cup plus 1 tablespoon yellow mustard
2 teaspoons Worcestershire sauce

Pour beans into stockpot. Slice hot dogs 1/2-inch thick and add to beans with onions, catsup, brown sugar, mustard and Worcestershire sauce. Cook over medium heat until heated through, stirring often, 15-20 minutes.

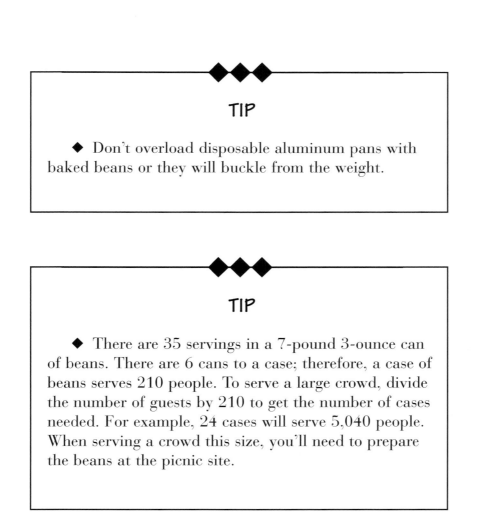

## TIP

◆ Don't overload disposable aluminum pans with baked beans or they will buckle from the weight.

## TIP

◆ There are 35 servings in a 7-pound 3-ounce can of beans. There are 6 cans to a case; therefore, a case of beans serves 210 people. To serve a large crowd, divide the number of guests by 210 to get the number of cases needed. For example, 24 cases will serve 5,040 people. When serving a crowd this size, you'll need to prepare the beans at the picnic site.

# Swedish Baked Beans

*Yield: 10 servings (one 9 x 5-inch loaf pan)*
*Cooking time: 25 minutes*

1/2 pound seasoned bulk pork sausage
1 apple
1/4 cup diced onions
2 tablespoons raisins
1 tablespoon brown sugar
1 tablespoon molasses
2 tablespoons catsup
1 1/2 teaspoons yellow mustard
   Scant 1/4 teaspoon ground cloves
1 can (31 ounces) baked beans

*Yield: 20 servings (one 9 x 9-inch pan)*
*Cooking time: 35 minutes*

1 pound seasoned bulk pork sausage
2 apples
1/2 cup diced onions
1/4 cup raisins
2 tablespoons brown sugar
2 tablespoons molasses
1/4 cup catsup
1 tablespoon yellow mustard
1/4 teaspoon ground cloves
2 cans (31 ounces each) baked beans

*Yield: 50 servings*
*Cooking time: 45-55 minutes*

2 1/4 pounds seasoned bulk pork sausage
4 apples
1 cup diced onions
2/3 cup raisins
1/4 cup brown sugar
4 cup molasses
1/2 cup catsup
2 tablespoons yellow mustard
1/2 teaspoon ground cloves
1 No. 10 can (7 pounds 3 ounces) baked beans
1 can (53 ounces) baked beans

*Yield: 125 servings*
*Cooking time: 55-65 minutes*

4 1/2 pounds seasoned bulk pork sausage
8 apples
2 cups diced onions
1 1/3 cups raisins
1/2 cup brown sugar
1/2 cup molasses
1 cup catsup
3 tablespoons yellow mustard
1 teaspoon ground cloves
3 No. 10 cans (7 pounds 3 ounces each) baked beans

In a large skillet, brown sausage until cooked through. Drain off fat. Preheat oven to 350 degrees. Peel, core, and dice apples. Combine sausage, apples, onion, raisins, brown sugar, molasses, catsup, mustard and cloves with beans. Stir thoroughly. Place beans in baking pan and cover with foil. Bake for length of time indicated or until beans are heated through.

◆ If you buy a high quality seasoned bulk pork sausage there will not be enough grease or liquid to drain. Also you will get a higher yield of meat.

◆ When making larger portions of Swedish beans cut back on the amount of apples and sausage used. I use McIntosh apples in the Swedish baked bean dish.

# Texts Fire Beans

*Yield: 16 servings (one 9 x 2-inch square pan)*
*Cooking time: 35-40 minutes covered,*
*then 10 minutes uncovered*

1 can (15 ounces) chunky chili with beans
1 can (1 pound) baked beans
1 can (15.8 ounces) great Northern beans, drained and rinsed
1 can (15 ounces) lima beans, drained and rinsed
1/4 cup diced onions
1 teaspoon cumin
1 teaspoon cayenne
1 teaspoon chili powder
1 garlic clove, minced
2 tablespoons brown sugar
1/4 cup catsup
Tabasco sauce to taste
5 slices bacon

*Yield: 30 servings*
*(one 4-inch-deep half-size pan)*
*Cooking time: 45-50 minutes covered,*
*then 10 minutes uncovered*

2 cans (15 ounces each) chunky chili with beans
2 cans (1 pound each) baked beans
2 cans (15.8 ounces each) great Northern beans, drained and rinsed
2 cans (15 ounces each) lima beans, drained and rinsed
1/2 cup diced onions
2 teaspoons cumin
2 teaspoons cayenne
2 teaspoons chili powder
2 garlic cloves, minced
1/4 cup brown sugar
1/2 cup catsup
Tabasco sauce to taste
6 slices bacon

---

### ◆◆◆

### TEXAS FIRE BEAN TIPS

◆ For a low-fat version of Texas Fire Beans, substitute canned chili with turkey and beans (99% fat free) for the chunky chili with beans. Some regions of the country, such as Texas and Arizona, sell canned spicy hot chili with beans.

◆ Because canned lima beans are not very popular, many supermarkets sell lima beans in 8 1/2-ounce cans. You can purchase frozen lima beans in a 1-pound package. Thaw lima beans before adding to the Texas Fire Beans. I like the canned lima beans best in this dish.

*Yield: 60- 65 servings*
*Cooking time: 40-45 minutes covered,*
*then 10 minutes uncovered*

4 cans (15 ounces each) chunky chili with beans
2 cans (31 ounces each) baked beans
4 cans (15.8 ounces each) great Northern beans, drained and rinsed
4 cans (15 ounces each) lima beans, drained and rinsed
1 cup diced onions
1 tablespoon cumin
1 tablespoon cayenne
1 tablespoon chili powder
4 garlic cloves, minced
1/2 cup brown sugar
1 cup catsup
Tabasco sauce to taste
6 slices bacon

*Continued on next page*

*Texas Fire Beans, continued*

*Yield: 115 servings*
*(one 4-inch-deep full-size hotel pan)*
*Cooking time: 35-40 minutes covered,*
*then 10-15 minutes uncovered*

1 No. 10 can (6 pounds 12 ounces)
   chunky chili with beans
1 No. 10 can (7 pounds 3 ounces) baked
   beans
5 cans (15.8 ounces each) great Northern
   beans, drained and rinsed
4 cans (15 ounces each) lima beans,
   drained and rinsed

1 1/2 cups diced onion
1 1/2 tablespoons cumin
1 1/2 tablespoons cayenne
1 1/2 tablespoons chili powder
   5 garlic cloves, minced
 3/4 cup brown sugar
1 1/2 cups catsup
   Tabasco sauce to taste
  10 slices bacon

Combine chili, baked, great Northern and lima beans, onion, cumin, cayenne, chili powder, garlic, brown sugar, catsup, and Tabasco sauce. Place beans into baking pan. Lay strips of bacon on top of mixture. Cover with foil. Bake at 350 degrees for length of time indicated. Uncover baked beans and brown bacon for additional time indicated, or until bacon is crisp.

# Black Beans Southwestern Style

*Yield: 10 servings*
1 can (14.5 ounces) stewed tomatoes
1 can (15 ounces) black beans, drained and
   rinsed
1 cup quick-cooking rice
1 cup warm water
1/3 cup diced onion (1 small onion)
1/3 cup diced celery, optional
1/3 cup diced green pepper
1 clove garlic, minced
1/3 teaspoon onion salt
2 teaspoons cumin
1 teaspoon mesquite flavored seasoning

*Yield: 20-25 servings*
2 cans (14.5 ounces each) stewed tomatoes

2 cans (15 ounces each) black beans,
   drained and rinsed
2 cups quick-cooking rice
2 cups warm water
2/3 cup diced onions
2/3 cup diced celery, optional
2/3 cup diced green bell pepper
2 cloves garlic, minced
1/2 teaspoon onion salt
2 teaspoons mesquite flavored seasoning

*Yield: 50 servings*
4 cans (14.5 ounces each) stewed tomatoes
4 cans (15 ounces each) black beans,
   drained and rinsed

*Continued on next page*

*Black Beans Southwestern Style, continued*

> 4 cups quick-cooking rice
> 4 cups warm water
> 1¹/₃ cups diced onions
> 1¹/₃ cups diced celery, optional
> 1¹/₃ cups diced green bell pepper
> 3 cloves garlic, minced
> ³/₄ teaspoon onion salt
> 2 tablespoons cumin
> 1 tablespoon mesquite flavored seasoning

*Yield: 100 servings*

> 1 No. 10 can (102 ounces) stewed tomatoes
> 1 can (14.5 ounces) stewed tomatoes

> 1 No. 10 can (102 ounces) black beans, drained and rinsed
> 1 can (15 ounces) black beans, drained and rinsed
> 8 cups quick-cooking rice
> 8 cups (2 quarts) warm water
> 2 cups diced celery, optional
> 2 cups diced onions
> 2 cups diced green bell pepper
> 4 cloves garlic, minced
> 3 tablespoons cumin
> 4 teaspoons mesquite flavored seasoning

Stir tomatoes with liquid, black beans, rice, water, onion, celery, green pepper, garlic, onion salt, cumin, and mesquite seasoning in a saucepan or stockpot on the stove. Stir occasionally over medium-low heat until rice is soft and ingredients are heated through, 15-20 minutes. The rice will thicken the bean dish.

VARIATION:

Place hot, cooked Black Beans Southwestern Style into a 4-inch deep full-size hotel pan and add one of the following cooked and diced meats: turkey, chicken, Mexican sausage or ground beef. Top with mild Cheddar or taco cheese. Cover. Bake at 350 degrees for 5-10 minutes or until cheese melts.

### VARIATION QUANTITIES

| Servings | Meat, lbs. | Cheese, cups |
|----------|-----------|--------------|
| 10 | 1 | 2 |
| 20-25 | 1¹/₂ | 3 |
| 50 | 2¹/₄ | 3 |
| 100 | 3 | 4 |

## TIP

◆ This black bean dish is low in fat and is a great vegetarian dish. It is relatively inexpensive to serve. It is a good filler for a picnic buffet line and is outstanding for a Mexican theme picnic.

# El Mexican Pinto Beans

*Yield: 20-25 servings*
*Cooking time: 30-35 minutes*

- 1 pound ground beef
- 1/2 pound bacon
- 4 cans (15 ounces each) pinto beans, drained and rinsed
- 1 can (15 ounces) Southwestern corn, extra crispy, drained
- 1 can (14.5 ounces each) diced salsa tomatoes with green chilies
- 1 medium onion, sliced
- 3/4 cup diced green bell pepper
- 3/4 cup diced celery
- 1/2 teaspoon garlic powder
- 1/2 teaspoon onion powder
- 2 teaspoons chili powder
- 2 teaspoons cumin
- 1/2 teaspoon black pepper
- 2 cups (1/2 pound) shredded Monterey Jack/Cheddar cheese blend

*Yield: 50-55 servings*
*Cooking time: 45-55 minutes*

- 2 pounds ground beef
- 1 pound bacon
- 1 No.10 can (102 ounces) pinto beans, drained and rinsed
- 1 can (15 ounces) pinto beans, drained and rinsed
- 2 cans (15 ounces each) Southwestern corn, extra crispy, drained
- 2 cans (14.5 ounces each) diced salsa tomatoes with green chilies
- 2 medium onions, sliced
- 1 1/2 cups diced green bell pepper
- 1 1/2 cups diced celery
- 1 teaspoon garlic powder
- 1 teaspoon onion powder
- 4 teaspoons chili powder
- 4 teaspoons cumin

- 1 teaspoon black pepper
- 2 cups (1/2 pound) shredded Monterey Jack/Cheddar cheese blend

*Yield: 70-75 servings*
*Cooking time: 55-65 minutes*

- 3 pounds ground beef
- 1 1/2 pounds bacon
- 2 No. 10 cans (102 ounces each) pinto beans, drained and rinsed
- 3 cans (15 ounces each) Southwestern corn, extra crispy, drained
- 3 cans (14.5 ounces each) diced salsa tomatoes with green chilies
- 3 small onions, sliced
- 2 cups diced green bell pepper
- 2 cups diced celery
- 1 1/2 teaspoons garlic powder
- 1 1/2 teaspoons onion powder
- 2 tablespoons chili powder
- 2 tablespoons cumin
- 1 1/2 teaspoons black pepper
- 3 cups (3/4 pound) shredded Monterey Jack/Cheddar cheese blend

*Yield: 100 servings*
*Cooking time: 65-75 minutes*

- 4 pounds ground beef
- 1 1/2 pounds bacon
- 2 No. 10 cans (102 ounces each) pinto beans, drained and rinsed
- 4 cans (15 ounces each) pinto beans, drained and rinsed
- 4 cans (15 ounces each) Southwestern corn, extra crispy, drained
- 4 cans (15 ounces each) diced salsa tomatoes with green chilies
- 4 small onions, sliced
- 3 cups diced green bell pepper
- 3 cups diced celery

*Continued on next page*

*El Mexican Pinto Beans, continued*

- 2 teaspoons garlic powder
- 2 teaspoons onion powder
- 3 tablespoons chili powder
- 3 tablespoons cumin
- 2 teaspoons black pepper
- 4 cups (1 pound) shredded Monterey Jack/Cheddar cheese blend

*Yield: 115-120 servings*
*Cooking time: 45-55 minutes*

- 5 pounds ground beef
- 2 pounds bacon
- 3 No. 10 cans (102 ounces each) pinto beans, drained and rinsed
- 2 cans (15 ounces each) pinto beans, drained and rinsed
- 5 cans (15 ounces each) Southwestern corn, extra crispy, drained
- 5 cans (14.5 each) diced salsa tomatoes with green chilies
- 4 small onions, sliced
- 2 1/4 cups diced green bell peppers
- 1 cup diced celery
- 2 1/2 teaspoons garlic powder
- 2 1/2 teaspoons onion powder
- 4 tablespoons chili powder
- 4 tablespoons cumin
- 2 1/2 teaspoons black pepper
- 6 cups (1 1/2 pounds) shredded Monterey Jack/Cheddar cheese blend

In a skillet over medium heat, brown ground beef and drain. Cook bacon in a separate skillet and drain. Crumble bacon. Preheat oven to 350 degrees. Combine pinto beans, crispy corn and tomatoes with liquid. Add beef, bacon, onions, green pepper, celery, garlic powder, onion salt, chili, cumin and black pepper. Stir thoroughly. Place bean mixture into baking pans. Cover and bake for length of time indicated. Uncover pans and top with cheese. Cover again, turn off oven and let pans sit in oven until cheese melts, about 5 minutes.

# Field Peas with Snaps

*Yield: 5 servings*

- 1 can (15 ounces) field peas with snaps
- 1/4 cup bottled barbecue sauce
- 1/2 teaspoon cumin

*Yield: 20 servings*

- 4 cans (15 ounces each) field peas with snaps
- 1 cup bottled barbecue sauce
- 2 teaspoons cumin

Pour field peas with liquid into large saucepan. Add barbecue sauce and cumin. Heat over medium heat until hot (about 10 minutes).

*Note: I first tasted and enjoyed eating field peas in Mississippi. They are readily available in the South. I only make field peas with snaps in small quantities for small parties when I entertain in my home.*

# Grilling Corn on the Cob

A standard grill used for picnics is 2 feet by 5 feet.

You can fit 55-59 ears of corn on a standard grill depending on how they are positioned. Leave a little space in between the rows for the heat to come through. You can usually fit 11 ears of corn per row.

An ear of corn with husks, untrimmed, is about a foot long. A husked and trimmed ear of corn is about 10 to 11 inches long. A small ear of corn is 8 inches long.

Use 1 1/2 twenty-pound bags of charcoal on a commercial grill. It takes 30 minutes to get the coals hot. Soak the corn in a tub of cold water for about a half hour to an hour before grilling. Grill corn 20 to 25 minutes. Test an ear for doneness. (Husks get brown as the corn cooks.) Continue to turn the corn every 5 minutes or so to cook evenly. The weather has a lot to do with the timing. If it is a windy day the corn will take longer. Place the corn into an insulated hot box to keep it hot as it comes off the grill.

The corn can be preboiled in their husks for 5 minutes at the party site in a large pot of water heated with propane gas. Or the corn can be preboiled in the husks at the catering shop for 5 to 6 minutes and carried in insulated hot boxes to the party site. About 30 ears will fit in a single unit hot box. A 9-quart pot will hold 17 ears of corn with the husks; 24 ears will fit into a 4-inch deep full-size pan. The insert pan can be covered with foil and placed in the convection oven for 10 minutes.

For very large groups a large corn roaster should be rented from a local farmer or merchant. Eight hundred to one thousand ears of corn can be cooked in this large piece of equipment in 10 to 15 minutes.

Use a bain marie to melt 2 pounds of butter or margarine. Place water in the larger pan to not quite half full. Place margarine in the smaller pan. Insert the smaller pan into the large pan. This system acts like a double boiler. Place the bain marie on the grill to melt the butter or margarine while the corn is cooking.

To set up a corn station place a hot box of corn on the picnic table. Place the sterno under the butter or margarine on a round holder. Husk the corn to the end, wrap a napkin around the peeled husks and dip each ear of corn into the butter in the bain marie. Salt the corn per request and serve each guest as they go through the line.

If the crowd is large, extra corn stations should be added. One 2-sided corn station can service 200 people. Having a separate corn station keeps the main buffet line moving quickly. Many people will pass the corn by if they have to husk and butter their own corn. Figure one ear of corn per person. Use fresh locally grown corn picked not more than a day in advance for best taste. Corn shipped in from in other parts of the country is not as tasty. Corn on the cob lovers can tell the difference if the corn is not fresh or cooked properly. Corn lovers will eat two or three ears while others simply pass it up. Very young children and elderly people have problems eating off the cob.

If the corn is cooked properly the chef will receive many compliments.

# Stir-Fried Vegetables

## Harvest Vegetable Blend

*Yield — 6-8 servings*

1/4 cup (1/2 stick) margarine
2 red tomatoes, cut into wedges
2 green tomatoes, cut into wedges
1 large bell pepper, cut into strips
1 onion, sliced into rings
1 small zucchini, sliced
1 yellow squash, sliced
1/2 cup fresh chives, chopped
2 teaspoons Italian pasta seasoning
Pepper and seasoning salt to taste

Melt margarine in a large skillet. Add vegetables and seasonings and stir-fry 8-10 minutes or until vegetables are tender. (For fancy cutting techniques, see diagram on page 110.)

# Potatoes

I remember when my husband and I first planted and grew potatoes. I was so excited to see how large our potatoes were as we dug them up from the ground. Potatoes are healthy and low in calories. It is what you serve on the potato, such as butter, sour cream, bacon, sauce, and gravy, that makes the potato dish high in fats and calories. I usually make German potato salad, French potatoes, baked potatoes, Valley Forge Potatoes and Loaded Potatoes at my picnics. I serve Valley Forge Potatoes with the Red, White and Blue picnic and the Loaded Potatoes for the Western picnics. I serve baked potatoes with butter and sour cream at theme picnics such as the Executive Picnic, T-bone Feast, and My Lord and My Lady Surf and Turf.

## PURCHASING BAKING POTATOES IN QUANTITY

Potatoes are sold by the count in 50-pound boxes. Potatoes come in 40, 50, 60, 70, 80, 90, 100, 110, 120-count and utility mix. A 50-count potato weighs 1 pound. A 120-count potato is the smallest size potato. It is wise to contact a pro-

duce sales representative to learn more about the sizes and their appropriate uses.

I usually use 80-count potatoes for baking. They are 6-ounce, medium-large potatoes, the size used in many restaurants. It is very important to buy baking potatoes that are uniform in size. Whether you bake a potato in a convection oven or a regular oven you need to have them baked through all at the same time. Also when you serve uniformly sized baked potatoes in a buffet line, each guest will get the same size. Making the right impression on the guests is crucial.

When serving baked potatoes it is wise to have two extra dishes of butter, one on each side of the buffet line, next to the baked potatoes, along with two dishes of sour cream. People go through the line and only take butter for their rolls, forgetting to take extra for potatoes.

Do not put potatoes on a baking sheet or in a hotel pan, or the potatoes will cook properly. It is best to place potatoes on the baking rack so the air can circulate around the potato while cooking.

(See diagram on page 109.)

Bake 80-count potatoes at 350 degrees in a convection oven, or 400 degrees in a conventional oven, for 1 hour or until soft.

## FOIL SHEETS FOR BAKING POTATOES

It is wise to buy precut foil sheets, 9 x 10¾ inches, to wrap potatoes. Five hundred sheets come to a box, 6 boxes per case. Gold foil wrap looks very nice, but is almost double in price. There are 200 sheets of gold foil per box, 12 boxes per case.

Be sure to wash, scrub, and dry potatoes before you wrap them. I am very surprised at how many restaurants do not wash potatoes before baking them. In fact there are wholesale produce vendors that pre-wrap the potatoes without washing them. The pre-wrapped potato is then shipped to restaurants ready for baking.

Approximately 120 baking potatoes (80 count) will fit in an insulated hot box. Fifty potatoes will fit into a 4-inch deep full size hotel pan.

## *The Baked Potato Panic Story*

I experienced baked potato panic when I first began to cater because I did not know how to properly bake potatoes in the convection oven. The party was 30 minutes from the shop. Everything that had to be heated in the convection oven had been checked off the list. Suddenly I realized that the potatoes were not baking properly—I had put the potatoes in a pan to bake, instead of on the rack in the oven, and the pan blocked the heat from the potatoes. I sent the crew on to the party with the rest of the food. Meanwhile, back at the shop I dumped the foil-wrapped potatoes into big pots of boiling water and cooked them at a rapid boil for 30 minutes. I drained the foil-covered potatoes and placed them into an insulated hot box. The potatoes arrived minutes before the guests were to be served. Everyone at the party was having a good time. I placed the potatoes on the grill. The chef used a little showmanship. I then placed the potatoes into a 4-inch deep full-size hotel pan. I slit each potato and served them with a smile and a sigh of relief. Once again, a disaster was foiled.

# Loaded Potatoes

A loaded potato is a baked potato served with butter, sour cream, Cheddar cheese, bacon bits, sliced mushrooms, and green onions. Salsa is also a good, low-fat, low-calorie alternative to offer. Carry plain baked potatoes in insulated hot boxes, and the toppings in separate containers. Carry serving dishes and fill with toppings at the party. Use one serving dish per line per ingredient. (Most buffets are two-sided).

**Baked Potato Toppings, per Person:**
• Butter: 2 pats
• Sour cream: 2-3 ounces
• Cheddar cheese: 2 ounces
• Bacon bits: 1 ounce
• Sliced fresh mushrooms: 1 ounce
    (or 2 ounces fried mushrooms)
• Sliced fresh green onions: 1/2 ounce

If cost is a factor, skip the mushrooms and green onions.

# Valley Forge Potatoes

*Yield: 40 servings*

20  potatoes
 1  cup (2 sticks) butter or margarine, melted
    Barbecue seasoning spice to taste

*Toppings*
2 1/2  pounds Cheddar cheese, shredded
2 1/2  pounds sour cream
      Extra butter pats

Preheat oven to 350 degrees. Grease an 18 x 24-inch baking sheet. Scrub potatoes; cut in half lengthwise. Place potato halves cut side up on the baking sheet. Brush butter over cut side of each potato. Sprinkle barbecue seasoning spice over the buttered potatoes. Cover the entire baking sheet with foil and bake for 30 minutes or until tender. Poke a potato with a fork or paring knife to test. Serve with sour cream and Cheddar cheese. For a browner potato take off the foil for the last 10 minutes of baking. You can fit 100 Valley Forge Potatoes in a 4-inch deep full-size hotel pan.

# Sauerkraut

Sauerkraut is a regional dish, and goes well with bratwurst. There are many Germans living in Wisconsin. Many Wisconsinites are sauerkraut and brat lovers. When serving brats, sauerkraut is expected on the buffet line. One No. 10 can of sauerkraut will serve 70 to 80 people, as not everyone will take some.

There are six No. 10 cans of sauerkraut per case (102 ounces per can). Sauerkraut to be served with bratwurst is just heated through and not seasoned. Three No. 10 cans will fit into a 4-inch deep full-size hotel pan. One and a half cans (153 ounces) will fit into a 4-inch deep half-size hotel pan. Cover filled pan with foil and bake at 350 degrees until just heated, 20-30 minutes. You can carry the sauerkraut along and heat through on the grill depending on size of the crowd and space on the grill. Place sauerkraut down the center of the pan and the grilled brats on the sides. (See illustration on page 84.) Serve.

How to place potatoes for baking (page 106)

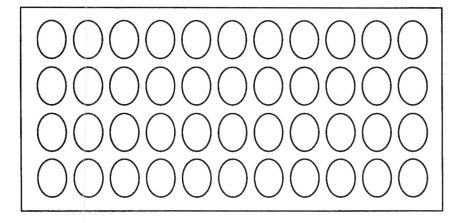

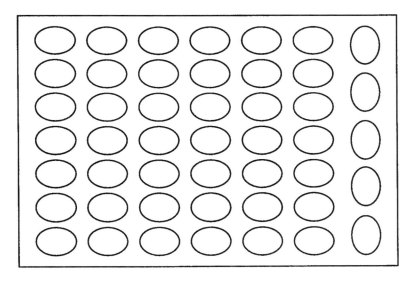

## How to cut vegetables for stir-fry (page 105)

Insert knife at an angle to the center of the vegetable. Make a second diagonal cut at an opposite angle to form a V. Continue around vegetable until circle is completed. Cut sections 1½ to 2 inches thick.

A

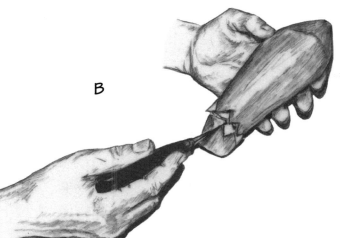

B

C

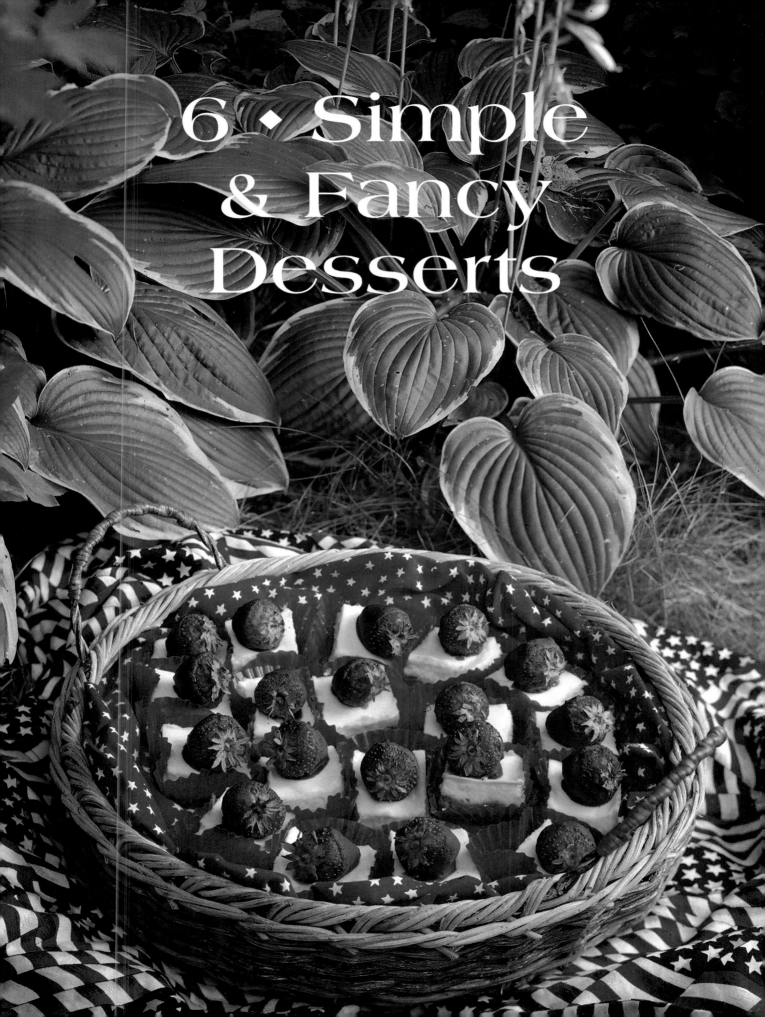

# 6 • Simple & Fancy Desserts

# Simple & Fancy Desserts

If you get a chance to tour a large bakery operation, you will be totally blown away. I remember watching a lady on an assembly line making frosting roses on a stick. If you blinked, you missed seeing her make one. The mixers are so big you can sit in one and get lost. The conveyor belts take the unbaked goodies to the huge ovens. Everything is made on an assembly line.

Large bakeries make mistakes, too. One time, one of the night crew mixed the bread dough and made a big mistake. Instead of wasting the dough, they spent time to make up Christmas bread sculptures, which were sold through grocery stores. The next year customers were asking for bread sculptures. Wherever possible, a good business will turn a mistake into a profit.

A picnic is not a picnic without dessert. I usually serve a variety of pan desserts at my catered picnics and have always received rave reviews. For the My Lady and My Lord Surf and Turf party I serve fancy tortes and pies. I began my business by making my own 9-inch pies. As the business grew, I bought frozen pies and baked them at the shop. For any two-crusted pies I use an egg wash and sprinkle sugar on the top crust (see page 161 for details). For the Hawaiian Luau I serve Hawaiian cheesecake (see recipe on page 160). I decorate the dessert table at each party in a theme mode to look very special. It is a great way to get people's attention. I let people take two or three desserts. They recognize that my desserts were special. I developed a reputation for my efforts. I also had a cake decorator on staff who would decorate company logos for sheet cakes. People like to see their company name on a sheet cake. It was a good attention-getter. When your catering service runs that extra mile by making desserts special, your company certainly will be called for repeat business or new business. Remember the dessert is the last course of the meal. While the entire meal must be tasty, the dessert is a terrific way to end a great picnic. I cut desserts and dessert bars into small portions for a dessert buffet table. I also have a server at the buffet table to control the serving of the desserts.

As your catering firm grows, you may not have the time to bake everything from scratch. So some shortcuts for baking must be made in order to save time. You can make some desserts and buy some desserts. Cake mixes are a great way to save time as they have been tested and are fairly foolproof. While I could put about anything together without a recipe, I use measuring cups and spoons for baking cakes and cookies from scratch. However, I could estimate how to make many of the crusts for bars. Bars make great picnic desserts. As a youngster, I used to watch my grandmother bake, and she could use a pinch of this and a dash of that, or a handful of flour, and her baking was so good. Through experimenting, I perfected my desserts in quantity. I use an 11 x 17 x 1-inch aluminum half-sheet cake pan to bake the majority of my picnic desserts. (I use a full sheet cake pan only for making simple sheet cakes.) I prefer the half-sheet cake pan for several reasons. The packed dessert was easier to handle and transport. Also, there is a psychological aspect to consider: When people go through a buffet line and see full-size sheet cakes, they are apt to take more. In addition, a full sheet cake pan takes up too much room on the buffet table.

I usually offered three choices of desserts per picnic buffet, but you can get by with two or even one. On less expensive picnics where you can afford only one kind of dessert, a chocolate, strawberry, cherry or lemon dessert usually

pleases most picnickers. For a more formal picnic, I place the desserts on trays with doilies or in baskets when I arrived. The pan bar desserts remain in the pan for a more casual party. You can sometimes cut a half-sheet cake recipe in half to make a 9 x 13 x 2-inch pan or double it for a full sheet cake pan; check with each recipe for instructions. Refer to the cake chart on page 122 for more information and baking times.

Do not divide or double the bar recipes; they will not work except in the quantities given.

This chapter will give you information on ingredients, measurements, and recipes. There are also several charts to assist you to make beautiful bakery products. So bake up a storm and eat your heart out with tasty and tempting desserts.

## TIPS

◆ As you read through the recipes you will see that I explained the recipes' sizes. A 9 x 13-inch pan is usually not enough servings for a catered picnic. If you make two half-sheet cakes rather than one full-sheet cake, you can put out one of each variety at a time. Then if you don't need the second one, you can use it for another party provided you never unwrapped it or set it out on the table.

◆ For more elegant picnics, I use risers and glass mirrors to impress guests. The decorations set the mood and accent the desserts. Setting up and serving a dessert buffet is truly a great joy to me because I make my guests very happy. I also make money for my efforts.

◆ Helpful cutting charts are provided for cakes, bars and pies on pages 124 and 145.

# GENERAL INFORMATION ON BAKING INGREDIENTS AND MEASUREMENTS

BAKING POWDER: 7 ounces baking powder equals 1 cup or 16 tablespoons or 48 teaspoons

BAKING SODA: 1 pound baking soda equals 2 cups or 32 tablespoons or 96 teaspoons

BUTTER OR STICK MARGARINE: 1 pound butter equals 16 ounces (4 sticks) or 32 tablespoons

CHOCOLATE: 1 square of chocolate equals 1 ounce (TIP: Substitute 2 tablespoons plus 2 teaspoons cocoa for 1 ounce chocolate); Nestlé Chocobake pre-melted unsweetened chocolate 8 ounces per box; 1 can of cocoa (8 ounces) equals 2 1/2 cups

CHOCOLATE CHIPS: 6 ounces chocolate chips equals 1 cup

CHOCOLATE M&M's: 1 bag (12 ounces) mini M&M's equals 2 cups

COCONUT: 1 bag (7 ounces) shredded coconut equals 2 2/3 cups; 1 bag (14 ounces) coconut equals 5 1/3 cups

CREAM CHEESE: 1 package (8 ounces) cream cheese equals 1 cup

EGGS: 1 large egg equals 1/4 cup; 4 eggs equal 1 cup; 6 medium eggs weigh 8 ounces; 6 large eggs weigh 10 ounces; 6 extra-large eggs weigh 12 ounces; 6 jumbo eggs weigh 14 ounces

FLOUR: 1 pound flour equals 4 cups

GRAHAM CRACKERS: 1 box (16 ounces) graham crackers contains 3 packs of 10 large crackers each or a total of 30 crackers; 1 box (16 ounces) whole graham crackers equals 5 3/4 cups graham cracker crumbs; 5 1/2 whole graham crackers make 1 cup graham cracker crumbs

GRAHAM CRACKER CRUMBS: 1 box (15 ounces) graham cracker crumbs equal a little less than 4 cups, enough for three (8- or 9-inch) graham cracker piecrusts.

LEMON: Juice of 1 lemon equals 2-3 tablespoons

LEMON PIE FILLING: 1 can (15.75 ounces) equals approximately 2 cups

MOLASSES: 1 1/2 cups molasses is the equivalent of 1 cup sugar

NUTS (shelled):
1 bag (10 ounces) walnuts equals 2 1/2 cups
1 bag (2.5 ounces) walnut pieces equal 1/2 cup
1 bag (2 ounces) slivered almonds equals 1/3 cup
1 bag (2.5 ounces) sliced almonds equals 1/2 cup
1 bag (8 ounces) whole pecans equals 2 cups
1 bag (1 pound) whole pecans equals 4 cups

ORANGE: Juice of 1 orange equals 6-8 tablespoons

SALT: 1 box (1 pound 10 ounces) equals 2 2/3 cups

SHORTENING (solid vegetable shortening): 1/4 pound shortening equals 1 cup

SUGAR: 1 pound granulated sugar equals 2 1/2 cups 1 pound brown sugar equals 2 cups firmly packed; 1 pound powdered sugar equals 4 cups

SWEETENED CONDENSED MILK: 1 can (14 ounces) equals 1 cup

UNFLAVORED GELATIN: 1 tablespoon unflavored gelatin thickens 2 cups liquid; 1 box (1 ounce) unflavored gelatin contains 4 envelopes Each envelope contains 1/4 ounce gelatin (2 1/2 teaspoons)

## MEASUREMENTS

1/8 cup equals 2 tablespoons (1 fluid ounce)
1/4 cup equals 4 tablespoons
1/3 cup equals 5 tablespoons plus 1 teaspoon
1/2 cup equals 8 tablespoon
3/4 cup equals 12 tablespoons
1 cup equals 16 tablespoons
16 ounces by weight equals one pound or 454 grams
16 liquid ounces equals 2 cups
1 cup equals 1/2 pint
4 cups (2 pints) equals 1 quart (32 fluid ounces)
2 quarts (1/2 gallon) equals 64 fluid ounces
4 quarts equal one gallon
8 quarts equals 1 peck
4 pecks equals one bushel

# How to Purchase Foods in Quantity for Baking

When you purchase items in large quantities you can save some money. However, it is very important to check prices. For example, sweetened condensed milk is cheaper when purchased at the local grocery store than the wholesale house. Work with a sales representative from a wholesale foods operation. Use a couple of wholesale vendors to ensure competitive pricing. Spend the time to get to know quantity sizes. Make a list that you can operate from on a weekly basis. Place this form on your computer and run off several sheets at a time. It is important to know weights and quantity food packaging. This knowledge will help you buy precise quantities for all your parties. With this knowledge you will buy successfully to make a profit.

Too many new catering businesses over-buy and prepare too much food because they do not know enough about cooking in quantity. The fear is not having enough food. Quantity baking takes practice and experience. It is important to prepare extra—5 to 10 percent over the final count is a good estimate.

## HOW TO HANDLE DELIVERIES

Whenever you get a delivery in, check each item. It is a hassle to be short of an item or to have a mix-up especially in your busy season. Rotate old items to the front and new items to the back of the shelf. Rotate frozen and refrigerated foods as well.

---

## TIP

 It's very important to use high quality baking ingredients. Fresh baking powder and baking soda make a difference. And powdered sugar or cocoa with lumps will yield an inferior product. If you use ingredients with lumps, be sure to sift them well. Moisture in the air can make powdered sugar become lumpy. Most enriched flours do not need to be sifted provided the flour is fresh. I recommend using only grade A large eggs for baking, because they have a higher yield.

---

## TIP

You can make up your own single acting baking powder.

**Homemade Single Acting Baking Powder**
*Yield: ¼ cup*

2 tablespoons cream of tartar
1 tablespoon baking soda
1 tablespoon cornstarch

Mix together cream of tartar, baking soda and cornstarch. Store in a clean dry glass container with cover. Keep in container stored in a dry area.

# PURCHASE SHEET FOR ORDERING BAKING SUPPLIES IN QUANTITY

| | *Quantity* | | *Quantity* |
|---|---|---|---|
| **BAKING POWDER** | | **COMMERCIAL SHORTENING** | |
| 6 cans (5 pounds each) per case | _____ | 35-pound box (bulk) | _____ |
| 25 pounds bulk | _____ | | |
| 4 containers (10 pounds each) | _____ | **COMMERCIAL WHIPPED TOPPING** (frozen) | |
| | | 12 cartons (2 pounds each) per case | _____ |
| **BAKING SODA** | | | |
| 12 boxes (2 pounds each) per case | _____ | **COCONUT** | |
| | | 10 pounds | _____ |
| **BUTTER** | | 25 pounds | _____ |
| 36 packages (1 pound each) per case | _____ | 50 pounds | _____ |
| | | | |
| **BUTTERSCOTCH CHIPS** | | **CORN SYRUP** | |
| **REGULAR AND MINI SIZE** | | 1 gallon | _____ |
| 10 pounds per case | _____ | | |
| 25 pounds per case | _____ | **CREAM CHEESE** | |
| | | one 3-pound block | _____ |
| **CHOCOLATE CHIPS** | | 10 blocks (3 pounds each) per case | _____ |
| **REGULAR AND MINI SIZE** | | | |
| 10 pounds per case | _____ | **CREAM OF TARTAR** | |
| 25 pounds per case | _____ | 1 container (26 ounces) | _____ |
| 50 pounds per case | _____ | 1 container (5 pounds) | _____ |
| | | 1 container (50 pounds) | _____ |
| **CHOCOLATE BAKING SQUARES** | | | |
| 6 packages (1 pound each) per case | _____ | **EGGS** | |
| | | 1 case (144 eggs) | _____ |
| **CHOCOLATE PIE SHELLS** | | 1 case egg whites (30 pounds) | _____ |
| 24 (9-inch) pie shells per case | _____ | 1 case eggs whites (50 pounds) | _____ |
| | | | |
| **COCOA** | | **ALL-PURPOSE FLOUR** | |
| 6 cans (5 pounds each) per case | _____ | 1 bag (25 pounds each) | _____ |
| | | 1 bag (50 pounds each) | _____ |
| **COMMERCIAL CAKE MIXES** | | 1 bag (100 pounds each) | _____ |
| 6 boxes (5 pounds each) per case | _____ | | |
| (White, yellow, chocolate) | | **FLAVORINGS** | |
| | | Almond extract: 1 quart bottle | _____ |
| **COMMERCIAL OIL SPRAY** | | Vanilla extract: 1 quart bottle | _____ |
| 6 cans (17 ounces each) per case | _____ | 1 gallon bottle | _____ |
| | | | |
| **COMMERCIAL SALAD OIL** | | **FROSTING (READY-MADE)** | |
| one 5-gallon container | _____ | 1 container (30 pounds) buttercream | _____ |
| 6 bottles (1 gallon each) per case | _____ | 1 container (22 pounds) glossy fudge | _____ |

## GRAHAM CRACKER CRUMBS

10 pounds _____

25 pounds _____

50 pounds _____

## GRAHAM CRACKER PIECRUST

Twenty-four 9-inch piecrusts per case _____

## GRAHAM CRACKER TART SHELL

144 shells (3 inches) per case _____

## MARGARINE

Yellow margarine: 31 pounds per case _____

White margarine: 24 pounds per case _____

## MARASCHINO CHERRIES

1 gallon _____

4 gallons per case _____

## PEANUT BUTTER

6 pails (5 pounds each) per case _____

12 containers (16 ounces each) per case _____

35 pounds smooth peanut butter _____

35 pounds crunchy peanut butter _____

## PIES (FROZEN UNBAKED)

Blueberry, cherry, apple, Dutch apple,
   pumpkin, strawberry rhubarb
   6 pies (8-inch) per case _____

## PIES (READY TO SERVE)

Coconut cream, vanilla cream,
   chocolate cream, pecan _____

## PIE FILLING

6 No. 10 cans
   (6 pound 8 ounces each) per case _____

Cherry, blueberry, peach apple,
   pineapple, strawberry, lemon
   20-pound tubs _____
   40-pound tubs _____

## SALT

1 bag (50 pounds) _____

## SHELLED NUTS

### ALMOND SLICES

1 box (10 pounds) _____

1 box (25 pounds) _____

### ALMOND SLIVERS

1 box (10 pounds) _____

### CASHEWS

1 case (25 pounds)
   (whole 240 count) _____

### FINE CRUSHED PEANUT TOPPING

1 case (30 pounds) _____

### PECAN HALVES

1 box (5 pounds) _____

1 box (30 pounds) _____

### PECAN PIECES

1 box (5 pounds) _____

1 box (30 pounds) _____

### WALNUTS

1 box (5 pounds) _____

1 box (30 pounds) _____

## SPICES

Allspice, cinnamon, cloves, nutmeg,
   pumpkin pie spice
   1 can (1 pound) _____

## BROWN SUGAR

1 box (40 pounds) _____

1 bag (50 pounds) _____

1 bag (100 pounds) _____

## GRANULATED SUGAR

1 bag (50 pounds each) _____

1 bag (100 pounds each) _____

## POWDERED SUGAR

1 box (40 pounds) _____

1 bag (100 pounds) _____

## DOILIES

1 box (10- or 12-inch) doilies (5000) _____

1 box (14-inch) doilies (2500) _____

1 box (12-, 14-, or 15-inch) (500)  _____
1 box (16-inch) (2500)  _____

CAKE BOXES
    QUARTER SHEET CAKE BOX
      100 per case  _____
    HALF SHEET CAKE BOX
      50 per case  _____
    FULL SHEET CAKE BOX
      50 per case  _____

CAKE DOME COVERS
    QUARTER SHEET CAKE DOME
      50 per case  _____
    HALF SHEET CAKE DOME
      50 per case  _____
    FULL SHEET CAKE DOME
      35 per case  _____

SHEET CAKE PANS
    QUARTER SHEET CAKE PANS
      100 per case  _____
    HALF SHEET CAKE PANS
      50 per case  _____
    FULL SHEET CAKE PANS
      50 per case  _____

FOIL
1 roll (12-inch, 18-inch, 24-inch)  _____

PLASTIC WRAP
1 roll (12-inch, 18-inch, 24-inch)  _____

DISPOSABLE ALUMINUM CAKE PANS
1 square pan (8 x 8 x $1^3/_4$ inches)  _____
1 pan ($9^1/_2$ x $6^1/_2$ x $4^1/_2$ inches)  _____
1 biscuit pan ($11^1/_4$ x $7^1/_4$ inches)  _____
1 dessert pan (13 x 9 x 2 inches)  _____
1 oblong cake pan ($8^1/_4$ x $12^1/_4$ inches)  _____
1 cake pan ($8^1/_2$ x $1^1/_2$ inches)  _____
1 half-size cake pan (11 x 17 x 1 inch)  _____
1 full-size cake pan (17 x 24 x 1 inch)  _____

DISPOSABLE ALUMINUM PIE PANS
1 pan ($8^3/_4$ x $1^1/_2$ inch)  _____
1 pan (9 x 1 inch)  _____
1 pan (10 x 1 inch)  _____

OTHER:

---

### TIP

Now that I have a list started for you, you can add on your own baking supplies that you use. When the sales representative comes in person or calls your catering service by telephone have your list ready. It is important to take an inventory list before you talk with the salesperson. Do not get pressured into buying items you do not use. Watch the cash flow in your catering business.

# Chocolate Brownies

*Yield: one 8 x 8 x 2-inch square pan*

2 squares (1 ounce each) unsweetened chocolate
2 tablespoons shortening
1/4 cup margarine
1 cup sugar
2 eggs
1 teaspoon vanilla
3/4 cup flour
1/2 teaspoon salt
1/2 teaspoon baking powder
1/2 cup chopped walnuts, optional

*Yield: 1 half-sheet cake pan*

8 squares (1 ounce each) unsweetened chocolate
1/3 cup shortening
1/2 cup margarine
4 cups sugar
8 eggs
2 teaspoons vanilla
3 cups flour
2 teaspoons baking powder
1 teaspoon salt
1 1/2 cups chopped walnuts, optional

Preheat oven to 350 degrees. Spray a baking pan with nonstick cooking spray. Melt chocolate, margarine, and shortening together. Cool slightly. Beat sugar, eggs and vanilla. Stir in chocolate mixture. Add flour, baking powder and salt and combine well. Pour into prepared pan and bake 22-27 minutes for 8 x 8-inch pan, or 25-30 minutes for 11 x 17-inch half-sheet pan. Cool.

### TIP

◆ Melt margarine or shortening in the microwave for 30-50 seconds, depending on the amount and on your style of microwave.

### EASY CHOCOLATE FROSTING
*Yield: 8 ounces frosting for one 8 x 8 x 2-inch square pan*

1 1/2 squares (1 1/2 ounces) semisweet chocolate
1 1/2 cups powdered sugar
3 tablespoons margarine
3 tablespoons half-and-half
1/2 teaspoon vanilla
Pinch of salt (optional)
1/2 cup chopped walnuts (optional)

*Yield: 1 1/2 pounds frosting for 1 half-sheet cake pan*

1/2 cup margarine
4 squares (1 ounce each) semisweet chocolate
4 cups powdered sugar
1/4 cup half-and-half
1 teaspoon vanilla
1/4 teaspoon salt
1 cup chopped walnuts (optional)

Melt margarine and chocolate together. Add remaining ingredients. Beat until smooth and creamy. Frost brownies. Sprinkle nuts over frosted brownies. Cover and refrigerate. *Note:* I use nuts on only half the brownies, as some people don't like them.

### TIPS

◆ You can substitute milk for half-and-half for the easy chocolate frosting. In smaller amounts of frosting I usually leave out the salt. The sugar flavors the frosting.

◆ It's more expensive to make brownies from scratch than from a box mix. Therefore I use box mixes to make my brownies. I use quick and easy homemade frostings to give a homemade taste.

# Double Fudge Brownies with Chocolate Topping Garnish

*Yield: 1 half-sheet pan*

1 half-sheet pan double fudge brownies, from mix*
2 cups chocolate chips
1 tablespoon water
1 tablespoon margarine
1 batch frosting of choice
1 cup chopped pecans

(*Make brownies using 2 boxes double-fudge brownie mix according to directions on package, using eggs, water and oil for 2 batches. Bake batter in a an 11 x 17-inch half-sheet pan for 30 minutes.)

Microwave chocolate chips and margarine until melted. Add water and stir thoroughly. Score 10 diagonal lines about 2 inches apart on frosted brownies. Using a number 126 (large rose) tip, fill pastry bag with chocolate topping. Squiggle tip back and forth to make a ruffle effect. Sprinkle nuts in between the decorated chocolate ruffles. Place into a half-sheet cake box. Refrigerate.

## TIP

◆ Appearance, touch or toothpick test do not indicate when brownies are done. For drier brownies bake 28 minutes and more moist brownies bake 24 minutes for a 9 x 13 x 2-inch pan. For a 11 x 17 x 1-inch pan bake for 30-35 minutes. When cutting brownies dip a sharp knife into warm water.

# Butterscotch Brownies

*Yield: one 8 x 8 x 2-inch square pan*

1/4 cup margarine, softened
1 cup light brown sugar, packed
1 egg
3/4 cup flour
1/2 teaspoon baking powder
1/4 teaspoon salt
1/2 teaspoon vanilla

Preheat oven to 350 degrees. Grease an 8 x 8 x 2-inch pan. Cream margarine with sugar and egg. Blend flour, baking powder and salt. Add vanilla. Blend all ingredients thoroughly. Pour batter into prepared pan and spread evenly. Bake for 22-27 minutes. Cool.

*Note:* Do not overbake butterscotch brownies. For contrast use caramel fudge frosting on chocolate brownies or chocolate frosting on butterscotch brownies.

### CARAMEL FUDGE FROSTING
*Yield: frosting for one 8 x 8 x 2-inch square pan*

1/2 cup caramel fudge, softened
1 tablespoon margarine
3/4 cup powdered sugar

*Garnish*
1/4 cup mini chocolate chips
1/4 cup mini butterscotch chips

Microwave caramel fudge and margarine together. Add powdered sugar and beat until smooth and creamy. Frost the butterscotch brownies and refrigerate to set frosting. Garnish with chocolate and butterscotch chips. Cut bars into desired size. Cover and refrigerate.

# Cakes

Marble, chocolate, and yellow cakes are favorite desserts of picnickers, and a basic boxed cake mix with a simple buttercream frosting is the least expensive dessert to serve.

Batter from 6 cake mixes or two 5-pound cake mixes will fit in one 12-quart mixer. When I make 3 or more cake mixes at once, I lessen the amount of oil (see chart following). Too much oil makes a cake soggy. Follow directions for the amount of water and eggs on the package directions. (Always use large eggs when baking.) The amount of water and oil may vary from different flavors and brands of cake mixes.

### CHART FOR 18.25-OUNCE CAKE MIXES

| Quantity | Eggs | Vegetable Oil |
|---|---|---|
| 1 cake mix | 3 eggs | 1/3 cup oil |
| 2 cake mixes | 6 eggs | 2/3 cup oil |
| 3 cake mixes | 9 eggs | 2/3 cup + 2 tablespoons oil |
| 4 cake mixes | 12 eggs | 1 cup oil |
| 5 cake mixes | 15 eggs | 1 1/3 cups oil |
| 6 cake mixes | 18 eggs | 1 2/3 cups oil |

### CHART FOR ROUND CAKE PANS

| Pan Size | Batter | Baking Time (at 350°) |
|---|---|---|
| 6 x 2" round | 2 cups | 20-25 minutes |
| 8 x 2" round | 2 3/4 cups | 30 minutes |
| 9 x 2" round | 2 3/4 cups | 30 minutes |
| 10 x 2" round | 5 1/2 cups | 40-45 minutes |
| 12 x 2" round | 7 1/2 cups | 45-50 minutes |
| 14 x 2" round | 10 cups | 55-60 minutes |
| 16 x 2" round | 13 3/4 cups | 65-80 minutes |

### CHART FOR RECTANGULAR CAKE PANS

| Pan Size | No. of Cake Mixes | Batter | Baking Time (at 350°) |
|---|---|---|---|
| 13 x 9 x 2" | 1 | 5 1/2 cups | 30 minutes |
| 11 x 17 x 1" | 2 | 11 cups | 30-35 minutes |
| 18 x 14 x 2" | 4 | 22 cups | 55 minutes |

## GENERAL INFORMATION

### USING A CONVECTION OVEN TO BAKE CAKES

If you use a convection oven, lower the temperature by 50 degrees, and bake cakes at 300 degrees. Sheet cakes bake for 27 minutes, while 8- or 9-inch round or square layer cakes bake for 25 minutes. For best results, rotate sheet cakes one-half turn after 10 minutes of baking. If a wooden pick inserted in the center of cake comes out clean, the cake is done. Cupcakes take 13 to 19 minutes.

### INFORMATION ON COMMERCIAL BOXED CAKE MIXES

One commercial boxed cake mix weighs 5 pounds, and there are 6 commercial cake mixes to a case. A commercial cake mix calls for cool water only. For high altitudes, there are special directions on the box that are necessary for you to follow.

### COMMERCIAL CAKE MIX

One 5-pound commercial cake mix makes:
   eight 8 x 2-inch or 9 x 2-inch round cakes
   OR four 8 x 2-inch or 9 x 2-inch round cakes
   OR 56 cupcakes (3 ounces each)
   OR two 11 x 17 x 1-inch half-sheet cakes
   OR one 18 x 24 x 1-inch full-sheet cake

### GENERAL INFORMATION ON TYPES OF MIXERS

**Small Commercial Mixers**

There are several sizes of commercial countertop mixers. I owned one 4-quart and one 5-quart mixer. I not only use the mixers for baking, but also for general mixing. The small mixers usually have 10 speeds. I would be lost without my mixers!

**Medium Commercial Mixers**

There are 12-quart and 20-quart mixers. It is wiser to purchase a 20-quart mixer even if it seems too big when you first start your business, as there is very little difference in price between the two. The 20-quart mixer is very popular in most food operations, and it can be set on a bench with rollers for easy access. Twelve- and 20-quart mixers have 3 speeds.

**Large Commercial Mixers**

Eighty- or 140-quart mixers are found in bakery companies. These mixers are floor models.

### FROSTING

There are many varieties of frosting. It is very important to place the proper frosting with the right cake. Some cakes taste best with a light and less sweet frosting. There are very sweet and sugary frostings, cream cheese frosting, and a variety of chocolate and flavored frostings. There are whipped cream and non-dairy whipped toppings. The icing is the life of the cake for most dessert lovers, and a decorated cake will win the hearts of most picnickers. I use buttercream frosting, an excellent picnic pleaser, most of the time on basic cakes.

You can purchase frosting, if you wish, from a bakery distributor. The advantage of the ready-made frosting is consistency and saving labor. I like making my own frostings, however, and I have a reputation for my tasty frostings. Find your niche.

I use solid white vegetable shortening and white margarine to get a pure white frosting. Sometimes your local grocery store may not carry white margarine. You may have to use all solid white vegetable shortening and butter flavoring to get a pure white frosting. Frosting made with all butter or margarine or half butter and half margarine is very tasty. However, butter and margarine-based frosting does not hold up in the heat. Regular brown vanilla tints white frosting off-white, so you may wish to use clear vanilla extract. I use almond extract instead of

vanilla in buttercream frosting. It is a personal preference. Try half vanilla and half almond extract for a distinct taste.

Try adding two cups of commercial whipped topping to a 10-pound batch of frosting. This topping will help stabilize the frosting somewhat for a hot summer day. It also somewhat cuts down the sweetness.

A 5-quart mixer will hold 2 pounds of frosting, while a 10- to 12-quart mixer will hold 10 pounds of frosting. If you own only a small home-style mixer, make 1 pound of frosting at a time. This method is time-consuming and not very efficient.

## CAKE CUTTING INFORMATION

*Note:* I usually cut a half-sheet cake into 35 pieces and a full-sheet cake into 72 or 80 pieces. Picnickers waste cake if the pieces are too large.

13 x 9-INCH CAKE: On the 9-inch side, score 4 sections. On the 13-inch side, score 6 sections. Serves 24 ($2^1/_4$ x $2^1/_4$-inch pieces).

11 x 17 x 1-INCH HALF-SHEET CAKE: On the 11-inch side, score 5 sections. On the 17-inch side, score 5 sections. Serves 25 ($2^1/_2$ x $3^1/_2$ inch pieces)

OR: On the 11-inch side, score 5 sections. On the 17-inch side, score 6 sections. Serves 30 ($2$-$^1/_2$ x $2^3/_4$ inch pieces).

OR: On the 11-inch side, score 5 sections. On the 17-inch side, score 7 sections. Serves 35 ($2^1/_2$ x $2^1/_2$ inch pieces).

OR: On the 11-inch side, score 5 sections. On the 17-inch side, score 8 sections. Serves 40 ($2^1/_8$ x $2^1/_2$ inch pieces).

18 x 24 x 1-INCH FULL SIZE SHEET CAKE: On the 18-inch side, score 9 sections. On the 24-inch side, score 8 sections. Serves 72 (2 x 3-inch pieces).

# Black Forest Cake

*Yield: 1 half-sheet cake*

2 boxes (18.25 ounces each) chocolate fudge cake mix
  Water (for mix)
  Eggs (for mix)
  Oil (for mix)
2 cans (1 pound each) pitted black cherries, well drained
1½ pounds frozen commercial whipped topping, thawed
1 cup chocolate jimmies, for garnish
15 whole Maraschino cherries with stems, drained, for garnish

Preheat oven to 350 degrees. Grease an 11 x 17-inch half-sheet cake pan. In a 5-quart bowl, mix cake mixes with enough water, eggs and oil for 2 mixes, following directions on package. Beat until smooth. Scatter black cherries over the bottom of prepared pan. Pour batter over cherries. Bake for 30-35 minutes or until wooden pick inserted in center of cake comes out clean. Cool.

Chill a 5-quart mixing bowl. Beat commercial whipped topping until peaks form. Spread whipped topping over Black Forest cake. Pipe on a border with a number E1 star tip. Pipe 15 stars on cake (3 across and 5 down). Sprinkle chocolate jimmies over top of cake. Place one whole Maraschino cherry in the middle of each star. Place cake into half-sheet cake box. Refrigerate. Black Forest pan cake will keep in the refrigerator up to 3 days. I generally make the cake in advance. Freeze the cake, then frost and garnish it on the day of party.

# Carrot Cake

I generally use 2 cake mixes (18.25 ounces each). I do not add raisins, walnuts, or crushed pineapple to the batter, because I would lose profit from them. The cream cheese frosting makes a very tasty topping to enhance the carrot cake mix. Carrot cake made from scratch is heavier in texture and the ingredients and labor are more expensive. The walnut garnish is optional, since walnuts add to the cost. However, the walnut garnish is visually appealing and flavorful. I use the walnuts unless the customer requests me to leave the nuts off.

To save time, bake and garnish several carrot cakes in advance. Place each carrot cake into a half-sheet cake box. Cover each box with a plastic bag and freeze.

## Carrot Cake
### Yield: 1 half-sheet cake

2 cups sugar
1 1/2 cups oil
8 eggs
4 jars (6 ounces each) baby food carrots
5 cups flour
3 teaspoons cinnamon
2 teaspoons baking soda
2 teaspoons baking powder
1 teaspoon salt
1 batch Cream Cheese Frosting (page 126)
1 cup walnuts, chopped

Preheat oven to 350 degrees. Grease an 11 x 17-inch half-sheet pan. In a 5-quart mixing bowl, beat sugar, oil, eggs, and carrot baby food together. Add flour, cinnamon, baking soda, baking powder, and salt. Blend together until smooth. Pour batter into prepared pan. Bake for 35-45 minutes or until wooden pick inserted in center of cake comes out clean. Cool.

Frost with Cream Cheese Frosting. Sprinkle walnuts on top. Place cake into half-sheet cake box. Refrigerate. Carrot cake will keep in the refrigerator up to 5 days.

TIP: To save time, make one half-sheet cake from 2 mixes. Prepare according to package directions. Frost and decorate as above.

## Pineapple Carrot Cake
### Yield: 1 half-sheet cake

2 boxes (18.25 ounces each) carrot cake mix
2 cups water
2/3 cup oil
6 eggs
1 cup crushed pineapple, drained
1 cup carrots, finely grated
1/2 cup raisins
1 batch Cream Cheese Frosting (page 126)
1 cup walnuts, chopped

Preheat oven to 350 degrees. Grease an 11 x 17-inch half-sheet pan. Review package directions. In a 5-quart mixing bowl, add water, oil, and eggs to the cake mixes. Beat until smooth. Fold in pineapple, carrots and raisins. Pour batter into prepared pan. Bake for 30 to 35 minutes or until wooden pick in center of the cake comes out clean. Cool.

Frost with Cream Cheese Frosting. Sprinkle with walnuts. Place cake into half-sheet cake box. Carrot cake will keep in refrigerator up to 5 days.

## CREAM CHEESE FROSTING

*Yield: frosting for 1 half-sheet cake*

- 1 package (8 ounces) cream cheese, softened
- 1/2 cup (1 stick) margarine, softened
- 2 pounds powdered sugar
- 1/3 cup evaporated milk
- 1 teaspoon salt
- 1 teaspoon vanilla

Blend together cream cheese and margarine. Add powdered sugar alternately with evaporated milk. Add salt and vanilla. Beat until smooth. Frost carrot cake. Cream cheese frosting will keep in the refrigerator up to 5 days.

## ALTERNATE GARNISH FOR CARROT CAKE

Make 2 pounds of Buttercream Frosting (page 133). Divide frosting into 3 bowls. Color 6 ounces of frosting green and 10 ounces orange. Leave 1 pound white. Frost cake with thin layer of white frosting. Score the cake 5 rows across and 7 down. Fill 1 pastry bag with white frosting, and using a number 28 tip, pipe in lines over the scored lines and pipe a border. Fill 1 pastry bag with orange icing using number 28 tip. Form a carrot in the middle of each piece (35 pieces total). Fill 1 pastry bag with green frosting using a number 3 tip. Pipe on 3 lines to form carrot top. The disadvantage of this garnish is that it takes extra time and extra frosting. The advantage is it looks very attractive.

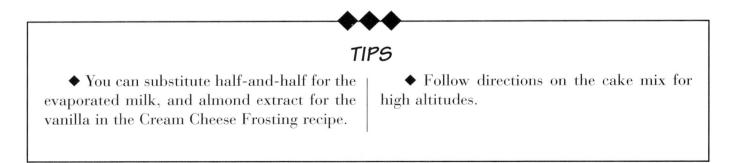

## TIPS

◆ You can substitute half-and-half for the evaporated milk, and almond extract for the vanilla in the Cream Cheese Frosting recipe.

◆ Follow directions on the cake mix for high altitudes.

# Cherry Cakes

A variety of cherry cakes (my personal favorite!) make a big hit at a picnic. The following sheet cakes are so easy to make but they look like you worked a long time to complete the job.

# Maraschino Cherry Cake

*Yield: 1 half-sheet cake*

1²/₃ cups water
³/₄ cup Maraschino cherries
1 cup Maraschino cherry juice
²/₃ cup oil
6 egg whites
2 boxes (18.25 ounces each) French vanilla cake mix
³/₄ cup almonds, chopped
1 batch Egg White Frosting (page 128)

*Garnish*

15 whole Maraschino cherries
75-90 almond slices or slivers (2-3 ounces)

Cut cherries into eighths. Set aside.

Preheat oven to 350 degrees. Grease an 11 x 17-inch half-sheet cake pan. In a 5-quart mixing bowl add water, Maraschino cherry juice, oil, and egg whites to the cake mixes. Beat until smooth. Fold in reserved cherries and almonds. Pour batter into prepared pan. Bake for 35-40 minutes. Cool. Frost with Egg White Frosting. Garnish with 15 Maraschino cherries (3 across and 5 down). To make a flower, form 5 or 6 petals by standing almond slivers up around each cherry. If you use 5 almond slices per flower, you need at least 75 almond slices. (Drain Maraschino cherries well before placing on the cake with frosting, as excess cherry juice will run on the frosting.)

Place cake into half-sheet cake box.

Refrigerate. You can freeze this cake without the frosting. Be sure cake is covered tightly before freezing. The frosted Maraschino cherry cake will keep fresh in the refrigerator up to 3 days, with plastic bag over cake box.

# Wild Cherry Cake

The wild cherry cake is less expensive to make than a Maraschino cherry cake because the almonds and Maraschino cherries are not in the cake batter. You will still get the same effect. Use the egg white frosting for the wild cherry cake, also.

Make a wild cherry half-sheet cake with 2 boxes (18.25 ounces each) wild cherry cake mix. Follow package directions. Pour batter into a 11 x 17-inch half-sheet pan and bake for 30-35 minutes. Frost with Egg White Frosting (page 128).

## Maraschino Cherry Cake Story

When I was a little girl, I always asked Mom to make my favorite Maraschino cherry cake for my birthday. In the Maraschino batter you can use 1 cup of Maraschino cherry juice and 1¹/₃ cups of water, or use 2²/₃ cups water and 2 to 3 drops red food coloring to make the cake batter a soft pink. Add chopped almonds and Maraschino cherries to make a delicious and festive cake.

# Yellow Cherry Cake

*Yield: 1 half-sheet cake*

2 boxes (18.25 ounces each) yellow cake mix
2²/₃ cups water
²/₃ cup vegetable oil
6 eggs

*Topping*
1 container (1 pound 8 ounces) non-dairy
 whipped topping, thawed
2 cans (20 ounces each) cherry pie filling

Preheat oven to 350 degrees. Grease an 11 x 17-inch half-sheet cake pan. In a 5-quart mixing bowl, add water, oil, and eggs to cake mixes. Beat until smooth. Pour batter into prepared pan. Bake for 30-35 minutes. Cool.

Spread non-dairy whipped topping over the cake. Dab cherry pie filling gently over topping. Pipe on a border of whipped topping with a number E1 star tip. Place cake into half-sheet cake box. Refrigerate. Yellow cherry cake will stay fresh in refrigerator up to 5 days. Do not freeze cake with cherry pie filling.

## TIP
◆ An 11 x 17 x 1-inch half-sheet pan will fit in a home-style oven, but an 18 x 24 x 1-inch full sheet pan will not.

## EGG WHITE FROSTING

If you double this frosting recipe use only 5 egg whites. A 5-quart mixer holds only a triple batch of egg white frosting. If you do not have a commercial mixing bowl place ingredients into a saucepan. Follow directions. Return the ingredients to a regular mixer. It is very important to add the cream of tartar to the egg white mixture in the beginning. If you forget to do so the end product will not hold up nor become stiff. You can use the buttercream frosting recipe on the Maraschino cake instead of the egg white frosting. I like the egg white frosting because of its bright white color and light texture. You can make egg white frosting one day in advance; store in an airtight container in the refrigerator. Do not freeze or it will break down.

*Yield: frosting for 1 half-sheet cake (1 pound)*
3 egg whites
1¹/₂ cups sugar
¹/₃ cup water
¹/₄ teaspoon cream of tartar
1 teaspoon almond extract

In a 5-quart mixing bowl, mix egg whites, sugar, water, and cream of tartar. Place 2 inches of water in skillet and bring to a boil. Place mixing bowl with ingredients over boiling water. Beat with a wire whisk for 2-3 minutes or until ingredients are heated and egg whites are frothy. Return mixing bowl to mixer. Beat mixture at highest speed until mixture is stiff and stands in peaks (about 5-7 minutes), scraping bottom and sides of the bowl occasionally. Fold in almond extract.

# Chocolate Cakes

## Chocolate Cherry Cake

The chocolate cherry cake is very moist and tasty and is simple to make. The Fluffy Light Frosting adds a silky, whipped cream taste. The water in the chocolate cake mixes is less than what is called for on the boxed mix.

*Yield: one 13 x 9-inch cake*
1 box (18.25 ounce) fudge chocolate
   cake mix
2 eggs
1 can (21 ounces) cherry pie filling
1/4 cup water
1 teaspoon almond extract

*Yield: 1 half-sheet cake*
2 boxes (18.25 ounces each) fudge
   chocolate cake mix
4 eggs
1 can (1 pound 14 ounces) cherry pie filling
2 1/2 cups water
1/3 cup vegetable oil
1 teaspoon almond extract

Preheat oven to 350 degrees. Grease a cake pan. In a 5-quart mixing bowl, blend cake mix with eggs, pie filling, water, oil and almond extract. Beat ingredients for 5 minutes or until smooth. Pour batter into prepared pan. Bake 13 x 9-inch cake for 30-35 minutes or half-sheet cake for 40-45 minutes, or until wooden pick comes out clean. Cool. Frost with Fluffy Light Frosting (right). Place cake in cake box. Refrigerate. The chocolate cherry cake will keep in the refrigerator up to 3 days.

*Note*: You only need to add oil to the large size (half-sheet) cake.

TIP: You can substitute 1 can (21 ounces) of raspberry filling for the cherry pie filling.

### FLUFFY LIGHT FROSTING

Eight to 12 ounces of frosting will frost a 9 x 13-inch cake. One and a half to 2 pounds of frosting will frost one 11 x 17-inch half-sheet cake. This frosting really makes the cake.

TIP: You can use margarine or half butter and half margarine. However there is nothing better than the taste of butter in this recipe.

TIP: On a hot day keep cakes with this frosting cold or the frosting will not withstand the heat.

*Yield: frosting for one 9 x 13 x 2-inch cake*
5 tablespoons flour
1 cup whole milk
1 cup (2 sticks) butter softened
1 cup granulated sugar
1/4 teaspoon salt
1 teaspoon almond extract

In a small saucepan, beat flour and milk with wire whisk until smooth. Cook mixture until thick. Set aside and let cool. (If the flour-milk mixture is added to the butter mixture before it has cooled, the butter will melt and curdle. Cool the flour mixture bowl in ice water to speed up the process.) Cream butter, sugar, salt and almond extract. Beat flour-milk mixture into butter-sugar mixture at high speed for about 15 minutes or until smooth and creamy.

TIP: Substitute amaretto liqueur for the almond extract.

## LIGHT COOKED FROSTING
*Yield: frosting for 1 half-sheet cake*
*(2 1/2 pounds)*

1/2 cup 2% milk
2 1/2 tablespoons flour
1/2 cup (1 stick) butter or margarine,
    softened
1/2 cup sugar
1/4 teaspoon salt
  1 teaspoon vanilla
  1 container (12 ounces) non-dairy whipped
    topping, thawed

*Garnish*
  24 whole Maraschino cherries, drained
  24 whole pecans

Blend the milk and flour in a small saucepan. Cook on low heat, stirring constantly with a whisk, until thick. Cool. In a 5-quart mixing bowl, cream at high speed butter, sugar, salt, and vanilla. Add the cooled flour-milk mixture. Beat at high speed to a creamy consistency (8-10 minutes). Place mixture into the refrigerator for about 45 minutes. Add 1 cup of the whipped topping to the frosting mixture. Blend together. Spread the frosting over the cake. Place the remaining whipped topping in a pastry bag. Using a number 28 star tip, pipe on a border. Pipe on 24 stars on the cake (4 across and 6 down). Place one whole Maraschino cherry in the middle of each whipped topping star. Place pecans in between the rows next to the Maraschino cherries (4 down and 6 across).

# Chocolate Fudge Cake Variations

Prepare a full-sheet fudge cake using four 18.25-ounce mixes, or a half-sheet cake using 2 mixes. Follow package directions. Bake at 350 degrees in an 18 x 24-inch full-sheet pan for 45-55 minutes, or an 11 x 17-inch half-sheet pan for 30-35 minutes, or until wooden pick in center of cake comes out clean. Cool.

◆ Frost with Easy Chocolate Chip Frosting (page 131). Score full-sheet cake into 70 squares, or half-sheet cake into 35 squares. Pipe non-dairy whipped topping on scored lines with a number 30 tip. Pipe 1 star in the middle of each piece of cake. Stand up 1 cashew in the middle of each star. Place cake in at cake box. Refrigerate. The chocolate fudge cake will keep in the refrigerator up to 4 days.

◆ OR frost cake with Peanut Butter Frosting (page 131). Score as above, and pipe non-dairy whipped topping over score lines. Garnish each square with a chocolate kiss.

◆ OR frost with Chocolate Cream Cheese Frosting (page 131). Score as above, and pipe non-dairy whipped topping over score lines. Garnish each square with a pecan half.

◆ OR use 2 cans (21 ounces each) raspberry pie filling for a half-sheet cake, or 4 cans for a full-sheet cake. Spread on top of cooled cake. Score cake as above. Pipe stars with non-dairy whipped topping on scored lines using number E1 star tip. Pipe on border. Place 1 fresh whole raspberry on each star to complete the cake.

◆ OR frost cake with Pistachio Frosting (page 131). Sprinkle mini chocolate chips and chopped walnuts over cake.

## EASY CHOCOLATE CHIP FROSTING

One and a half pounds of frosting will cover 1 half-sheet cake. One pound of frosting will cover a 9 x 13 x 2-inch cake.

You can use cream or 2 percent milk instead of evaporated milk. The chocolate chip frosting is great not only for cakes, but also for brownies. Place leftover frosting in an airtight container and freeze up to 30 days.

*Yield: frosting for 1 full-sheet cake
and one 9 x 13 x 2-inch cake (4 pounds)*

1 package (24 ounces) chocolate chips
  (4 cups)
1/2 cup (1 stick) margarine
1 1/4 cups evaporated milk
2 pounds powdered sugar
1 teaspoon vanilla
1 teaspoon salt

Combine chocolate chips, margarine and half the milk in double boiler. Stir over low heat until chocolate chips are melted. Remove from heat. In a 5-quart mixing bowl, mix together powdered sugar and remaining milk; beat well. Add chocolate mixture to powdered sugar mixture. Add vanilla and salt. Beat until smooth and creamy.

## PEANUT BUTTER FROSTING

*Yield: frosting for 1 half-sheet cake and
one 13 x 9 x 2-inch cake (2 3/4 pounds)*

1/2 cup (1 stick) margarine, softened
1/2 cup creamy peanut butter
1/2-3/4 cup half-and-half
2 pounds powdered sugar

In a 5-quart mixer, beat margarine and peanut butter together. Add cream alternately with powdered sugar. Beat until smooth. Frost cake. Garnish.

*Note:* One and one-half pounds of peanut butter frosting will cover 1 half-sheet cake. One pound of peanut butter frosting will cover one 9 x 13 x 2-inch cake. You can refrigerate leftover frosting in an airtight container for 4 days. Do not freeze.

*Note:* To make **Chocolate Peanut Butter Frosting**, add 2 packages (1 ounce each) pre-melted chocolate to frosting and mix well.

## CHOCOLATE CREAM CHEESE FROSTING
*Yield: frosting for 1 half-sheet cake*

1/2 cup cream cheese (1/2 of an 8-ounce
  package)
1/2 cup (1 stick) margarine, softened
4 packets (1 ounce each) pre-melted
  unsweetened chocolate
2 pounds powdered sugar
1/2 cup milk
1 teaspoon almond extract
1/4 teaspoons salt

Beat cream cheese and margarine together. Add pre-melted chocolate to cream cheese mixture. Add powdered sugar, milk, almond extract and salt. Beat until smooth and creamy.

This frosting is very tasty on the Chocolate Cherry Cake (page 129).

## PISTACHIO FROSTING
Try this frosting on a chocolate fudge cake.

*Yield: frosting for 1 half-sheet cake*
1 box (3/4 ounce) instant pistachio pudding
  mix
1 pound frozen non-dairy whipped topping,
  thawed

In a large bowl mix pistachio pudding mix with whipped topping and beat until smooth. Spread over cake. Frosting will keep in refrigerator up to 3 days. Do not freeze.

# German Chocolate Cake with Broiled Frosting

*Yield: 1 half-sheet cake*

1 German chocolate half-sheet cake*
3/4 cup margarine, melted
1 1/2 cups brown sugar
2 cups coconut
2 cups pecans
2 teaspoons vanilla
1/2 cup 2% milk

(*Prepare German chocolate cake using 2 cake mixes, following package directions. Bake in an 11 x 17-inch half-sheet pan at 350 degrees for 30-35 minutes, or until wooden pick inserted in center comes out clean.)

To make **Broiled Frosting**, in a 5-quart mixing bowl, mix margarine, brown sugar, coconut, pecans, vanilla, and milk together. Pour over slightly cooled cake. Put under the broiler for 2 to 3 minutes. Place cake into half-sheet cake box. Refrigerate German chocolate cake up to 5 days. Do not freeze—broiled frosting loses flavor if frozen.

# Lemon Cake with Lemon Cream Cheese Frosting

*Yield: 1 half-sheet cake*

1 half-sheet lemon cake*
1 package (8 ounces) cream cheese, softened
1/2 cup (1 stick) butter or margarine, softened
2 pounds powdered sugar, divided
1/4 cup half-and-half or 2% milk
3 tablespoons lemon juice

Garnish
15 lemon gumdrops
75-90 almond silvers or slices
(approximately 2 ounces)

(*Prepare lemon cake using 2 cake mixes, following package directions. Bake in an 11 x 17-inch half-sheet pan at 350 degrees for 30-35 minutes, or until wooden pick inserted in center comes out clean.)

To make **Lemon Cream Cheese Frosting**, in a 5-quart bowl beat cream cheese and margarine together. Add half the powdered sugar and beat well. Add cream and continue to beat. Add remaining powdered sugar. Beat slowly. Add lemon juice. Continue to beat until smooth and creamy.

Frost the cake. Garnish with 15 gumdrops (3 across and 5 down). Form daisy petals around each gumdrop by standing up 5 or 6 almond slices or slivers around each gumdrop. Place cake into half-sheet cake box. Refrigerate. Lemon cake will keep in refrigerator up to 5 days. Freeze cake before garnishing.

## BUTTERCREAM FROSTING

*Yield: frosting for 1 half-sheet cake*
- 1 cup white vegetable shortening
- 1 cup white margarine, softened
- 1 bag (2 pounds) powdered sugar
- $1/3$ cup water
- $1^1/2$ teaspoon salt
- 2 teaspoons almond extract

*Yield: frosting for 5 half-sheet cakes*
- 3 cups white solid shortening
- 2 cups white margarine, softened
- 10 pounds powdered sugar
- $1^1/3$ to $1^1/2$ cups water
- 1 teaspoon salt
- $1/4$ cup almond extract

In a mixing bowl, cream shortening and margarine together. Alternately add powdered sugar and water. Beat. Add salt and extract. Beat until smooth and creamy.

TIP: You can use yellow margarine in the buttercream frosting. I prefer white margarine to maintain a pure white color.

TIP: You can substitute brewed coffee (flavored coffees are nice) of your choice in place of water. Be sure the coffee is cold or the margarine will melt. My favorite flavored coffees are cinnamon and hazelnut.

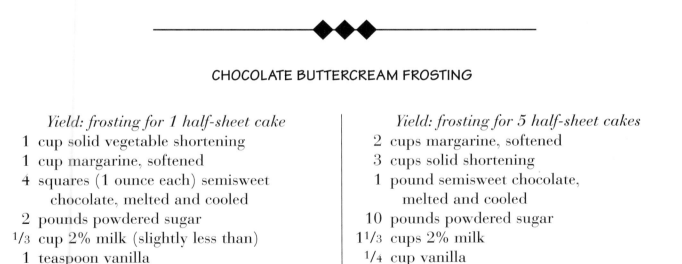

## CHOCOLATE BUTTERCREAM FROSTING

*Yield: frosting for 1 half-sheet cake*
- 1 cup solid vegetable shortening
- 1 cup margarine, softened
- 4 squares (1 ounce each) semisweet chocolate, melted and cooled
- 2 pounds powdered sugar
- $1/3$ cup 2% milk (slightly less than)
- 1 teaspoon vanilla
- $1/2$ teaspoon salt

*Yield: frosting for 5 half-sheet cakes*
- 2 cups margarine, softened
- 3 cups solid shortening
- 1 pound semisweet chocolate, melted and cooled
- 10 pounds powdered sugar
- $1^1/3$ cups 2% milk
- $1/4$ cup vanilla
- 1 teaspoon salt

In a mixing bowl cream shortening and margarine together. Add chocolate to shortening mixture. Add powdered sugar, a little at a time, alternately with milk. Beat. Add vanilla and salt. Beat until smooth and creamy.

## TIP
◆ One 18.25 ounce cake mix equals $5^1/2$ cups

# Oatmeal Cake

*Yield: 1 half-sheet cake*

2¹/₂ cups hot water
2 cups quick oats
1 cup vegetable shortening
2 cups sugar
2 cups brown sugar
2 teaspoons baking soda
¹/₂ teaspoon salt
2 teaspoons cinnamon
1 teaspoon nutmeg
1 teaspoon cloves
4 eggs
2 teaspoons vanilla
2²/₃ cups flour

Preheat oven to 350 degrees. Grease an 11 x 17-inch half-sheet cake pan. Pour hot water over the oats. In a separate bowl, cream together shortening, sugar, brown sugar, baking soda, salt, cinnamon, nutmeg, cloves, eggs and vanilla. Add to oatmeal mixture and beat well. Add flour and blend well. Pour batter into prepared pan and bake for 30-35 minutes or until wooden pick comes out clean. Cool. Frost with Broiled Frosting (page 132), substituting walnuts for pecans, and cream for 2 percent milk.

◆◆◆

## TIP

◆ One (18.25 ounces) cake mix makes 24-28 cupcakes filled ²/₃ full. Fill cupcakes with a number 12 scoop.

# Plantation Cake

*Yield: 1 half-sheet cake*

1 box (18.25 ounces) yellow cake mix
1 box (18.25 ounces) butter cake mix
2²/₃ cups water
¹/₃ cup oil
¹/₂ cup (1 stick) margarine
6 eggs
*Topping*
1 pound frozen commercial non-dairy whipped topping, thawed
1 can (20 ounces) crushed pineapple, well drained

*Garnish*
1 can (15 ounces) mandarin oranges, well drained
20 whole pecan halves

Preheat oven to 350 degrees. Grease an 11 x 17-inch half-sheet cake pan. In a 5-quart mixing bowl place both cake mixes; add water, oil, margarine and eggs. Beat until smooth. Pour batter into prepared pan. Bake for 30-35 minutes, or until wooden pick inserted in center comes out clean.

Chill a 5-quart bowl. Beat commercial whipped topping until stiff peaks form. Fold in crushed pineapple. Spread mixture over cake. Arrange mandarin orange sections on cake (7 across and 9 down). Arrange pecans (5 across) every other row. Stand pecan halves up in each row to give the cake height. Place cake into half-sheet cake box. Refrigerate. Plantation cake will stay fresh in refrigerator up to 3 days. Do not freeze.

# Strawberry Picnic Cake

*Yield: 1 half-sheet cake*

1　half-sheet French vanilla cake*

*Topping*

1　container (16 pound) non-dairy
　　whipped topping, thawed

*Garnish*

3　pints fresh strawberries

1/2-3/4　cup sugar

(*Prepare a half-sheet French vanilla cake using 2 mixes, following package directions. Bake at 350 degrees for 30-35 minutes or until wooden pick in center of cake comes out clean. Cool.)

Spread whipped topping over cake. Place cake into half-sheet cake box. Score cake into 2 1/2-inch squares. Refrigerate. Slice strawberries and mix with sugar. Carry sweetened strawberries in a sealed container to the party. Top cake with sweetened strawberries as served. Cake will keep in refrigerator up to 4 days without strawberries. Bag the cake box and freeze up to 7 days without strawberries.

◆◆◆

# Strawberry Rhubarb Cake

Depending on the time of the year and the geographic location, fresh and frozen rhubarb can be hard to locate. I use frozen rhubarb. The impressive strawberry rhubarb cake is an attractive Fourth of July cake, and is an ideal cake for an upbeat picnic party.

*Yield: 1 half-sheet cake*

1　bag (20 ounces) frozen, unsweetened
　　rhubarb, thawed

1/3　cup sugar

2 1/2　cups water

1/2　cup oil

6　eggs

2　boxes (18.25 ounces each) yellow cake mix

*Topping*

1　pound non-dairy whipped topping, thawed

2　containers (14 ounces each) strawberry
　　glaze

1　quart fresh strawberries, halved

1　pint fresh blueberries

1　bag (3 ounces) almond slices

Preheat oven to 350 degrees. Grease an 11 x 17 x 1-inch half-sheet cake pan. Squeeze juice from rhubarb; add sugar. In a 5-quart mixing bowl add water, oil, and eggs to cake mixes. Beat until smooth. Fold in rhubarb. Pour cake batter into prepared pan. Bake for 35-45 minutes, or until wooden pick inserted in center comes out clean. Cool for 5-8 minutes. Turn cake onto a 12 x 18-inch piece of cardboard. Cool 2 hours longer.

Frost sides of cake with whipped topping. Spread strawberry glaze on top of cake. Pipe whipped topping on sides and border of cake with E1 star tip. Pipe 6 rows of whipped topping across the top of the cake. Place strawberry halves on glaze on top of cake. Place blueberries on whipped topping stars. Place 1 almond slice on each side of each blueberry. (Refer to picture on page 122.) Place cake into half-sheet cake box. Refrigerate. Strawberry rhubarb cake will keep in refrigerator for 3 days. Do not freeze with topping.

# Mile High Very Berry Shortcake

*Yield: one 9 x 13 x 2-inch cake*
*(24 servings)*

1 box (18.25 ounces) yellow cake mix
2²/₃ cups water
²/₃ cup vegetable oil
3 eggs
2¹/₂ cups all-purpose baking mix

*Topping*
2¹/₂ cups non-dairy whipped topping, thawed
1 cup raspberries, frozen, thawed and
    drained

*Garnish*
2 cups fresh raspberries
2 cups fresh blueberries
1 pint fresh strawberries, halved

Preheat oven to 350 degrees. Grease a 13 x 9 x 2-inch baking pan. In a 5-quart mixing bowl, blend cake mix, water, oil, and eggs. Batter will be runny. Add the all-purpose baking mix to thicken mixture. Beat until smooth for 1 minute. Pour batter into prepared pan. Bake for 35-40 minutes or until wooden pick comes out clean. Cool.

Mix thawed raspberries into non-dairy whipped topping. Spread topping on cake. Garnish with fresh raspberries, blueberries, and strawberries. Serve with a scoop of ice cream or whipped topping.

*Note:* This cake should only be made in the 13 x 9 x 2-inch pans, as you need the 2-inch depth to get a nice high cake.

◆◆◆

## SLICED AND SWEETENED FROZEN STRAWBERRIES

Sliced and sweetened frozen strawberries can be purchased from wholesale vendors by the case. One case will contain 24 containers (1 pound each), 6 containers (6¹/₂ pounds each), or one 30-pound container. Sometimes wholesale food vendors will sell you a half-case of 3 containers weighing 6¹/₂ pounds each. You can also buy only 1 or 2 containers at a time. The 30-pound case is the least expensive to purchase, and is best when feeding a large crowd. Consider storage when purchasing frozen strawberries in quantity. Turn over frozen strawberries as quickly as possible. Inventory sitting around is money out of your pocket.

Sliced and sweetened frozen strawberries can be purchased at the grocery store in 12-ounce or 1-pound containers. 1 pound of frozen strawberries will serve 4 to 5 people.

## FRESH STRAWBERRIES

Buy strawberries in quantity by the flat (12 pints per flat), or purchase strawberries at the grocery store by the pint, quart, or pound. One quart yields 4 cups, and serves 6 to 8 people.

Fresh strawberries are labor-intensive to clean, hull, and slice. I serve fresh, sliced strawberries only upon the customer's request and if I get my price.

# Pound Cakes

Strawberry shortcake is a very popular summer picnic dessert. Pound cake is sometimes served in place of biscuits, and is quick and easy to make. I like making pound cake from scratch because it rises more than a mix, and the yield on the homemade pound cake is greater. There are 16 to 18 slices per pound cake made from a boxed mix versus 18 to 20 slices per homemade pound cake. Of course, this also depends upon how you slice the cake. You can add grated lemon or orange peel to the batter, and orange extract or orange juice can be used in pound cake, too. If you are in a high altitude (over 3,500 feet) adjust the recipe: Preheat oven to 375 degrees. When blending the batter, increase milk to 1 cup and add 3 tablespoons all-purpose flour. Bake for 45-50 minutes. For a different look, use a bundt pan and bake at 350 degrees for 45-50 minutes. You can make 2 pound cakes at a time with a 5-quart mixer.

---

# Old-Fashioned Pound Cake

*Yield: one 9 x 5-inch loaf cake*

1 cup solid vegetable shortening
1 1/2 cups sugar
1 teaspoon vanilla
2 teaspoons lemon extract
6 eggs
2 cups flour
1 teaspoon baking powder

Preheat oven to 325 degrees. Grease and flour a 9 x 5 x 3-inch loaf pan. In a mixing bowl, cream shortening, sugar, vanilla, and lemon extract together until fluffy. Add eggs and beat well. Add flour and baking powder and mix well. Pour batter into prepared pan. Bake for 1 1/2 hours or until wooden pick in center of cake comes out clean. Cool pound cake in pan for 15 minutes. Loosen edges with spatula or knife and remove from pan. Cool on wire rack, wrap, and refrigerate. Slice pound cake before serving. Serve with sliced, sweetened strawberries and whipped cream.

# Pound Cake

*Yield: one 9 x 5-inch loaf cake*

1 box (16 ounces) pound cake mix
3/4 cup evaporated milk
2 eggs
2 teaspoons lemon extract

Preheat oven to 350 degrees. Grease and flour a 9 x 5 x 3-inch loaf pan. In a 5-quart mixing bowl, blend milk, eggs, and lemon extract into cake mix. Beat for 4 minutes with mixer on medium speed. Pour batter into prepared pan. Bake for 60-65 minutes or cake is golden brown and top springs back when lightly touched. A crack in the center of the pound cake is normal. Cool pound cake in pan for 15 minutes. Loosen edges with spatula or knife and remove from pan. Cool on wire rack, wrap, and refrigerate. Slice pound cake before serving. Serve with sliced, sweetened strawberries. Garnish with whipped topping.

# Pan Shortcake

*Yield: 1 half-sheet cake pan*

2 cups evaporated milk
3/4 cup sugar
3/4 cup (1 1/2 sticks) margarine, melted
10 cups all-purpose baking mix

Preheat oven to 350 degrees. Lightly grease an 11 x 17-inch half-sheet pan. In a 5-quart mixing bowl, stir milk, sugar, and margarine into all-purpose baking mix. Beat for 2 minutes. Spread dough evenly into prepared pan. Bake for 25-30 minutes or until wooden pick in center comes out clean. Cool, wrap, and refrigerate.

## Using Biscuits for Strawberry Shortcake

Biscuits are universal and served in many different dishes, including strawberry shortcake. It is too time-consuming to make biscuits from scratch for a large crowd. You can buy frozen prepared biscuits by the case. Each biscuit will be uniform in size.

## How to Purchase All-Purpose Baking Mix

Grocery stores sell 40-ounce or 60-ounce boxes of baking mix. Wholesale food vendors sell six 5-pound boxes per case. If you are going to make a lot of shortcakes, it is wise to buy baking mix by the case, as it is very expensive to buy it at the grocery store. It is smart to buy an off-brand name of baking mix wholesale, and use milk and a good grade of margarine to make the less expensive mix tasty. The strawberries and whipped topping will add flavor to the shortcake.

## Biscuits by the Case

140 biscuits (1 1/2 ounces each) per case
120 biscuits (2 ounces each) per case
120 biscuits (2 1/2 ounces) per case

I never purchase frozen biscuits by the case. Instead, I make shortcake in an 11 x 17-inch pan and cut it into 35 squares (2 1/2 inches each) at the party. It works very well for my picnics, served with thawed, frozen strawberries and a bowl of non-dairy whipped topping. I refill items as needed. When I set up a strawberry shortcake dessert bar, I have strawberry patterned tablecloths and some small baskets of fresh strawberries for display. There is just something visually appealing about big, fresh strawberries spilling out of a basket on a glass mirror. Sometimes I served vanilla ice cream with the strawberry shortcake, depending on the customer's request and willingness to pay the price.

# Upside-Down Cakes

## Fruit Cocktail Upside-Down Cake

Fruit cocktail can be used in a yellow upside-down cake. Three 1-pound cans of fruit cocktail yield 2 pounds of drained fruit, enough for one 11 x 17-inch half-sheet cake pan. Two No. 10 cans of fruit cocktail make five 11 x 17-inch half-sheet cakes.

*Yield: 1 half-sheet cake*
- 2 boxes (18.25 ounces each) yellow cake mix
- 1/2 cup (1 stick) margarine
- 3 cups brown sugar
- 3 cans (1 pound each) fruit cocktail, drained
- 2 2/3 cups water
- 2/3 cup vegetable oil
- 6 eggs
- 1 container (1 pound) non-dairy whipped topping

Preheat oven to 350 degrees. Melt margarine and pour into an 11 x 17-inch half-sheet cake pan. Pack brown sugar into pan. Place fruit cocktail over brown sugar. In a 5-quart mixing bowl, add water, oil, and eggs to cake mixes. Beat until smooth. Pour batter over fruit cocktail. Bake for 35-45 minutes or until wooden pick in center of cake comes out clean. Cool for 5-8 minutes. Turn out cake onto a 12 x 18-inch piece of cardboard. Place into a half-sheet cake box. Refrigerate. Cake will keep in the refrigerator for 3 days. Serve cake with non-dairy whipped topping. Do not freeze.

## Peach Spice Upside-Down Cake

*Yield: 1 half sheet-cake*
- 1/2 cup (1 stick) margarine
- 3 cups brown sugar
- 3 cups pecans, chopped
- 3 cans (15 ounces each) sliced peaches, drained
- 2 2/3 cups water
- 2/3 cup oil
- 6 eggs
- 2 boxes (18.25 ounces each) spice cake mix
- 1 container (16 ounces) non-dairy whipped topping

Preheat oven to 325 degrees. Melt margarine and pour into an 11 x 17-inch half-sheet cake pan. Pack brown sugar into pan. Spread pecans over brown sugar. Place peach slices over pecans (5 across and 7 down).

In a 5-quart mixing bowl, add water, oil, and eggs to cake mixes and beat until smooth. Pour batter over peaches. Bake for 45-50 minutes or until wooden pick in center comes out clean. Cool 5-8 minutes. Turn out onto a 12 x 18-inch sheet of cardboard. Cool. Place in a half-sheet cake box. Refrigerate. Upside-down cake will keep in refrigerator up to 3 days. Serve cake with non-dairy whipped topping. Do not freeze this cake.

*Note:* One No. 10 can of sliced peaches makes two 11 x 17-inch half-sheet cakes or 1 full-size sheet cake.

# Pineapple-Carrot Upside-Down Cake

Three 20-ounce cans of crushed pineapple, drained, yield only 30 ounces fruit, as half of the weight per can of crushed pineapple is juice. Three 20-ounce cans of crushed pineapple are used for one 11 x 17 x 1-inch half-sheet cake.

*Yield: 1 half-sheet cake*

 2 boxes (18.25 ounces) carrot cake mix
 1/2 cup (1 stick) margarine
 3 cups brown sugar
 3 cans (20 ounces) crushed pineapple, well drained
2 2/3 cups water
 2/3 cup vegetable oil
 6 eggs
 1 container (1 pound) non-dairy whipped topping

Preheat oven to 325 degrees. Melt margarine. Pour margarine into an 11 x 17-inch half sheet cake pan. Pack brown sugar into pan. Spread pineapple over brown sugar. In a 5-quart mixing bowl, add water, oil, and eggs to cake mixes. Beat until smooth. Pour batter over pineapple. Bake for 50-55 minutes or until wooden pick in center comes out clean. Cool 5 - 8 minutes. Turn out onto a 12 x 18-inch cardboard. Cool. Place in a half-sheet cake box. Refrigerate. Upside-down cake will keep in refrigerator up to 3 days. Serve cake with non-dairy whipped topping. Do not freeze this cake.

# Pineapple Upside-Down Cake

There are 10 pineapple rings to one 20-ounce can. Two 20-ounce cans are used per 11 x 17-inch pineapple upside-down cake. A No. 10 can of pineapple slices should make three 11 x 17 x 1-inch cakes. Three cups of firmly packed brown sugar equals 24 ounces. To save money, use a half of a Maraschino cherry per pineapple ring, cavity of the cherry facing down.

*Yield: 1 half-sheet cake*

 2 boxes (18.25 ounces each) yellow cake mix
 1/2 cup (1 stick) margarine
 3 cups brown sugar
 2 cans (20 ounces each) pineapple rings, drained
 20 whole Maraschino cherries, stems removed
2 2/3 cups water
 2/3 cup vegetable oil
 6 eggs
 1 container (1 pound) non-dairy whipped topping

Preheat oven to 350 degrees. Melt margarine and pour into an 11 x 17 -inch half-sheet cake pan. Pack brown sugar into pan. Place 20 pineapple slices on brown sugar (4 across and 5 down). Place 1 Maraschino cherry in center of each pineapple slice. In a 5-quart mixing bowl, add water, oil, and eggs to cake mixes. Beat until smooth. Pour cake batter over pineapple rings and cherries. Bake for 35-45 minutes or until wooden pick in center comes out clean. Cool for 5-8 minutes. Turn out cake onto a 12 x 18-inch cardboard. Place in a half-sheet cake box. Refrigerate. Pineapple upside down cake will keep in refrigerator up to 3 days. Serve cake with non-dairy whipped topping. Do not freeze.

# Cookies

SCOOP SIZE FOR MAKING COOKIES—To get uniform size cookies use a scoop. I use three different size scoops for making cookies. The smaller the number of the scoop the larger the cookie.

| Scoop Size | Batter | Cookie Size | Baking Time |
|---|---|---|---|
| No. 12 | 4 tablespoons (4 oz.) | large 5" baked | 15-18 min. |
| No. 24 | 2 tablespoons (2 oz.) | medium 3¹/2" baked | 10-12 min. |
| No. 40 | 1 tablespoon (1 oz.) | small 2¹/2" baked | 8-10 min. |

Number of cookies, by scoop size

| Batches | No. 12 | No. 24 | No. 40 |
|---|---|---|---|
| 1 | 7 | 13 | 32 |
| 2 | 14 | 26 | 68 |
| 3 | 21 | 39 | 92 |
| 4 | 28 | 52 | 138 |
| 5 | 35 | 65 | 160 |
| 6 | 42 | 78 | 184 |

## Chocolate Chip Story

I had a worker that made wonderful chocolate chip cookies. One day she put 2 cups of salt instead of sugar into the cookie dough. The cookies baked up beautifully. I happened to taste a cookie just moments before leaving for the party. We frantically whipped up two new batches of cookies, and I bought some extra cookies from the store on the way to the party. Luckily the party was for only 100 people. We arranged the warm, just-baked cookies at the party. The guests were impressed with our great chocolate chip cookies. If they only knew the truth. Oh, well!

The problem occurred because the sugar and salt were in big white bins next to each other. The bins were not marked and looked alike. After that we color-coded the bins. The problem never happened again. This mistake was another great learning experience.

# Baking Chocolate Chip Cookies on a 13½ x 17½-inch Cookie Sheet

Leave 2 inches space around each cookie so they won't run together. A No. 12 scoop yield 6 cookies per cookie sheet (2 across and 3 down). A No. 24 scoop yields 12 cookies per cookie sheet (3 across and 4 down). A No. 40 scoop yield 20 cookies per baking sheet (4 across and 5 down). On a 17½ x 25½-inch baking sheet, a No. 12 scoop yields 12 cookies per sheet (3 across and 4 down) A No. 24 scoop yields 24 cookies per sheet (4 across and 6 down). A No. 40 scoop yields 42 cookies per sheet (6 across and 7 down). (A 17½ x 24½ baking sheet will not fit in a home style oven.)

I use the No. 24 scoop to make cookies for picnic lunch boxes. The 3½ inch cookie is just right to top off a picnic lunch box or meal.

There are many varieties of bakery cookies on the market that are delicious. Also you can buy a variety of frozen cookies. There are also frozen diabetic and fat-free cookies on the market. Check with your local bakery or wholesale distributor for more information.

I make cookies in multiple batches. I would buy cookies for very large picnics, rather than making them, or make bars instead of cookies because they're less work: they don't have to be watched while they're baking, and they can be cut and served right from the baking pans, which makes transporting them easier. You have to watch cookies while they bake to be sure they do not burn. Cookies have to be removed from the baking sheets, cooled and arranged on trays. You need to pack cookies carefully so they do not break.

Follow directions carefully for salt and baking soda. Remember that in quantity cooking you do not increase salt or baking soda in larger batches.

As you are scooping the dough out of the bowl, run the filled scoop across the lip of bowl to level out scoop. When cookie dough is released from the scoop the dough forms a half ball. Flatten dough lightly with the heel of your hand or a spatula before baking for thin cookies. If you like cookies to be a little thicker do not press the cookie down. Cookies will flatten somewhat while baking. If you want extra-crisp cookies double the margarine and shortening and add ½ cup flour per single batch.

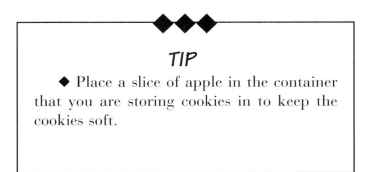

## TIP

◆ Place a slice of apple in the container that you are storing cookies in to keep the cookies soft.

# Chocolate Chip Cookies

### Yield: 1 double batch
*(2 pounds 12 ounces cookie dough)*

1/2 cup (1 stick) margarine, softened
1/2 cup solid vegetable shortening
2/3 cup sugar
3/4 cup brown sugar
2 eggs
1 teaspoon vanilla
2 1/4 cups flour
1 teaspoons baking soda
1/2 teaspoon salt
1 package (12 ounces) chocolate chips (2 cups)

### Yield: 3 single batches
*(4 pounds 2 ounces cookie dough)*

3/4 cup (1 1/2 sticks) margarine, softened
3/4 cups solid vegetable shortening
1 cup sugar
1 1/2 cups brown sugar
3 eggs
1 1/2 teaspoons vanilla
3 1/4 cups plus 2 tablespoons flour
2 1/2 teaspoons baking soda
1 teaspoons salt
1 package (6 ounces) plus 1 package (12 ounces) chocolate chips (3 cups)

### Yield: 2 double batches
*(5 pounds 8 ounces cookie dough)*

1 cup (2 sticks) margarine, softened
1 cup solid vegetable shortening
1 1/3 cups sugar
2 cups brown sugar
4 eggs
2 teaspoons vanilla
4 1/2 cups flour
2 teaspoons baking soda
1 teaspoons salt
1 package (24 ounces) chocolate chips (4 cups)

### Yield: 5 single batches
*(6 pounds 14 ounces cookie dough)*

1 1/4 cups (2 1/2 sticks) margarine, softened
1 1/4 cups solid vegetable shortening
1 2/3 cups sugar
2 1/2 cups brown sugar
5 eggs
2 1/2 teaspoons vanilla
5 1/2 cups plus 2 tablespoons flour
2 1/2 teaspoons baking soda
1 1/2 teaspoons salt
1 package (24 ounces) plus 1 package (6 ounces) chocolate chips (5 cups)

### Yield: 3 double batches or 6 single batches
*(8 pounds 4 ounces cookie dough)*

1 1/2 cups (3 sticks) margarine
1 1/2 cups solid vegetable shortening
2 cups sugar
3 cups brown sugar
6 eggs
1 tablespoon vanilla
6 3/4 cups flour
3 teaspoons baking soda
1 teaspoon salt
3 packages (12 ounces each) chocolate chips (6 cups)

Preheat oven to 375 degrees. Beat margarine, shortening, sugar, brown sugar, eggs and vanilla in large mixer. Add flour gradually to mixture. Add baking soda and salt and beat until smooth. Stir in chocolate chips by hand. Use a scoop for desired cookie size. Place cookies on ungreased cookie sheet. Flatten out cookie with palm of hand or spatula if desired. Refer to chart for baking time on page 141.

# Peanut Butter Cookies

### Yield: 1 single batch
### (1¹/₂ pounds cookie dough)

¹/₄ cup solid vegetable shortening
¹/₄ cup (¹/₂ stick) margarine, softened
¹/₂ cup peanut butter
¹/₂ cup sugar
¹/₂ cup brown sugar
1 egg
1 teaspoon vanilla
1¹/₄ cups flour
¹/₂ teaspoon baking powder
¹/₂ teaspoon baking soda
¹/₄ teaspoon salt

### Yield: 1 double batch
### (3 pounds cookie dough)

¹/₂ cup solid vegetable shortening
¹/₂ cup (1 stick) margarine, softened
1 cup peanut butter
1 cup sugar
1 cup brown sugar
2 eggs
1 teaspoon vanilla
2¹/₂ cups flour
1 teaspoon baking powder
1 teaspoon baking soda
¹/₂ teaspoon salt

### Yield: 3 single batches
### (4¹/₂ pounds cookie dough)

³/₄ cup solid vegetable shortening
³/₄ cup (1¹/₂ sticks) margarine
1¹/₂ cups peanut butter
1¹/₂ cups sugar
1¹/₂ cups brown sugar
3 eggs
2¹/₂ teaspoons vanilla
3³/₄ cups flour
2 teaspoons baking powder
2 teaspoons baking soda
¹/₂ teaspoon salt

### Yield: 4 single or 2 double batches
### (6 pounds cookie dough)

1 cup shortening
1 cup (2 sticks) margarine, softened
2 cups peanut butter
2 cups sugar
2 cups brown sugar
4 eggs
2 teaspoon vanilla
5 cups flour
2 teaspoon baking powder
2 teaspoons baking soda
¹/₂ teaspoon salt

### Yield: 5 single batches
### (7¹/₂ pounds cookie dough)

1¹/₄ cups shortening
1¹/₄ cups (2¹/₂ sticks) margarine, softened
2¹/₂ cups peanut butter
2¹/₂ cups sugar
2¹/₂ cups brown sugar
5 eggs
1 tablespoon vanilla
6¹/₄ cups flour
1 tablespoon baking powder
1 tablespoons baking soda
³/₄ teaspoon salt

### Yield: 6 single or 3 double batches
### (9 pounds cookie dough)

1¹/₂ cups shortening
1¹/₂ cups (3 sticks) margarine, softened
3 cups peanut butter
3 cups sugar
3 cups brown sugar
6 eggs
1 tablespoon vanilla
7¹/₂ cups flour
4 teaspoons baking powder
4 teaspoon baking soda
1 teaspoon salt

*Continued on next page*

*Peanut Butter Cookies, continued*

Mix shortening, peanut butter, sugar, brown sugar, eggs and vanilla thoroughly. Add flour, baking powder, baking soda and salt to shortening mixture. Blend. Use a scoop to make uniform size cookies. Flatten crisscross-style with fork. Refer to chart for baking time of cookies according to size of cookie and yield on page 141.

◆◆◆

# Bars

◆◆◆

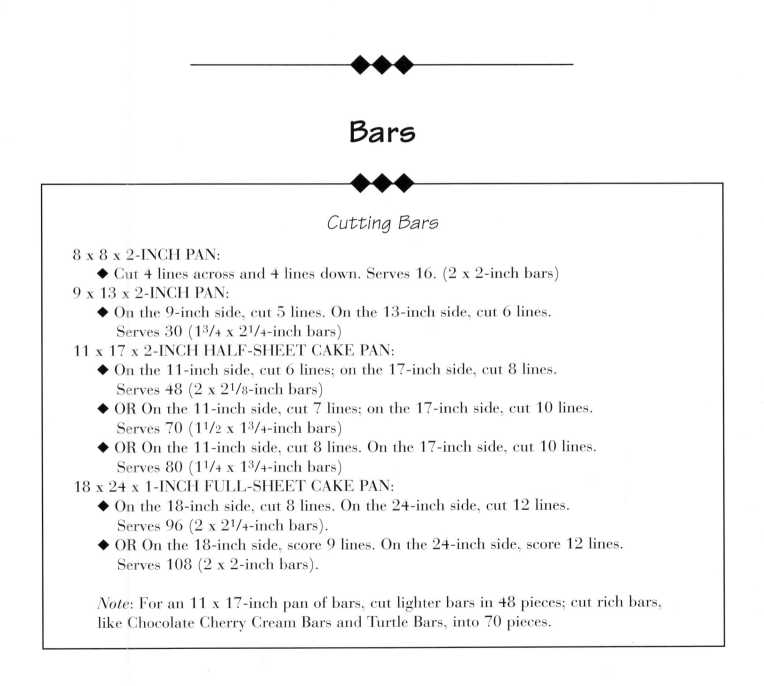

### Cutting Bars

8 x 8 x 2-INCH PAN:
  ◆ Cut 4 lines across and 4 lines down. Serves 16. (2 x 2-inch bars)

9 x 13 x 2-INCH PAN:
  ◆ On the 9-inch side, cut 5 lines. On the 13-inch side, cut 6 lines.
    Serves 30 ($1^3/_4$ x $2^1/_4$-inch bars)

11 x 17 x 2-INCH HALF-SHEET CAKE PAN:
  ◆ On the 11-inch side, cut 6 lines; on the 17-inch side, cut 8 lines.
    Serves 48 (2 x $2^1/_8$-inch bars)
  ◆ OR On the 11-inch side, cut 7 lines; on the 17-inch side, cut 10 lines.
    Serves 70 ($1^1/_2$ x $1^3/_4$-inch bars)
  ◆ OR On the 11-inch side, cut 8 lines. On the 17-inch side, cut 10 lines.
    Serves 80 ($1^1/_4$ x $1^3/_4$-inch bars)

18 x 24 x 1-INCH FULL-SHEET CAKE PAN:
  ◆ On the 18-inch side, cut 8 lines. On the 24-inch side, cut 12 lines.
    Serves 96 (2 x $2^1/_4$-inch bars).
  ◆ OR On the 18-inch side, score 9 lines. On the 24-inch side, score 12 lines.
    Serves 108 (2 x 2-inch bars).

*Note*: For an 11 x 17-inch pan of bars, cut lighter bars in 48 pieces; cut rich bars, like Chocolate Cherry Cream Bars and Turtle Bars, into 70 pieces.

# Hello Dolly Bars

TIPS: Picnickers clamor for these rich and tasty, but expensive to make, bars. They are quick and easy to make and transport. To get a variety of desserts, be creative—substitute butterscotch chips or peanut butter chips for the chocolate chips and almonds for the walnuts or pecans. Hello Dolly bars will keep in the freezer for up to 30 days. Make these bars in advance and keep on hand for surprise guests.

### *Yield one 9 x 9 x 2-inch pan*

*Crust*
- 1/2 cup (1 stick) margarine, melted
- 1 cup graham cracker crumbs

*Topping*
- 1 cup coconut
- 1 cup pecans or walnuts, chopped
- 1 cup semisweet mini chocolate chips
- 1 can (14 ounces) sweetened condensed milk
- 1 cup colored mini M&M's, optional

### *Yield: One 13 x 9 x 2-inch pan*

*Crust*
- 1 cup (2 sticks) margarine, melted
- 2 cups graham cracker crumbs

*Topping*
- 2 cups coconut
- 2 cups pecans or walnuts, chopped
- 2 cups semisweet mini chocolate chips
- 2 cans (14 ounces each) sweetened condensed milk
- 2 cups colored mini M&M's, optional

### *Yield: 1 half-sheet cake pan*

*Crust*
- 2 cups (4 sticks) margarine, melted
- 4 cups graham cracker crumbs
- 3 cups coconut
- 2 cups pecans or walnuts, chopped
- 3 cups semisweet mini chocolate chips
- 3 cans (14 ounces each) sweetened condensed milk
- 2 cups colored mini M&M's, optional

Preheat oven to 350 degrees. Melt margarine in microwave and pour into pan. Spread graham cracker crumbs evenly over melted butter to form a crust. Top with coconut. Top with nuts. Sprinkle chocolate chips over nuts. Pour sweetened condensed milk evenly over top of chocolate chips. Sprinkle M&M's on top, if desired. Bake for 25-30 minutes or until golden brown. Cool slightly. Cut into bars (see chart on page 145). Cover and refrigerate.

# Lemon Bars

Lemon bars are very simple and inexpensive to make. I prefer using butter in the crust instead of margarine, but you can use half butter and half margarine or all margarine if you prefer. Do not overbake lemon bars. The filling puffs during baking, but flattens when cooled. I have given you measurements for powdered sugar for the topping for the lemon bars, but you may need to use more. If you are serving lemon bars on a hot summer day, it is best to carry the powered sugar with you to the party and put it on there. Humidity makes the powdered sugar sticky.

### *Yield: one 8 x 8 x 2-inch pan*

*Crust*
1 cup flour
1/4 cup powdered sugar
1/2 cup (1 stick) butter, melted

*Filling*
2 eggs
1 cup granulated sugar
1/2 teaspoon baking powder
1/8 teaspoon salt
2 tablespoons lemon juice

*Topping*
3 tablespoons powdered sugar

### *Yield: one 13 x 9 x 2-inch pan*

*Crust*
2 cups flour
1/2 cup powdered sugar
1 cup (2 sticks) butter, melted

*Filling*
5 eggs
3 cups granulated sugar
3/4 teaspoon baking powder
1/4 teaspoon salt
1/3 cup lemon juice

*Topping*
1/3 cup powdered sugar

### *Yield: 1 half-sheet pan*

*Crust*
3 cups flour
3/4 cup powdered sugar
1 1/2 cups (3 sticks) butter, melted

*Filling*
8 eggs
4 cups sugar
2/3 cup lemon juice
1 teaspoon baking powder
1/4 teaspoon salt

*Topping*
1/2 cup powdered sugar

Preheat oven to 350 degrees. In a bowl, stir flour and powdered sugar together. Blend in butter thoroughly. Press evenly into ungreased pan. Bake for 12-15 minutes. In a mixing bowl, beat eggs, sugar, baking powder, salt, and lemon juice together. Pour over crust and bake for 25-30 minutes more. Refrigerate overnight. Cut into bars (see chart on page 145). Sift powdered sugar over bars just before serving.

# Turtle Bars

You can substitute walnuts for pecans to save money; however, a true turtle bar has pecans. There are about 50 caramels in one 14-ounce bag. It takes two 14-ounce bags to make the filling for one half-sheet pan. When you use caramel squares you need to add evaporated milk to get a creamy consistency. If you are making several batches of turtle bars, as it is best to purchase No. 10 cans of caramel fudge; it is too labor-intensive to unwrap individual caramels. Each can weighs 96 fluid ounces, and there are 12 cups per can (6 cans per case). Four half-sheet pans of turtle bars can be made from one No. 10 can. Use 3 cups of caramel fudge or caramel syrup per half sheet-cake pan. Each cup of caramel weighs 10 ounces. For smaller recipes, purchase caramel syrup at your local grocery store in 20-ounce containers. For each half-sheet pan use 1¹/₂ containers of caramel syrup (30 ounces), or 30 ounces of institutional caramel fudge. It is best to weigh out the 30 ounces of caramel rather than using a measuring cup. If you do use a cup, grease it with margarine so the caramel slides out easily. Omit evaporated milk when using caramel fudge or syrup. Use caramel fudge or syrup at room temperature to get a good pouring consistency. I cut a half-sheet pan of turtle bars into 70 pieces because they are very rich and expensive to make. If you are going to spend the time and energy to do turtle bars, it is best to make larger quantities. Extra bars freeze well.

### TURTLE BARS (Method I)
*Yield: one 9 x 13 x 2-inch pan*
*Crust*
  1 box (18.25 ounces) German chocolate
     cake mix
  ¹/₃ cup evaporated milk
  ¹/₂ cup (1 stick) margarine, melted
  1 cup chopped pecans

*Filling*
  1 package (14 ounces) caramels
  ¹/₂ cup evaporated milk
  1 package (12 ounces) chocolate chips
     (2 cups)

*Yield: 1 half sheet-cake pan*
*Crust*
  2 boxes (18.25 ounces each) German
     chocolate cake mix
  ²/₃ cup evaporated milk
  1 cup (2 sticks) margarine, melted
  2 cups chopped pecans
*Filling*
  2 packages (14 ounces each) caramels
  1 cup evaporated milk
  3 cups chocolate chips

Preheat oven to 350 degrees. Grease baking pan. Mix cake mix with evaporated milk, margarine, and nuts until it holds together. Divide dough in half. Spread and press half of dough evenly into bottom of prepared pan. Bake 8 to 10 minutes. Melt caramels with evaporated milk in top of a double boiler. Using a wire whisk, beat mixture until smooth and creamy. Sprinkle chocolate chips over warm dough. Pour warm caramel mixture over entire surface of chocolate chips. Sprinkle remaining dough on top of caramel mixture and chocolate chips. Bake 20-25 minutes longer. Cool. Cut into bars (see page 145). Cover and refrigerate.

### TURTLE BAR FILLING (Method II)
For filling, instead of caramels and evaporated milk, use 1 container (15 ounces) caramel syrup or caramel fudge (1¹/₂ cups) for a 9 x 13-inch pan, or 3 cups (30 ounces) for a half-sheet cake pan. Proceed as above.

# Almond Coconut Bars

### Yield: one 8 x 8 x 2-inch pan

**Crust**

- 1/4 cup (1/2 stick) butter or margarine, softened
- 1/4 cup solid white vegetable shortening
- 2 tablespoons brown sugar
- 2 tablespoons sugar
- 1 cup plus 2 tablespoons flour

**Filling**

- 2 eggs, well beaten
- 1/2 cup brown sugar
- 1/2 teaspoon vanilla
- 1 tablespoon flour
- 1/2 teaspoon baking powder
- 1/4 teaspoon salt
- 3/4 cup coconut
- 3/4 cup slivered almonds

### Yield: one 13 x 9 x 2-inch pan

**Crust**

- 1/2 cup (1 stick) butter or margarine, softened
- 1/2 cup solid white vegetable shortening
- 1/4 cup brown sugar
- 1/4 cup sugar
- 2 1/4 cups flour

**Filling**

- 3 eggs, well beaten
- 1 cup brown sugar
- 1 teaspoon vanilla
- 3 tablespoons flour
- 1 teaspoon baking powder
- 1/4 teaspoon salt
- 1 1/2 cups coconut
- 1 1/2 cups slivered almonds

### Yield: 1 half-sheet pan

**Crust**

- 1 cup (2 sticks) butter or margarine, softened
- 1 cup solid white vegetable shortening
- 1/2 cup brown sugar
- 2 1/4 cups flour

**Filling**

- 6 eggs, well beaten
- 2 cups brown sugar
- 3 teaspoons vanilla
- 6 tablespoons flour
- 3 teaspoons baking powder
- 1/2 teaspoon salt
- 3 cups coconut
- 3 cups slivered almonds

Preheat oven to 350 degrees. In a small bowl, cream butter, shortening and brown sugar. Stir in flour. Press into bottom of ungreased pan. Bake 12-15 minutes.

To make filling, in a separate bowl mix eggs, brown sugar, and vanilla. Add flour, baking powder and salt; blend well. Stir in coconut and almonds by hand. Spread filling over crust. Bake 15-20 minutes for 8 x 8-inch pan, or 20-25 minutes for 13 x 9-inch pan, or 30-35 minutes for half-sheet pan, or until golden brown. Cool. Cut into bars (see chart on page 145). Refrigerate.

# Cherry Coconut Bars

Cherry Coconut Bars are gooey and wonderful. Make these one day in advance to allow them time to firm up. They freeze well.

*Yield: one 8 x 8 x 2-inch pan*

Crust
  1 cup flour
  1/2 cup (1 stick) butter, melted
  1/4 cup powdered sugar

Filling
  1 cup granulated sugar
  2 eggs, slightly beaten
  1/4 cup flour
  1/2 teaspoon baking powder
  1/4 teaspoon salt
  1 teaspoon vanilla
  1/2 cup chopped walnuts
  1/2 cup coconut
  1/2 cup Maraschino cherries,
    drained and cut into eighths

*Yield: one 13 x 9 x 2-inch pan*

Crust
  2 cups flour
  1 cup (2 sticks) butter, melted
  1/2 cup powdered sugar

Filling
  2 cups granulated sugar
  4 eggs, slightly beaten
  1/2 cup flour
  1 teaspoon baking powder
  1/2 teaspoon salt
  2 teaspoons vanilla
  1 cup chopped walnuts
  1 cup coconut
  1 cup Maraschino cherries, drained and cut
    into eighths

*Yield: 1 half-sheet pan*

Crust
  3 cups flour
  1 1/2 cups (3 sticks) butter, melted
  3/4 cup powdered sugar

Filling
  4 cups granulated sugar
  8 eggs, slightly beaten
  1 cup flour
  2 teaspoons baking powder
  1 teaspoon salt
  3 teaspoons vanilla
  2 cups chopped walnuts
  2 cups coconut
  2 jars (1 pound each) Maraschino cherries,
    drained and cut into eighths

Preheat oven to 350 degrees. In a bowl, mix flour, butter, and powdered sugar with an electric mixer until well blended. Press crust evenly into an ungreased pan. Bake for 8-10 minutes until golden brown. In a separate bowl, mix sugar, eggs, flour, baking powder, salt, walnuts, coconut, and cherries; blend well. Pour over crust and bake for 25-30 minutes. Cool, cut into bars (see chart on page 145) and refrigerate.

## TIP

◆ There are approximately 38 whole cherries in a 1-pound jar of Maraschino cherries.

◆ Do not automatically double salt or baking powder when doubling a recipe.

# Chocolate Cherry Cream Bars

These bars are candylike and very rich; you should cut them into very small pieces. Dip a knife into hot water to cut. Chocolate Cherry Cream Bars do not freeze well.

### Yield: one 8 x 8 x 2-inch pan

*Crust*
- 3/4 cup flour
- 1/2 cup (1 stick) margarine, melted
- 1/3 cup powdered sugar
- 2 tablespoons cocoa

*Topping*
- 16 large whole Maraschino cherries, drained
- 1 cup coconut
- 1 can (14 ounces) sweetened condensed milk

*Chocolate Frosting*
- 2 tablespoons margarine, melted
- 1 ounce (1 square) semisweet chocolate
- 1 cup powdered sugar
  - Pinch of salt, optional
- 1/4 teaspoon vanilla
- 2 tablespoons evaporated milk

### Yield: one 13 x 9 x 2-inch pan

*Crust*
- 1 1/2 cups flour
- 1 cup (2 sticks) margarine, melted
- 3/4 cup powdered sugar
- 1/4 cup cocoa

*Topping*
- 35 large whole Maraschino cherries, drained
- 2 cups coconut
- 2 cans (14 ounces each) sweetened condensed milk

*Chocolate Frosting*
- 1/4 cup (1/2 stick) margarine, melted
- 2 squares (1 ounce each) semisweet chocolate
- 2 cups powdered sugar
  - Pinch of salt, optional
- 1/2 teaspoon vanilla
- 1/4 cup evaporated milk

### Yield: 1 half-sheet pan

*Crust*
- 3 1/4 cups flour
- 1 1/2 cups (3 sticks) margarine, melted
- 1 cup powdered sugar
- 1/3 cup cocoa

*Topping*
- 80 large whole Maraschino cherries, drained
- 3 cups coconut
- 3 cans (14 ounces each) sweetened condensed milk

*Chocolate Frosting*
- 1/2 cup (1 stick) margarine, melted
- 4 ounces (4 squares) semisweet chocolate
- 4 cups powdered sugar
- 1/8 teaspoon salt
- 1 teaspoon vanilla
- 1/3 cup plus 2 tablespoons evaporated milk

Preheat oven to 350 degrees. Pour flour into a large bowl and add margarine, powdered sugar, and cocoa. Beat ingredients thoroughly. Spread crust evenly in an ungreased pan. Bake for 8-10 minutes. Place cherries evenly on crust. Top with coconut. Drizzle sweetened condensed milk over coconut. Bake 20-25 minutes for 8 x 8-inch pan, 25-30 minutes for 13 x 9-inch pan, or 30-35 minutes for half-sheet pan, or until golden brown. Cool slightly. In a saucepan over low heat or in the microwave, melt margarine and chocolate. Add mixture to bowl with powdered sugar, salt, vanilla and evaporated milk. Beat until smooth and creamy. Frost bars, cover, and refrigerate. Cut into tiny bars when cooled.

# Pecan Bars

*Yield: one 13 x 9-inch pan*

**Crust**
- 2 cups flour
- 1 cup (2 sticks) butter, melted
- 1/2 cup powdered sugar

**Filling**
- 6 eggs
- 2 cups sugar
- 2 cups corn syrup
- 1/3 cup butter, melted
- 2 cups finely chopped pecans
- 2 teaspoons vanilla
- 1/3 cup flour

*Yield: one 11 x 17-inch half-sheet pan*

**Crust**
- 3 cups flour
- 1 1/2 cups (3 sticks) butter, melted
- 3/4 cup powdered sugar

**Filling**
- 9 eggs
- 3 cups sugar
- 3 cups corn syrup
- 1/2 cup (1 stick) butter, melted
- 1 pound finely chopped pecans
- 1 tablespoon vanilla
- 1/2 cup flour

Preheat oven to 350 degrees. In a large bowl, mix together flour, butter and powdered sugar until well blended. Press dough evenly into ungreased pan. Bake for 12-15 minutes or until golden brown. In a separate bowl, mix eggs, sugar, corn syrup, butter, pecans, vanilla and flour together until smooth. Pour on top of crust. Bake 9x13 pan for 25-35 minutes, or 11x17 pan for 45-55 minutes. Cut into bars when completely cool. Refrigerate.

---

# Dessert Bar Crisp

A fruit crisp is a cross between a bar and a cake. Crisps are simple to make and are a popular picnic dessert. Serve with non-dairy whipped topping or ice cream. For a simple picnic, carry and serve the crisp right from the pan. For a fancier picnic, cut into 1 1/2-inch squares. Place each piece into a paper cupcake liner and, with a number 28 tip, pipe a whipped topping star in the middle of each piece. Top with a drained Maraschino cherry with stem, and serve them from a flat, round basket. It looks like you worked all day on this dessert! Presentation is everything. (See picture on page 122.)

# Peach Crisp

*Yield: 1 half-sheet pan*
- 2 cans (29 ounces) sliced peaches in heavy syrup, undrained
- 2 boxes (18.25 ounces) spice cake mix
- 1 cup (2 sticks) margarine
- 3 cups coconut
- 2 cups chopped pecans

Preheat oven to 350 degrees. Pour peaches with syrup into ungreased 11 x 17-inch pan. Sprinkle dry cake mix over peaches. Cut margarine into 50 slices; place squares in rows 5 across and 10 down over cake mix. Sprinkle with coconut and nuts. Bake for 55-60 minutes or until golden brown. Serve warm or cold with ice cream or non-dairy whipped topping.

# Strawberry Rhubarb Crisp

*Yield: 1 half-sheet pan*

1 package (20 ounces) frozen rhubarb, unsweetened
1 package (20 ounces) frozen strawberries, unsweetened
1 box (6 ounces) strawberry gelatin
1 cup boiling water
2 boxes (18.25 ounces each) white cake mix
1 cup (2 sticks) margarine
3 cups coconut
2 cups almond slivers

Preheat oven to 325 degrees. Thaw frozen strawberries and rhubarb. Cut strawberries into quarters; dice rhubarb. Mix strawberries and rhubarb together with their juices and pour into an ungreased 11 x 17-inch half-sheet pan. Pour the boiling water over the gelatin, and pour it over the strawberry-rhubarb mixture. Sprinkle dry cake mix over fruit in pan. Cut margarine in 50 squares; place squares evenly over cake mix. Sprinkle coconut and almond slivers over top. Bake for 60-75 minutes or until golden brown. Serve warm or cold with whipped topping or ice cream.

# Rhubarb Squares

These delicious bar is a favorite among seniors, although many children may not like them. Use fresh rhubarb when possible. If you use frozen rhubarb, be sure to squeeze out the excess liquid.

*Yield: one 8 x 8-inch pan*

*Crust*
1 cup flour
1/4 cup confectioner's sugar
1/2 cup (1 stick) butter, melted

Filling
1 1/2 cups sugar
2 eggs
1/2 cup flour
3/4 teaspoon cinnamon
1/2 cup chopped walnuts
2 cups fresh or frozen rhubarb, diced

Preheat oven to 350 degrees. For the crust, mix flour, confectioner's sugar and margarine until it holds together. Spread and press evenly into ungreased pan. Bake 8-10 minutes. Beat eggs and sugar together. Add flour, baking powder, cinnamon and walnuts. Stir in drained rhubarb. Bake for 30-35 minutes. Cool; cover with plastic wrap and refrigerate.

# Fancy Picnic Cakes and Tortes

Fancy tortes and cakes not only can be served at a Hawaiian Luau or an executive picnic but also at any function. These desserts make a big impression on guests. Each dessert is easy to make.

# Black Forest Torte

One 18.25-ounce cake mix made into batter is approximately 40 ounces total weight. Use a scale and place approximately 13$^1$/$_3$ ounces of batter in each of three 9-inch cake pans. If you are going to do a lot of Black Forest tortes, buy chocolate jimmies and Maraschino cherries in quantity. A Black Forest torte serves 12 to 14 guests. You can freeze the whole torte in a box. Place the box in a bag to insure freshness. I generally make the cakes ahead of time and freeze them without toppings or garnishes.

*Yield: one 9-inch torte (12-14 slices)*

3 eggs
  Vegetable oil for mix
  Water for mix
1 can (15 ounces) dark sweet cherries, pitted
1 box (18.25 ounces) chocolate fudge
  cake mix
1 container (2 pounds) commercial
  whipped topping, thawed and whipped,
  or 1 pound frozen ready-to-use
  non-dairy whipped topping, thawed
5 Maraschino cherries with stems, drained
$^1$/$_2$ cup chocolate jimmies

Preheat oven to 350 degrees. Grease three 9 x 1$^1$/$_2$ inch round cake pans. In a large mixing bowl, add eggs, oil, and water to cake mix and prepare according to directions on box. Drain juice from cherries. Scatter the cherries on the bottoms of the 3 prepared pans. Divide the batter evenly among the pans (13-14 ounces each). Bake for 20 minutes. Cool for 5 minutes. Turn cakes onto 9-inch circles of cardboard. Refrigerate. Place a dab of whipped topping into center of a 12-inch tray. Place first cake with cardboard onto tray. (The whipped topping holds the cake layer to the tray.) Spread whipped topping over top of first cake. Place second cake (without cardboard) on top, and spread with whipped topping. Place third cake (without cardboard) on top. Frost entire torte with whipped topping. Pipe a border on the top and bottom of torte using number E1 star tip. Pipe 5 stars on top of torte to form an X. Place a Maraschino cherry in the center of each star. Garnish the cake sides and top with chocolate jimmies.

# Flan Cake

A flan pan is raised in the middle and has fluted sides. The baked cake is served upside-down, creating a well in the center to be filled. Each flan cake serves 10. One pound of commercial whipped topping will cover three 10 x 2-inch flan cakes.

You could serve all flan tortes and make each one look different. Use your imagination. I like to mix and match desserts. A variety of desserts is the spice of life!

HOW TO CARRY A FLAN CAKE TO A PARTY—Place a 12-inch dome cover over each flan cake. Place each flan cake into a bakery container or insulated box with rollers. Station the container in the truck for safe traveling. I did not freeze flan cakes because I made them to order. You can make the flan cakes ahead of time and freeze without the filling and topping.

## Cherry Flan Cake

*Yield: three 10-inch flan cakes*

1 box (18.25 ounces) chocolate fudge
   or yellow cake mix
3 eggs
1 1/3 cups water
1/3 cup oil
3 cans (20 ounces each) cherry pie filling
1 container (1 pound) commercial whipped
   topping, thawed and whipped,
   or 1 pound frozen non-dairy whipped
   topping, thawed

Preheat oven to 350 degrees. Grease and flour three 10 x 2-inch flan cake pans. Add eggs, oil, and water to cake mix and prepare according to package directions. Divide the batter evenly among the prepared pans (13-14 ounces each). Bake for 10-15 minutes until wooden pick inserted in center comes out clean. Cool 5 minutes. Remove cake from pans.

Turn each cake on a 10-inch circle of cardboard. Cool. For each cake, place a dab of whipped topping onto a 12-inch serving tray. Place the cake, on its cardboard, onto tray. Fill each cake cavity with a third of the cherry pie filling. With an E1 star tip pipe on whipped topping on the side and place on top border. Two rows of whipped topping will cover top and sides of the flan cake.

*Variations:*
◆ 1 box (18.25 ounces) spice cake mix with 3 cans (20 ounces each) peach pie filling.
◆ 1 box (18.25 ounces) carrot cake mix with 3 containers (4.5 ounces each) ready-to-use vanilla pudding. Add 1 1/2 cups drained, crushed pineapple to the pudding.
◆ 1 box (18.25 ounces) French vanilla cake mix with 3 cans (20 ounces each) raspberry or strawberry pie filling.
◆ 1 box (18.25 ounces) white cake mix with 3 cans (20 ounces each) blueberry pie filling.
◆ 1 box (18.25 ounces) lemon cake mix with 3 containers (4.5 ounces each) lemon pie filling and 60 almond slices (looks like porcupine needles standing up on the sides of cake).
◆ 1 box (18.25 ounces) banana cake mix with 3 containers (4.5 ounces each) vanilla pudding Slice 3 large bananas into cavities of flans and spread pudding over the bananas. Sprinkle 1 1/2 cups coconut over pudding. Garnish with 18 Maraschino cherries with stems, drained.

# Flan Cake

*Yield: one 10-inch cake*

3/4  cup sugar
1/4  cup (1/2 stick) butter
 2  eggs
11/4  cups cake flour
 2  teaspoon baking powder
1/2  teaspoon salt
1/2  cup milk
1/2  teaspoon almond extract

Preheat oven to 350 degrees. Grease and flour a 10-inch flan pan. In a mixing bowl, beat butter, sugar, and eggs until fluffy. Sift dry ingredients; add alternately with almond extract and milk; blend well. Pour into prepared pan. Bake for 15-20 minutes or until wooden pick inserted in center comes out clean. Cool for 5 minutes. Remove from pan. Fill cavity with favorite filling. Cut into 10 pieces.

# Cheesecake

TO CUT CHEESECAKE: Dip a knife in hot water before slicing.

9-INCH CHEESECAKE, IN PIE PAN: Cut in 8 to 10 pieces.

9 X 13-INCH PAN: On the 9-inch side score 4 rows; on the 13-inch side score 6 rows.
   Serves 24 (21/4 x 21/4-inch pieces.)

11 X 17-INCH HALF-SHEET PAN: On the 11-inch side score 5 rows; on the 17-inch side score
   7 rows. Serves 35 (21/2 x 21/2-inch pieces.) OR On the 11-inch side score 5 rows; on the
   17-inch side score 8 rows. Serves 40 (21/2 x 21/8-inch pieces.)

# Icebox Cheesecake

*Yield: one 13 x 9-inch cheesecake*

Crust
 2  cups graham cracker crumbs
1/4  cup sugar
 1  cup (2 sticks) margarine, melted

Filling
 2  envelopes (1/4 ounce each) unflavored
      gelatin
 2  cups cold water
 4  packages (8 ounces each) cream cheese,
      softened
 1  cup sugar
 1  teaspoon vanilla

Topping
 1  can (21 ounces) blueberry pie filling

*Yield: 1 half-sheet cheesecake*

Crust
 4  cups graham cracker crumbs
1/2  cup sugar
11/2  cups (3 sticks) margarine, melted

Filling
 3  envelopes (1/4 ounce each) unflavored
      gelatin
 3  cups cold water
 6  packages (8 ounces each) cream cheese,
      softened
 2  cups sugar
 2  teaspoons vanilla

Topping
 2  cans (21 ounces each) blueberry pie
      filling

Preheat oven to 350 degrees. In a large bowl, mix crumbs, sugar, and margarine. Press into bottom of pan. Bake for 5-6 minutes.

Sprinkle gelatin over a quarter of the water; let stand 4 minutes. Microwave on high 40-60 seconds until gelatin is completely dissolved.

In mixing bowl beat cream cheese, sugar and vanilla until smooth. Add gelatin-water mixture. Gradually add remaining water and blend until smooth. Pour into crust; top with blueberry pie filling. Cover and refrigerate until set.

# Diabetic Velvet Cheesecake

*Yield: one 13 x 9-inch cheesecake*

*Crust*
- 2 cups crushed lowfat graham crackers
- 1 packet granulated sugar substitute
- 1/2 cup lowfat margarine, melted

*Filling*
- 4 packages (8 ounces each) reduced-fat cream cheese, softened
- 1 teaspoon granulated sugar substitute
- 6 eggs
- 2 teaspoons lemon juice

*Topping*
- 1 pint fresh strawberries, sliced

*Yield: 1 half-sheet cheesecake*

*Crust*
- 4 cups crushed lowfat graham crackers
- 4 packets granulated sugar substitute
- 1 cup lowfat margarine, melted

*Filling*
- 6 packages (8 ounces each) reduced-fat cream cheese, softened
- 2 teaspoons granulated sugar substitute
- 9 eggs
- 4 teaspoons lemon juice

*Topping*
- 2 pints fresh strawberries, sliced

Preheat oven to 300 degrees. In a large bowl, combine graham cracker crumbs, sugar substitute and margarine. Press into bottom of pan. In a large mixing bowl, beat cream cheese until smooth. Add sugar substitute and eggs, one at a time. Add lemon juice. Beat until creamy. Pour over crust. Bake for 55 minutes. Turn off oven; leave pan in oven with door ajar for 30 minutes. Remove pan from oven and refrigerate. Serve cheesecake with sliced strawberries. You can serve this cake to diabetic guests.

# Velvet Cheesecake

This baked cheesecake is time-consuming, but simple to make. You can use sweetened sliced frozen strawberries instead of fresh strawberries to save money. Also, frozen strawberries are available all year, in any part of the country. If you prefer more sour cream topping you can multiply the sour cream, sugar and vanilla one and a half times.

12 x 8-inch disposable pans are available at your grocery store.

*Yield: one 12 x 8-inch cheesecake*

**Crust**
- 2 cups graham cracker crumbs
- 1/4 cup sugar
- 3/4 cup (1 1/2 sticks) margarine, melted

**Filling**
- 2 pounds cream cheese, softened
- 1 cup sugar
- 2 teaspoons lemon juice
- 6 eggs

**Topping**
- 1 cup sour cream (room temperature)
- 2 tablespoons sugar
- 1 teaspoon vanilla
- 1 pint strawberries, sliced

*Yield: 1 half-sheet cake*

**Crust**
- 4 cups graham cracker crumbs
- 1/2 cup sugar
- 1 1/2 cups (3 sticks) margarine, melted

**Filling**
- 3 pounds cream cheese, softened
- 2 cups sugar
- 1 tablespoon lemon juice
- 9 eggs

**Topping**
- 2 cups sour cream (room temperature)
- 3 tablespoons sugar
- 2 teaspoon vanilla
- 2 pints strawberries, sliced

Preheat oven to 300 degrees. In a bowl combine graham cracker crumbs, sugar and margarine. Press into bottom of pan. In a separate bowl, beat cream cheese until smooth; gradually add sugar, beating until fluffy. Add lemon juice and eggs, beating well. Pour over crust. Bake 9 x 13 pan 45-50 minutes; half-sheet pan 55-60 minutes. Shut off oven and leave pan inside, with door ajar, 25 minutes. Combine sour cream, sugar and vanilla. Carefully spread over cheesecake. Immediately return to oven, leaving door ajar, 25 minutes longer. Refrigerate cake. Serve with sliced strawberries.

TIP: Make sure sour cream is room temperature or it will tear the cake.

*Note:* You can substitute 1 can (21 ounces) raspberry pie filling for each pint of strawberries, as topping.

## TIP

◆ You can buy a packaged mix for a no-bake cherry cheesecake that's made in a 9-inch pie pan and will serve 8. It contains mixes for the crust, filling and topping. You can also purchase 9-inch graham cracker crusts by the case (20 per case), and 6 cheesecake filling mixes (4 pounds each) per case—enough to make 48 cheesecakes. When making 9-inch cheesecakes, us the disposable aluminum pie pans, so you won't have to collect all your pans after the party.

# Black Forest Cheesecake

*Yield: one 13 x 9-inch cheesecake*

**Crust**
- 2 cups chocolate cookie crumbs
- 1/2 cup sugar
- 3/4 cup (1 1/2 sticks) margarine, melted

**Filling**
- 2 tablespoons water
- 1/2 envelope (1 1/2 teaspoons) unflavored gelatin
- 3 packages (8 ounces each) cream cheese, softened
- 1 can (14 ounces) sweetened condensed milk
- 1/4 cup lemon juice
- 1 teaspoon vanilla

**Topping**
- 1 can (30 ounces) cherry pie filling

*Yield: 1 half-sheet cake*

**Crust**
- 4 cups chocolate cookie crumbs
- 1 cup sugar
- 1 1/4 cups (2 1/2 sticks) margarine

**Filling**
- 1/4 cup water
- 1 envelope (1/4 ounce) unflavored gelatin
- 5 packages (8 ounces each) cream cheese, softened
- 2 cans (14 ounces each) sweetened condensed milk
- 1/2 cup lemon juice
- 2 teaspoons vanilla

**Topping**
- 2 cans (30 ounces) cherry pie filling

In baking pan, mix cookie crumbs, sugar and margarine. Press into pan to cover bottom. Chill for 8-10 minutes. In a measuring cup, sprinkle gelatin over water. Let stand 2 minutes; microwave on high for 40 seconds or until gelatin is dissolved. Stir well to completely dissolve gelatin. In a large bowl, beat cream cheese. Add condensed milk, gelatin mixture, lemon juice and vanilla, and continue to beat until smooth. Pour into crust. Refrigerate at least 2 hours or until filling is set. Spread with cherry pie filling. Cover and refrigerate. Cut just before serving.

## TIP

◆ The Black Forest Cheesecake can be turned into a Blueberry Icebox Cheesecake by changing the crust and the topping.

For a 13 x 9-inch crust, mix together 2 cups graham cracker crumbs, 1/4 cup sugar and 1 cup (2 sticks) margarine, melted; press into pan and refrigerate. Make filling for the 13 x 9-inch Black Forest Cheesecake, above. Pour over chilled crust and top with 1 can (21 ounces) blueberry pie filling. Cover and refrigerate.

# Hawaiian Cheesecake

The Hawaiian cheesecake is impressive and yet it is so simple to make. You can get a premium price for this elegant masterpiece. Slice this cheesecake into 16 pieces, using a sharp knife dipped in hot water. A frozen cheesecake must be thawed before removing from the pan. Set bottom of the pan of cheesecake on a stemmed glass. Push up pan sides holding cake pan. The cheesecake will be released from the pan and remain on the cardboard. Place a 12-inch dome cover over cheesecake.

*Yield: One 10-inch cheesecake (16 servings)*
- 1 frozen, prebaked 10-inch cheesecake, thawed
- 1 container (4.5 ounces) ready-to-serve vanilla pudding
- 2 kiwi fruit
- 1 can (15 ounces) mandarin oranges, drained
- 10-14 strawberries, halved
- 1 container (1 pound) commercial whipped topping, thawed and whipped, or 1 pound frozen non-dairy whipped topping, thawed.

Follow package directions for taking cheesecake out of the pan. Place a dab of whipped topping on a 12-inch serving tray. Place the cheesecake with cardboard on tray. Spread vanilla pudding over the top of the cheesecake. Peel and slice kiwi fruit. Form a circle of kiwi slices on outer edge of cheesecake. Form a circle of mandarin oranges inside the kiwi fruit. Fill in center with strawberry halves. Place one kiwi slice in the center. Pipe a border on top and bottom with a number 1E star tip. Do not freeze this cake.

# Lemon Angel Torte

Purchase a bakery chiffon or angel food cake. This cake is very light. Carry cake in a bakery box. You can freeze the plain angel food cake, but do not freeze after assembling.

*Yield: one 9 inch torte (14 slices)*
- 1 prepared angel food cake
- 1 box (1³/₄ ounces) instant lemon pudding mix
- 1 container (1 pound 8 ounces) commercial whipped topping, thawed and whipped, or 1 container (1 pound) plus 1 container (12 ounces) frozen ready-to-use non-dairy whipped topping, thawed
- 1 package (2.5 ounces) almond slices (30 pieces)
- ¹/₂ lemon, sliced

Slice the angel food cake horizontally to form 4 circles. Prepare pudding according to package directions. Fold half of whipped topping into pudding. Spread bottom layer of cake with pudding mixture. Place next layer on top; spread with more pudding. Continue with all layers. Do not spread top of cake with pudding. Place torte on the foam circle the cake was purchased with, or on a cardboard circle. Put a dab of whipped topping in the center of a 12-inch tray to hold the cake in place. Place assembled torte on tray. With remaining whipped topping frost the entire cake. Pipe a border on top and bottom with a number 1E star tip. Slice lemon half into 3 slices; cut each slice in half and place decoratively on cake so the rind on each half slice is facing up. Place almond slices at random sticking out of sides of cake, giving it a porcupine effect. Cover and refrigerate. The cake transports best in a 12-inch cake box.

# Pastry

## TIPS ON MAKING PIECRUST

1. Do not double salt if you decide to double a pastry recipe.
2. Butter makes a piecrust browner and less tender. Lard, commercial shortening and hydrogenated shortening make a tender, flaky crust.
3. Oil should make a tender crust but sometimes can make the crust tough or crumbly.
4. Mix and handle pastry as little as possible.
5. If piecrust is to be baked before filling, prick crust with fork to allow air and steam to escape. Pricking crust prevents blisters or bulging.
6. When a top crust is used, slit in several places to allow steam to escape.
7. Do not overfill a pie or top crust will bulge.
8. To flute a 2-crust pie leave $1/2$ to 1 inch extra pie dough around edges. Fold edges of pastry under to build a rim. Place thumb on edge of pie and press and twist the knuckle of the index finger toward the thumb. To flute a single pie crust leave $1/2$ to 1 inch extra dough on edges. Flute as directed above.
9. To prevent edge of crust from becoming too brown cover with a $11/2$-inch strip of aluminum foil.
10. Cut shapes out of top crust instead of cutting slits, for a decorative effect. Roll out top piecrust. With cookie cutter cut out design. If you are good at drawing you can make your own cutout designs.
11. A lattice top is very pretty. Line piecrust with bottom pastry shell, leaving a 1-inch overhang. Fill piecrust. Roll out top crust. Cut into $1/2$-inch strips with pastry wheel or sharp knife. Moisten edge of bottom pastry with water. Lay half of pastry strips across filling 1 inch apart. Weave first cross strip through center. Add another cross strip. Weave until lattice work is complete on entire pie. Fold lower crust over pastry strips. Press firmly around edge to seal.
12. For a golden brown crust beat together 1 large egg with 1 tablespoon milk to make an egg wash. Brush top of piecrust. This will make enough egg wash for six 9-inch glazed tops. Do not brush piecrust edges with egg wash or they will burn. Sprinkle 2 teaspoons to 1 tablespoon of sugar on center of crust. If you want a shiny top brush top crust with just milk before baking.

## GENERAL DIRECTIONS

Mix dry ingredients together. Add fat of choice. I prefer solid white shortening. I remember how tasty my grandmother's pies were—she used lard. Work quickly to get particles the size of a pea. Use ice-cold water. (I actually put ice cubes in the water.) Sprinkle water evenly on the flour-shortening mixture. Toss only until dough clings together to from a ball. Pie dough becomes tough if over-handled. All-purpose flour has a higher gluten content than pastry flour. If you get the pie dough too moist add 1 tablespoon shortening for every additional $1/4$ cup flour. Flour alone will result in tough crust.

Sprinkle flour on the countertop. Place the ball of dough on floured countertop, flatten slightly and sprinkle a little flour on top of dough; roll out. Or roll out dough between two sheets of waxed paper. Always use light, quick motions to prevent pie dough from sticking. Start from the center of the dough and roll out toward the edges until dough is $1/8$ inch thick. Roll dough loosely on rolling pin and unroll into bottom of pie pan, or fold dough into fourths or halves and place dough into pie pan. If using waxed paper, take off top layer and turn rolled dough upside down into pie pan. Take off second piece of waxed paper. Arrange dough in

pan. Do not stretch dough excessively while working with it. Patch any holes in crust. Be sure to pat dough carefully into the curves of the pan so that no air pockets remain.

When I was growing up my teacher said to use 2/3 of the dough for the lower crust and 1/3 for the top crust. I like to use ounces because it is more exact. Use 7 or 8 ounces pastry for the bottom crust for a 9 x 1-inch deep pan. Use 8 or 9 ounces pastry for a 10 x 1-inch pan or 10 ounces bottom crust of a 10 x 2-inch deep pan.

For a top crust use 6 ounces for a 9 x 1-inch deep or 8 ounces for a 10 x 2-inch or 10 x 1-inch deep pie pan. She use to tell me to roll the top crust thinner than the bottom crust. I roll out both bottom and top pretty much the same thickness. Raise the edge of the lower crust a little and fold the extra 1/4 to 1/2 inch of the upper crust under and press together to seal pie edges. This method will stop the juices from the filling from escaping. You then can press down the edge with tines of a fork or flute them.

◆◆◆

# Basic Piecrust I

*Yield: 1 double crust for 9- or 10-inch pie*

    3  cups flour
  3/4  teaspoon salt
    1  teaspoon sugar
 11/4  cups shortening
    2  teaspoons vinegar
    1  egg, beaten
  1/3  cup ice water

*Yield: 5 single crusts, or 2 double crusts and 1 single crust, for 9-inch pies*

    4  cups flour
    1  teaspoon salt
    2  teaspoons sugar
    2  cups shortening
    1  tablespoon vinegar
    1  egg, beaten
  1/2  cup ice water

In a large bowl, mix flour, salt and sugar. Blend shortening into flour mixture until pea-size crumbs form. Add vinegar and egg to water and blend into flour mixture until dough holds together.

# Basic Piecrust II

*Yield: 3 single crusts for 8- or 9-inch pies*

    3  cups flour
    1  teaspoon salt
    1  cup plus 3 tablespoons shortening
    6  tablespoons ice water

*Yield: bottom crust for one 11 x 17-inch pan*

    3  cups flour
 11/2  cups shortening
    1  teaspoon salt
1/3-1/2  cup ice water

*Yield: 2 double crusts for 9-inch pies*

 41/2  cups flour
    1  teaspoon salt
 13/4  cups plus 2 tablespoons shortening
  1/2  cup 1 tablespoon ice water

In a large bowl, add the shortening and salt to the flour. Blend until pea-size crumbs form. Add cup water and blend until dough holds together; add more water if necessary.

# Apple Pie

Fresh apple pie is a favorite pie of most picnickers. Apple pie was served as far back as 1630 in New England. The folks used up their apples from the orchards. It was a delicious treat enjoyed by all the townspeople. Baseball and apple pie are all American in today's market. Well, at least apple pie is unanimous. A tart cooking apple is a must for making an apple pie. Cortland, McIntosh, Granny Smith, Wealthy, or Rome Beauty are good pie apples. My favorite are McIntosh and Granny Smith. Granny Smiths are green apples that are very tart. McIntosh are red and firm. Avoid using a Delicious apple. It is a good eating apple but doesn't hold up well in pies.

For a 9 x 1-inch pie I use 5 large apples (6 ounces each). For a 10 x 2-inch pie I use 6 apples. Three medium apples equals 1 pound. Use 4 cups of apples for a 9 x 1-inch pie and 6 cups for a 10 x 2-inch pie.

*Yield: one 8 x 1-inch apple pie*
- 1 double piecrust recipe (page 162)
- 1/2 cup sugar
- 1/2 teaspoon cinnamon
- 3 3/4 cups apples peeled, cored, thinly sliced
- 1 tablespoon lemon juice
- 1 tablespoon cornstarch
- 1 tablespoon butter or margarine
- 1 egg
- 1 tablespoon milk
- 1 tablespoon sugar for top piecrust

*Yield: one 9 x 1-inch apple pie*
- 1 double piecrust recipe (page 162)
- 3/4 cup sugar
- 3/4 teaspoon cinnamon
- 2 tablespoons cornstarch
- 4 cups apples, peeled, cored, thinly sliced
- 1 tablespoon lemon juice
- 2 tablespoons butter
- 1 egg
- 1 tablespoon milk
- 1 tablespoon sugar for top piecrust

*Yield: one 10 x 2-inch pie*
- 1 double piecrust recipe (page 162)
- 1 cup sugar
- 1 teaspoon cinnamon
- 2 tablespoons cornstarch
- 6 cups apples, peeled, cored, thinly sliced
- 2 tablespoons lemon juice
- 2 tablespoons butter
- 1 egg
- 1 tablespoon milk
- 1 tablespoon sugar for top piecrust

Preheat oven to 425 degrees for aluminum pie pans and 400 degrees for glass pie pans. (I never use glass pie pans in my catering service for fear of the pan breaking on the way to the party. However, a glass pie pan is great for home use.) In a small bowl, mix sugar, cinnamon and cornstarch together. In a large bowl, pour lemon juice over sliced apples. Toss gently to coat; pat apples dry. Mix cinnamon and sugar mixture into apples. Place apples into pastry-lined pie pan. Dot with butter. Cover with top piecrust and cut slits in top to allow steam to escape. Mix together egg and milk; brush over top of crust. Sprinkle sugar over center of crust.

Bake pie for 15 minutes at 425 degrees. Turn down temperature to 375 degrees for aluminum and 350 for glass pan. Bake for 35-45 minutes more or until crust is golden brown and apples are tender.

## Cinnamon-Sugar Mixture Made in Quantity

12 cups sugar
3 tablespoons cinnamon
12 tablespoons cornstarch

Mix sugar, cinnamon and cornstarch together. You can make this batch ahead and store in a dry tight container. Use as needed. This mixture will keep for 60 days.

## Making Apple Pies in an Assembly Line

Make quantity batches of pie dough. Roll out all the crusts at once. Peel, core, and slice apples.

Toss all the apples in lemon juice. Pat apples lightly with paper towels. Place all bottom crusts into each pie pan. Measure apples for each pie. Sprinkle cinnamon-sugar mixture over apples. Dot with butter. Dampen edges of bottom pie crusts. Assemble top crusts. Seal. Cut steam slits on each pie. Brush egg wash over top of crusts and sprinkle with sugar.

## How to Freeze Apple Pie

Assemble apple pie. Do not put egg wash or sugar on top of pie. Do not cut steam slits or design in to crust. Place each pie in airtight plastic bag. Freeze. The pie will keep up to 6 months. Not only can you freeze fresh apple pie but also apple pie filling from a can. For best results do not thaw the pie before baking. It takes about one hour and 15 minutes to bake a frozen homemade pie at 375 degrees. Remember to put the egg wash and sugar on the apple pie before baking.

# Apple Pie with Streusel Topping

*Notes:* For a 11 x 17-inch pie use a No. 10 can of apple pie filling. The weight varies from 6 pounds 7 ounces to 7 pounds 3 ounces depending on the brand. If you buy apple pie filling at the grocery store, five 20-ounce cans are needed to make a pan pie. It is less expensive to use a No. 10 can of apple pie filling.

*Yield: one 11 x 17-inch pan pie*

*Crust*
1 1/2 cups shortening
1 teaspoon salt
3 cups flour
1/2 cup ice cold water

*Fresh Apple Filling*
5 pounds apples (12 large cooking apples)
1/2 cup lemon juice
3 cups sugar
1 tablespoon cinnamon
1/4 cup cornstarch
6 tablespoons margarine

*Topping*
1 cup brown sugar
1 cup (2 sticks) butter or margarine, softened
4 cups oatmeal
1 cup raisins
1 cup walnuts, chopped

Preheat oven to 350 degrees. To make crust, in a large bowl add shortening and salt to the flour. Blend with a 2-quart commercial mixer or with your fingers until shortening is a size of a pea. Add the water and blend until dough forms a ball.

Cut 2 pieces of waxed paper 12 1/2 x 16 inches each. Wet countertop with a damp cloth. Place 1 piece of waxed paper on countertop.

Place dough in middle of waxed paper. Place second piece of waxed paper over dough. Roll out dough to edges of waxed paper. Take off top piece of waxed paper. Place pie dough into the bottom of an ungreased 11 x 17-inch pan. Take off second piece of waxed paper. Pie crust should fit bottom of the half sheet cake pan, not the sides.

Peel and core, and quarter apples. Slice into thin slices. Pour lemon juice over the sliced apples. Toss gently until lemon juice coats the apple slices. Drain apples and pat dry with a paper towel. Set apples aside. Mix sugar, cinnamon, an cornstarch together. Pour over drained apples. Toss gently until apple slices are coated with the sugar and cinnamon mixture. Place coated apples over bottom piecrust. Slice 6 tablespoons of margarine into 15 squares. Place 3 across and 5 down over the apples. For streusel topping, stir together brown sugar, margarine and oatmeal. Blend in raisins.

Top apple pie with streusel topping. Bake at 350 degrees for 45 to 55 minutes. Cover the pie with foil and continue baking for 15 more minutes. or until apples are tender.

*Note:* You can substitute one No. 10 can (6 pounds 8 ounces) apple pie filling for the fresh apple filling in this recipe.

# Banana Cream Pie

*Yield: one 9-inch pie (8 servings)*

8 ounces piecrust dough
2 small to medium bananas, sliced
1 package (5.1 ounces) instant vanilla pudding mix
2³/₄ cups cold 2% milk
8 ounces non-dairy whipped topping, thawed
2 teaspoons lemon juice

Preheat oven to 400 degrees. Roll out crust between 2 pieces waxed paper to a circle about 1 inch larger than inverted pie pan. Take off top sheet of waxed paper. Place dough in pie pan waxed paper side up. Peel off second piece of waxed paper. Fold pastry edges under, even with edges of pan. Flute crust. To prevent edge of crust from becoming too brown cover with a 1¹/₂ inch strip of aluminum foil. With a fork prick pie shell. Bake for 20 minutes or until golden brown. Cool.

Sprinkle lemon juice over banana slices. Toss lightly. Pat bananas dry. Place bananas in bottom of cooled crust. In a 5-quart bowl mix milk with instant pudding mix. Beat for 3 minutes. Pour pudding over bananas. Fill pastry bag with non-diary whipped topping. Using a number E1 star tip, pipe non-dairy whipped topping over the top of the pie filling. Cover pie with dome lid and refrigerate.

## TIP

◆ Commercial whipped topping holds up in heat and travels well. Real whipping cream will melt in the heat. A topping piped on top of the banana cream pie is a nice decorative touch.

# Banana Cream Pie
## *11 x 17 x 1-inch Half-Sheet Pan*

*Note:* If you do not want to spend the time or labor to make a pastry crust from scratch, make a graham cracker crust. A 1-pound can of vanilla pudding can be purchased at the local grocery store. A No. 10 can of ready-to-serve vanilla pudding weighs 7 pounds 3 ounces (about 13 cups). Use 3¹/2 pounds of vanilla pudding per 11x 17-inch-half sheet pan. One No. 10 can is enough for 2 pan pies.

It takes a ¹/2 cup to 1 cup of whipped topping when piping on stars with a number E1 star tip depending on how big you make each star.

A banana cream pie must be refrigerated at all times. When you serve banana cream pie keep pie on ice packs and keep it cold. I generally serve banana cream pie for my Spring and Fall picnics, and avoided it on hot summer days. If banana cream pie is mishandled picnickers could get very sick. Beware!

*Note:* There is a recipe for a rolled pie crust and a graham cracker crust (below) for an 11 x 17-inch half sheet pan.

◆◆◆

# Banana Cream Pie

*Yield: 1 half-sheet pan pie*
1 pastry crust or graham cracker crust
6 bananas
3 tablespoons lemon juice
3 pounds 8 ounces ready-to-serve vanilla
   pudding
1¹/2 pounds commercial whipped topping

Slice bananas into a 5-quart bowl and toss with lemon juice; pat dry with paper towels. Spread banana slices in bottom of crust. Spread pudding on top of bananas.

Chill a 5-quart bowl. Beat commercial whipped topping in chilled bowl with a 2-quart commercial mixer until topping forms stiff peaks. Spread whipped topping over pie, or pipe on with a number E1 star tip. Cover with half-sheet cake plastic dome. Refrigerate.

## Graham Cracker Crust

*Yield: 1 crust for half-sheet pan*
2 cups (1 pound) butter, melted
¹/4-¹/3 cup sugar, or to taste
4 cups graham cracker crumbs

Preheat oven to 350 degrees. In a 5-quart bowl, add the melted butter and sugar to the graham cracker crumbs. Mix. Pack the graham cracker crumb mixture in the bottom of a half-sheet cake pan. Bake for 12-15 minutes. Cool.

# Double-Crust Canned Fruit Pie

*Yield: 1 half-sheet pan*

**Crust**

- 6 cups flour
- 1$\frac{1}{3}$ cups shortening
- 1 teaspoon salt
- 1 cup ice water
- 5 pounds pie filling, any fruit flavor
- 1 egg
- 1 tablespoon 2% milk
- 2 tablespoons to $\frac{1}{4}$ cup sugar

Preheat oven to 375 degrees. In a large bowl, add shortening and salt to the flour. Blend in mixer on low speed or by hand until shortening is a size of a pea. Add water and blend until the dough is shaped into a ball. Divide dough in half.

Cut 2 pieces of waxed paper 12$\frac{1}{2}$ x 16 inches each. Wet the countertop with a damp cloth. Place 1 piece of waxed paper on the dampened countertop. Place dough in middle of waxed paper. Place second piece of waxed paper over dough. Roll out to fit waxed paper. Take off top piece of waxed paper. Place dough into bottom of the pan. Peel off second piece of waxed paper. Fill pie pan with desired pie filling. Roll out top crust the same size and method used for bottom crust and place on top of filling.

Beat egg and milk together. Brush the egg mixture over top of piecrust. Sprinkle sugar over egg wash. Cut slits into top of crust to let steam escape. Bake for 25 minutes or until golden brown. Refer to cake cutting chart on page 122 for cutting pan pie.

# Pumpkin Pan Pie

*Yield: 1 half-sheet pan*

**Crust**

- 1 package (8 ounces) cream cheese
- $\frac{1}{2}$ cup (1 stick) margarine
- 2 eggs
- $\frac{1}{2}$ cup sugar
- 2 cups flour

**Filling**

- 1 can (29 ounces) pumpkin plus
- 1 can (15 ounces) pumpkin
- 6 eggs
- 2$\frac{1}{4}$ cups sugar
- 3 cans (12 ounces each) evaporated milk
- 1 teaspoon salt
- 1$\frac{1}{2}$ teaspoons ginger
- 3 teaspoons cinnamon
- 1 teaspoon ground cloves

Preheat oven to 350 degrees.

For crust, beat cream cheese and margarine until smooth. Add sugar and eggs and beat again. Add flour 1 cup at a time, beating well after each addition. Spread dough evenly into ungreased pan.

For filling, Beat pumpkin, eggs, sugar, evaporated milk, salt, ginger, cinnamon and cloves until smooth. Pour filling over piecrust.

Bake for 55-60 minutes or until knife inserted in center comes out clean. Cool and refrigerate.

TIP: Frost cooled pie with 12 ounces non-dairy whipped topping, sprinkle with 1 cup chopped pecans and 2 cups chocolate chips.

# Cherry Pie

*Yield: one 10 x 2-inch cherry pie*

**Crust**

   1¹/₄ cups solid shortening
   ³/₄ teaspoon salt
   3 cups flour
¹/₃ to ¹/₂ cup ice water

**Filling**

   1 can (21 ounces) plus 1 can
      (30 ounces) cherry pie filling
   1 egg
   1 tablespoon milk
   1 tablespoon sugar

Preheat oven to 400 degrees. In a medium bowl, add shortening and salt to flour. Blend with a mixer or by hand until shortening is the size of a pea. Add ¹/₃ cup water to the flour mixture and blend until dough is shaped into a ball, adding more water if necessary. Divide dough into 2 balls, one just slightly larger. Cut 4 pieces of waxed paper. Wet countertop with damp cloth. Place 1 piece of waxed paper on countertop. Place larger ball of dough onto waxed paper. Place second piece of waxed paper over dough. Roll out dough to a circle 1 inch larger than inverted pie pan. Take off top layer of waxed paper and place dough in pie pan. Take off second piece of waxed paper. Place both cans of cherry pie filling into bottom piecrust. Roll out second ball of dough just slightly larger than inverted pie pan. Moisten edges of bottom piecrust. Place top crust over cherry pie filling. Press edges together to seal; flute edges. To prevent edge of crust from becoming too brown cover with a 1¹/₂ inch strip of aluminum foil. Blend together egg and milk; brush egg wash over top of piecrust, avoiding edges. Sprinkle sugar over egg wash. Cut slits or a design in top crust to allow steam to escape. Bake for 20 minutes. Reduce temperature to 375 degrees and bake for 35-45 minutes longer or until golden brown.

## TIP

Because I live in Wisconsin, I get Door County cherries each year. I make a pie that, with these delicious cherries and the tender, flaky piecrust above, is outstanding. However, when fresh cherries aren't available, pie made with canned filling is tasty and has the added benefit of saving time and labor.

# Black Bottom Peanut Butter Cheesecake

There are approximately 4 cups chocolate cookie crumbs in a 25-ounce box of crumbs. You can substitute regular chocolate chips for the double chips. You can substitute lowfat cream cheese, peanut butter, and whipped topping for regular. Make this cheesecake 24 hours in advance for flavors to blend. I like to use glass pans for the 13 x 9-inch cheesecakes.

*Yield: one 8 x 8-inch square pan*
  3 tablespoons sugar
  1/4 cup (1/2 stick) butter, melted
  1 cup chocolate cookie crumbs
*Filling*
  1 envelope unflavored gelatin
  1/4 cup cold water
  2 packages (8 ounces each) cream cheese, softened
  1 cup powdered sugar
  1/3 cup creamy peanut butter
*Topping*
  3/4 cup non-dairy whipped topping
  1/2 cup unsalted peanuts, finely chopped
  1/2 cup double chocolate chips

*Yield: one 13 x 9-inch pan*
  1/3 cup sugar
  1/2 cup (1 stick) butter, melted
  2 cups chocolate cookie crumbs
*Filling*
  2 envelopes unflavored gelatin
  1/2 cup cold water
  4 packages (8 ounces each) cream cheese, softened
  2 cups powdered sugar
  2/3 cup creamy peanut butter
*Topping*
1 1/2 cups non-dairy whipped topping
  1 cup unsalted peanuts, finely chopped
  1 cup double chocolate chips

*Yield: 1 half-sheet pan*
  1/2 cup sugar
1 1/4 cups (2 1/2 sticks) butter, melted
  4 cups chocolate cookie crumbs
*Filling*
  3 envelopes unflavored gelatin
  2 cups cold water
  8 packages (8 ounces each) cream cheese, softened (4 pounds)
  4 cups powdered sugar
  1 cup creamy peanut butter
*Topping*
  3 cups non-dairy whipped topping
  2 cups unsalted peanuts, finely chopped
  2 cups mini chocolate chips

In a large bowl, add sugar and butter to cookie crumbs; mix thoroughly. Spread evenly and press mixture into ungreased pan. Chill or freeze crust 5 minutes. Meanwhile, dissolve gelatin in cold water. Let stand 2 minutes, then microwave for 40 seconds on high. Set aside to cool slightly. Beat cream cheese with mixer until fluffy. Beat in sugar and peanut butter. Slowly beat in gelatin mixture; blend thoroughly. Pour into crust. Spread whipped topping over filling. Sprinkle with nuts and chocolate chips. Refrigerate overnight.

TIP: You can sprinkle extra chocolate cookie crumbs over the whipped topping instead of the peanuts and chocolate chips for a simpler cheesecake. Or you can skip the toppings and serve the cheesecake plain.

You can also use margarine, or half margarine and half butter, for the butter in the crust.

# Lemon Meringue Pie

You can purchase frozen egg whites at a wholesale dealer or egg product distribution center. There are six 5-pound cartons per case of frozen egg whites. One 5-pound carton will make 5 half-sheet pan pies. Thaw amount needed up to 3 days before baking.

Use prepared lemon pie filling for consistency. There are 13 cups lemon filling in each No. 10 can, 6 cans to a case. One No. 10 can will make a half-sheet pan pie.

Lemon meringue pies will keep up to 5 days covered in the refrigerator.

If you cover the entire pie with meringue, including the edges of the crust, the meringue will not shrink. Keep this pie cold at all times.

## Lemon Meringue Piecrust I

*Yield: 1 crust for 11 x 17-inch half-sheet pan pie*

1 1/2 cups (3 sticks) margarine, softened
2 cups sugar
3 cups flour
1/4 cup half-and-half, or milk

Preheat oven to 350 degrees. Cream together margarine and sugar. Add flour and half-and-half and blend thoroughly. Press dough into ungreased half-sheet pan. Bake for 15-20 minutes. Cool.

## Lemon Meringue Piecrust II

*Yield: 1 crust for 11 x 17-inch half-sheet pan pie*

1 cup (2 sticks) margarine, softened
1 cup powdered sugar
4 cups flour

Preheat oven to 350 degrees. Cream margarine and sugar. Stir in flour until well-blended. Press crust into ungreased 11 x 17-inch half-sheet pan. Bake for 15-20 minutes. Cool.

## Lemon Meringue Pie

*Yield: 1 half-sheet pan pie*

1 baked Lemon Meringue Piecrust I or II
1 No. 10 can (7 pounds 6 ounces) French lemon filling
15 egg whites
1 1/4 teaspoons cream of tartar
2 2/3 teaspoons vanilla
1/2 cup plus 2 tablespoons sugar

Preheat oven to 350 degrees. Spread lemon filling evenly over baked crust. In a 5-quart bowl, mix cream of tartar, vanilla and egg whites. Beat egg whites, adding sugar gradually. Beat until egg whites form stiff peaks. Spread meringue over pie, making sure to cover all edges. Bake for 15 minutes or until meringue is golden brown. Cool. Store covered in refrigerator.

# Pecan Pie

*Yield: one 9-inch pie*

**Crust**

1 1/2 cups flour
1/2 teaspoon salt
1/2 teaspoon sugar
3/4 cup solid white shortening
1 egg, beaten
2-3 tablespoons ice water
1 teaspoon vinegar

**Filling**

3 eggs, beaten
1 cup sugar
1 cup light corn syrup
2 tablespoons butter, melted
1 teaspoon vanilla
1 3/4 cups pecan halves

Preheat oven to 350 degrees. In a medium bowl, mix flour, sugar and salt. Cut in shortening until pea-sized crumbs form. Add the beaten egg to the ice water along with the vinegar. Blend well; add to flour mixture and blend until dough holds together. Roll out dough between 2 pieces of waxed paper to 1 inch larger than inverted pie pan. Peel off top piece of waxed paper. Place dough in pie pan; remove remaining waxed paper. Tuck edges of dough under to form a border even with edges of pan. Flute crust. Cover edges with a 1 1/2-inch strip of foil. Set aside.

To make filling, in a 5-quart mixing bowl, beat eggs, sugar, corn syrup, butter and vanilla. Stir in pecans. Pour filling into prepared crust. Bake for 50 minutes. Cool for 8-10 minutes. Cover pecans with waxed paper to keep from becoming hard. Serve warm or cold with whipped cream or ice cream. Store in refrigerator.

# Raspberry Pie

*Yield: one 9-inch pie*

**Crust**

3 cups flour
3/4 teaspoon salt
1 teaspoon sugar
1 1/4 cups solid white shortening
2 teaspoons vinegar
1 egg, beaten
1/3 cup ice water

**Filling**

2 cans (21 ounces each) raspberry pie filling
1 egg
1 tablespoon milk
1 tablespoon sugar

Preheat oven to 400 degrees. In a 5-quart bowl, mix flour, sugar and salt. Cut in shortening until it forms pea-sized crumbs. Add egg and vinegar to ice water; mix until dough holds together. Divide into 2 balls. Roll out one ball to line bottom of pie pan. Roll out second ball to about 9 inches in diameter; set aside.

Preheat oven to 400 degrees. Pour raspberry filling into bottom crust. Moisten edges of bottom crust with water. Cover with top crust; seal edges together by pressing with fork. Trim excess dough. Cut slits or a design in top crust to allow steam to escape. In a small bowl, mix together egg and milk to form a wash. Brush over center of top crust, avoiding edges. Sprinkle egg wash with sugar. Bake for 20 to 25 minutes or until golden brown. Cool before cutting. Store in refrigerator.

# Puff Pastry Method
# for Making Pan Pie Crust

Use puff pastry sheets instead of homemade pie dough. It saves time. If you purchase puff pastry at the grocery store the size per sheet is smaller than from the wholesale vendor. One 1-pound box from the grocery store has two 10 x 15-inch puff pastry sheets. The 2 sheets are wrapped around a soft cardboard, folded in thirds. Use one 10 x 15-inch sheet to line a 11 x 17-inch half-sheet cake pan. Cut the puff pastry to 10 x 11 1/2 inches and a second sheet 7 1/2 x 11 1/2 inches. Overlap the dough by 1/2 inch. Repeat this again for the top crust. Or roll out each 10 x 15-inch sheet to 11 x 17 inches. I find it easier to cut the puff pastry dough when the dough is half-frozen. If the dough gets too soft, it becomes sticky and sometimes unmanageable. It takes approximately 2 1/2 boxes (1 pound 1 1/4 ounces) puff pastry to make one pan pie if you patch the crust together. The wholesale vendor sells twenty 10 x 15-inch sheets per case (30 pounds per case). If you are going to do a lot of pan pies or other items with puff pastry in your catering service it is wise to buy it by the case. It will save you money.

*Note:* 5 x 5-inch puff pastry squares are also available; they are ideal for individual desserts. Puff pastry is very easy to cut or roll to size.

1. Keep puff pastry frozen until ready to use. Thaw pastry sheets at room temperature for 20-30 minutes before unfolding the sheets. Try to thaw only what you need, and keep the rest frozen. If puff pastry is bought in quantity, sheets are laid out flat with cardboard in between.

2. Roll and shape dough on lightly floured surface. To seal cracks, sprinkle with water and press edges together.

3. Do not grease pan when using puff pastry.

4. Dark baking sheets may bake pastry faster. Lower temperature by 25 degrees, or watch carefully at suggested temperature.

5. Do not bake puff pastry in a toaster oven or microwave.

For each pan pie you will use four 10 x 15-inch sheets plus a 2 x 12-inch strip. Thirty pounds of puff pastry makes 8 pan pies if you cut and piece the bottom puff pastry sheet. If you need to do several pan pies, set up an assembly line—do all the bottom crusts first. Place filling on the bottom crusts. Then complete the top crust. If oven space permits bake all at one time.

*Notes:* Filling—Use cherry, strawberry, raspberry, apple or cherry pie filling to make a puff pastry pan pie. Buy pie filling in quantity for making several pan pies. Use the 40-pound tub for making 8 pan pies at a time. Use a 20-pound tub to make 4 pan pies at a time. Store pie filling in an airtight container and refrigerate. Once filling has been opened it will keep for 10 days.

*Note:* Four cups powdered sugar equals 1 pound. Two pounds powdered sugar will make glaze for 8 pan pies. Basically I just stir a little water into the powdered sugar until I get a thick glaze. Be careful that you do not make the powdered sugar-water mixture too runny. You can also add almond extract to taste, about 1/2 teaspoon per small batch of glaze.

# Puff Pastry Fruit Pan Pie

*Yield: 1 half-sheet cake pan*

Puff pastry (follow directions on
   page 172)

5  pounds canned fruit filling

*Icing*

1  cup powdered sugar

2  tablespoons water

1/2  teaspoon almond extract

1/4  teaspoon salt

Preheat oven to 400 degrees. Follow directions for puff pastry crust. Line the 11 x 17-inch half-sheet-cake pan with puff pastry cut to size. Fill with canned fruit pie filling of your choice. Place a top layer over the pie filling. Bake for 20-25 minute or until golden brown.

Mix powdered sugar, water, almond extract and salt together. When the pie comes out of the oven drizzle over the top of the baked crust.

# Filo Dough

You can purchase filo dough at the grocery store in a 1-pound box, containing approximately twenty 14 x 18-inch sheets. The sheets are paper-thin and fragile; keep unused dough in a sealed plastic bag while working to keep it from drying out. This dough works well for appetizers and main courses as well as desserts.

# Cherry Strudel

*Yield: 1 half-sheet pan*

1  box (8 ounces) filo dough

1/2  cup (1 stick) margarine, melted

2  cans (1 pound 14 ounces each) cherry pie
   filling

*Glaze*

1  cup powdered sugar

1/2  teaspoon almond extract

1/4  teaspoon salt

3  tablespoons water

Thaw filo dough; keep covered. Preheat oven to 400 degrees. Brush margarine over bottom of an 11 x 17-inch half-sheet pan. Cover bottom of pan with one layer of filo sheets, over-lapping if necessary. Brush with melted butter. Add 3 more layers of filo sheets, brushing each with more melted butter. Pour cherry pie filling over filo. Cover filling with a layer of filo sheets. Brush with melted butter. Repeat as with bottom crust, using remaining filo sheets. Brush top sheet with melted butter. Cover well and refrigerate overnight.

Preheat oven to 400 degrees. Bake for 20 to 25 minutes or until golden brown. In a small bowl, mix powdered sugar, almond extract, salt and water to form a glaze. Drizzle over strudel as soon as it comes out of the oven.

*Note:* You can substitute apple pie filling for the cherry pie filling.

How to cut a
pie into 8
servings

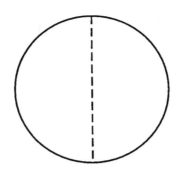

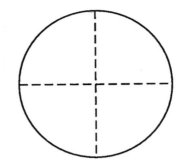

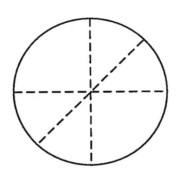

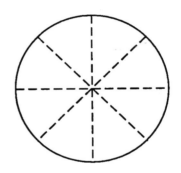

# 7 ♦ Picnics, Picnics, Picnics

# Picnics, Picnics, Picnics

THEME IDEA:
ROMANTIC PICNIC FOR TWO

Romance dates back to the beginning of man. A picnic is a great way for a couple to relax and get acquainted. They can be together in a romantic park scene.

I had a customer contact me to make a romantic picnic basket for two. He stated that he was going to propose on this date. He needed a beautiful picnic basket. Of course roses and wine were a must; he would supply them, and select just the right card for this occasion.

The staff was very excited about creating this basket. When he came to pick up the picnic basket he promised the staff he would let them know if his girlfriend accepted the proposal. Two weeks went by. We were sure she did not accept.

Finally he arrived in our shop. The secretary said, "Wait, I'll get Pat." The staff stopped working and whispered, "he's here!" I walked out into the office and said, "So, how did it go?" He smiled and said it worked. The staff cheered and came out and congratulated him. What a great memory!

Remember, the decorations play a very important part in creating a romantic picnic basket for two. Some suggestions: Tie a bow around a bottle of champagne. Use red cloth napkins with heart-shaped napkin rings. Slide a red rose through the napkin ring. Provide a bouquet of flowers inside the basket. Arrange selected food items neatly in the basket. Pack two champagne glasses and a fancy corkscrew with a ribbon printed with the word "Love." A card with the appropriate words from the suitor can be tucked into the basket. Food itself can be decorated nicely and act as part of the decorations.

THEME PICNIC BASKET

A theme picnic basket for two can be delight-

## ◆◆◆ PICNIC MENUS

**Fancy Romantic Picnic for Two**
Shrimp cocktail
Brie cheese with fancy crackers
Pineapple swan filled with fresh fruit
Heart-shaped finger sandwiches filled with chicken salad
Fresh vegetable sculptures with Dill Dip
Heart-shaped cake with red frosting roses
Bottled water
Champagne
A box of truffles and a bouquet of red roses

**Snack Picnic Basket**
Potato chips and dip
Taco chips and salsa
Gourmet pretzels with mustard
Lemonade and soda

**Lowfat Snack Picnic Basket**
Apple slices with caramel-apple dip
Raw vegetables with lowfat dill dip
Lowfat cheese slices with fat-free crackers
Bottled mineral water

**Simple Picnic Basket**
Ham and Swiss cheese on croissants
Condiments
Potato chips
Deviled Eggs
Relishes
Apples and chocolate chip cookies
Soda and juice
(A basket lined with checked fabric is excellent for this picnic.)

ful. Find out the interests of the person and create the theme around their hobbies. Find out what are the favorite foods of your date. Is he/she a vegetarian or a hearty or light eater? Is the person allergic to any foods. You certainly wouldn't make brownie points if the person got an allergic reaction from the food in your picnic basket. Theme suggestions:

Snack basket

Lowfat snack basket

Hawaiian picnic basket

Western basket

50th birthday theme

Family picnic basket for an outing at the zoo

So be creative and make up your own picnic basket to your taste. Have fun!

## ETHNIC PICNIC

The Ethnic Picnic is one of the most well-received. (See diagrams on page 188-191) It is best for large groups of 200 and up, although you can serve smaller groups. Large groups can go from buffet line to buffet line and select foods of choice. There is very little waiting in line because there are several tables of ethnic foods to select from. Guests can graze for up to three hours. The decorations and the costumes worn by the servers enhance each ethnic table greatly.

You need to charge properly for this style of party. The trick is not to cook every item for every person. In other words if you have 200 guests make 100 to 150 of each of five different entrees, although you may need to make 200 servings of very popular items. Let experience be your guide.

Depending on which part of the country you are in you may have to make more of a particular entree, such as bratwurst in Wisconsin. Figure two-thirds of the number of guests for most entrees and one third for hot dogs. Normally the ethnic picnic is served for adults; a child's menu could be added if necessary.

Keep in mind that sky is the limit. Each pic-

## ETHNIC THEME PICNIC MENUS

**German Theme**
Spanfurkel (whole roast pig)
Bratwurst and sauerkraut
German Potato Salad
Apple and Cherry Strudels

**Italian Theme**
Italian sausages
Crusty Italian buns with
   Chef's Romantic Sauce
Italian Vegetable Salad

**Mexican Theme**
Tortilla chips
Layered Cream Cheese Taco Salad Dip
Taco Refried Bean Dip
Avocado Salad
Mexican wedding cakes

**American Beach Theme**
Hot dogs & buns
Condiments
Potato chips
Deviled Eggs
Seven-Layer Salad
Fruit-Flavored Gelatin
Assorted dessert bars

**Spirit of '76 Theme**
Liberty Cheese Bell with assorted crackers
Colonial Chicken
Valley Forge Potatoes
Calico Beans
Old Glory Fruit Salad
Blueberry Pan Pie

## ETHNIC THEME PICNIC MENUS

**Southwestern Theme**
Tenderloin steak sandwiches
Condiments
Corn on the Cob
Black Beans Southwestern Style
Relishes

# PICNIC MENUS

**Red, White and Blue Picnic**
Liberty Cheese Ball and assorted crackers
Firecracker Chili Dip and taco chips
Colonial chicken
Constitution pork and Revolutionary
    barbecue sauce
Valley Forge Potatoes
Boston Baked Beans
Old Glory Fruit Salad
Apple, cherry and blueberry pan bars

**My Lady and My Lord**
**Surf and Turf Picnic**
Lobster boil and steak feast
Baked potatoes
Butter, sour cream & cheese
Large salad bar with French, ranch and
    Italian dressings
Rolls and butter
Assorted tortes and pies

**Old Fashioned Picnic Beverages**
Lemonade
Iced tea
Coffee
Assorted sodas

nic should ideally have three ethnic menus; for example, a German, Italian, and Mexican picnic. It is not uncommon to have 25 to 50 different dishes.

Organization is key. Pack a box for each ethnic menu and pretend that each country or region is an individual party. If you put all the decorations for each country in one box and the equipment used for that same country in another box.

Remember to pack in each box matches and pearl corsage pins for pinning on the table skirts. These are the two most frequently forgotten items.

It is important to have one person dressed in costume at each station to serve the food and fill the dishes. The extra food should be organized according to country, close to its station.

I have so much fun shopping for the decorations for ethnic picnics. I was able to purchase many decorations through my travels around the country. That made my buffet decorations unique.

Enjoy using your own imagination and create your own ethnic picnic buffet.

Many times companies celebrate a 10-, 25- or 50-year business anniversary party. The company is willing to spent the extra money to have a very special picnic party. However, the company is relying on you the caterer to put together a beautiful party. The guests will associate you with the company. Therefore, it is very important for you the caterer to make the right impression which means attending to every detail.

I once had the opportunity to do a My Lady and My Lord Surf and Turf picnic at a large stadium parking lot. We catered for a large well-known company that wished to entertain guests from all over the world. Our company set up a mini-restaurant, with round tables and fancy china. We also had a separate table with a large display of tortes and pies such as Black Forest

Tortes, various flan tortes, Lemon Angel Tortes, Hawaiian Cheesecakes, apple and cherry pie, strawberry cream pie, and banana cream pie. Other tailgaters came from all over the parking area to see our setup. We received rave reviews for a job well done.

We used propane to boil water for the frozen lobster tails. We used a huge kettle and added a bouquet garni of lobster/fish seasonings and lemon juice to the water in the pot. We brought the water to a boil and boiled the lobsters at the last minute for only 15 to 20 minutes depending on their size. We drained off the water as we went along and held the lobsters in a hot box. This is tricky, because lobster can not be held very long. We needed to do this task at the last minute, so it was important that the lobster was pre-thawed. We melted real butter in a container on top of the grill. Every person had a stand with a little dish of drawn butter with a candle under it. Each lobster was pre-cut down the center before being boiled to save time. Individual 10-ounce New York strip steaks were cooked on the grill on site.

A buffet table was set up with the large salad bar with every kind of salad fixing and style of lettuce to make a large salad while guests waited for the main course. Potatoes were made in the hot coals and stored in the hot boxes. Each table had a basket of piping hot rolls, butter roses, sour cream, and ice water with a lemon slice in every glass. Every guest table had a fancy bouquet of flowers in the center of the table. For the guests who did not want to select their steak or lobster we served them at the table; others came to the grill and lobster boil area to select their own entrees.

We had a guest who went up to the dessert table and let everyone know that the yummy black forest torte was all his. He was not kidding, either. He ran his finger straight across the cake and proceeded to lick it. He took this cake to his place setting. I remember taking a picture of this guest. This scene became quite a conversation

## PICNIC MENUS

### Economy Express Picnic
Hot dogs (all-beef)
Baked Beans
Buns & butter
Condiments
Chips
Lemonade

### Ballpark Tailgater Picnic
Fresh bratwurst & hot dogs
Potato Salad
Baked Beans
Buns & butter
Condiments
Dessert bars
Lemonade & iced tea

### All-American Picnic
Hamburgers & bratwurst
Potato Salad
Baked Beans
Buns & butter
Condiments
Dessert bars
Lemonade & iced tea

### Backyard Special Picnic
Chicken on the grill
Hot dogs
Potato Salad
Coleslaw
Baked Beans
Buns & butter
Condiments
Dessert bars
Lemonade & iced tea

## PICNIC MENUS

**Golfer's Delight Picnic**
Ribs, hot dogs & bratwurst
Potato Salad
Baked Beans
Deviled Eggs
Fresh fruit
Relishes
Buns & butter
Condiments
Black Forest Torte
Cheesecake
Lemonade & iced tea


**Simple Pig Roast 1**
Roast whole pig
Hot dogs
Bratwurst
German Potato Salad
Baked Beans
Coleslaw
Pickles, olives, diced onions
Rolls and buns with butter
Condiments
Chocolate Brownies
Coffee (reg/decaf) and milk

**Summer Dream Picnic**
Hamburgers, brats & hot dogs
Potato Salad
Coleslaw
Baked Beans
Relishes & condiments
Buns & butter
Watermelon
Dessert bars
Lemonade & iced tea

piece. Eventually a few others at his table did share the torte. Luckily we had other black forest tortes.

We received a letter of appreciation for a job well done. We also received additional catering jobs from this fancy picnic.

The disadvantage of this meal is the cost. It is always market price due to the cost of the lobster and steak.

## SETTING UP THE BUFFET

Arrive at the party site far enough in advance to ensure plenty of time to set up. The more people attending, the longer it will take to set up. (See diagrams on pages 191-198.)

Experienced staff usually need little guidance. They can follow a layout in writing and expedite the job quickly and smoothly. One waitperson for every fifty guests for a picnic will be enough help. If three or four people go early to the party in advance and decorate less help can be required. For example, a picnic of 1,500 a staff of ten to twelve including the grill staff can manage the party as long as guest and buffet tables are properly set up ahead of time. Make sure all packed boxes have been rechecked so all items have been shipped to the party. Forgotten items can cause a great deal of stress. You are responsible to supply all contracted items. Take extra money along and know where the closest grocery store is in case something is missing. Be prepared. Remember the party needs to be organized to be successful.

The lead caterer directing the party should have a layout sheet. The lead griller should direct the grill crew in the grill setup. Each worker should be assigned duties to help pull the buffet together. Refer to the layout sheet if unsure or ask the lead person for advice if in doubt.

## SETTING UP A TWO-LINE BUFFET
A. Cover and skirt the buffet tables.
B. At the beginning of the buffet set out dinner plates, napkins, forks, and knives.

C. Arrange breads, hamburger and hot dog buns on platters or in baskets. Butter goes after the breads.

D. Salads go next in line.

E. Near the meats are all the condiments.

F. Chafing dishes with hot foods go last in the buffet line.

TIP: I usually use a separate buffet table for a larger group to speed up the line. For a small group (up to 50) place the desserts before the chafing dishes. For a simple buffet line for a small gathering (up to 50), use two 8-foot tables, one for desserts and beverages.

TIP: The variety of foods and number of people served will determine the number of tables and buffet setups. It is best not to run any more than 75 to 100 per buffet line. When I serve even 40 to 50 I ran two lines. You want to serve people quickly.

## TABLE COVERING

White plastic is used the most. You can purchase a variety of colors in plastic. Paper table covering is the least expensive, but does not hold up as well. If someone spills on the paper table covering it is ruined whereas plastic can be wiped clean. There is also a coated cloth out that looks like regular cloth but is water-repellent and is easily wiped clean. You can get a price break if you purchase 12 rolls of plastic table covering at a time. The plastic is worth the few extra pennies to make a good impression. One roll equals 150 feet (1800 inches). Add on the drape, usually 8 inches per side, to the length of the table and divide the total number of inches by 1800 to figure out how many tables can be covered per roll. (It is easier to work with inches than feet.)

## COVERING BUFFET TABLES

The 8-foot table is used for the majority of banquets and picnics. One 150-foot roll of plastic table covering (40 inches wide) will cover:

• 16 individual 8-foot tables with an 8-inch

## PICNIC MENUS

**Elegant Hawaiian Spanfurkel**
Whole roast pig
Roast chicken
Gourmet mustard, regular mustard, and barbecue sauce
French or German Potato Salad
Oven Baked Beans
Garden Vegetable or Seafood Pasta Salad
Relishes
Fresh Fruit Tray with Pineapple Tree
Assorted dinner rolls with butter
Assorted homemade dessert bars
Coffee (reg/decaf) and iced tea

**Hawaiian Luau**
Spareribs on the grill (rack of ribs)
Breasts of chicken with Waikiki sauce
White rice with red and green pepper
Green beans with almonds
Relishes with palm trees
Fresh Fruit Tray with Pineapple Tree
Rolls and butter
Hawaiian Cheesecake and assorted cheesecakes
Black Forest Torte
Lemonade and iced tea

**Desserts that can be readily used in a picnic basket:**
Sweetheart Cake decorated with red frosting roses
Swan cream puffs
Heart-shaped sugar cookies
Small box of chocolates
(The box should be wrapped and adorned with a dainty bow.)

## PICNIC MENUS

**Executive Picnic**
Tenderloin Shish Kabobs
Baked Potatoes w/sour cream
Corn on the Cob
Tossed salad w/dressing
Rolls & butter
Condiments
Assorted pies & tortes
Lemonade & iced tea

**Bankers Outing**
Tenderloin steaks & ribs
Potato Salad
Coleslaw
Baked Beans
Corn on the cob
Rolls & butter
Relishes & condiments
Cheesecake
Lemonade & iced tea

**T-Bone Feast**
1-lb. T-bone steaks
Baked Potatoes w/sour cream
Make-your-own salads
Deviled Eggs
Assorted cheese tray
Rolls & butter
Assorted pies & tortes
Lemonade & iced tea

**Beverages that can be readily used in a picnic basket:**
Bottled mineral water
Bottled juices
Iced tea
Lemonade
Soda
Wine & champagne

draping on each end.
- 17 individual 8-foot tables with a 4-inch draping on each end.
- 8 sets of two 8-foot tables end to end.
- 5 sets of three 8-foot tables end to end and 1 set of two 8-foot tables end to end.
- 20 individual 6-foot tables with an 8-inch draping on each end.
- 22 individual 6-foot tables with a 4-inch draping on each end.
- 11 sets of two 6-foot tables end to end.
- 7 sets of three 6-foot tables end to end.
- 16 individual 36-inch round tables.
- 13 individual 48-inch round tables.
- 11 individual 60-inch round tables.

**6-Foot and 8-Foot Tables:** Many caterers will use a straight buffet of two to three 8-foot tables lined up one after another. For example you can place three 8-foot tables in a line to create one 24-foot (288-inch) table. Add 8 inches at each end for the tablecloth to drape and you need a 25-foot 4-inch-long (304 inches) table covering. When two 8-foot tables are placed together you have 16 feet (192 inches) plus 16 inches for draping, 8 inches on each end, to total 17 feet 4 inches (208 inches).

Two 6-foot banquet tables end to end, with 8 inches draping on each end, equals 13 feet 4 inches (160 inches). Three 6-foot tables end to end equals 19 feet 4 inches (232 inches).

A 52 x 108-inch tablecloth will cover one 8-foot table. Sometimes the picnic grounds will have 36-inch tables or 5-foot or 6-foot picnic tables. Be prepared to adjust to any size table.

**36-Inch Round Tables:** To use the 150-foot roll, cut 2 pieces, each 52 inches long. Lay them side by side over the table, overlapping approximately 12 inches. You will have an 8-inch drape.

Or you can use a 54-inch square tablecloth for each 36-inch round table.

**48-inch and 60-Inch Round Tables:** While a plastic table covering on a roll can be used in a

pinch to cover a 48-inch or 60-inch round table, the appearance is not as neat as individual round tablecloths. To cover a 48-inch round table with roll covering, cut 2 pieces each 5 feet 4 inches long (64 inches) and overlap them about 8 inches to create a square with an 8-inch draping. To cover a 60-inch round table, cut 2 pieces each 6 feet 4 inches long (76 inches) and overlap them about 4 inches to create a square with an 8-inch draping.

For a 48-inch or 60-inch round table it is best to buy round or square tablecloths. A 54-inch or 69-inch square is good for a 48-inch table. A 72-inch square tablecloth is a good size for a 60-inch round table. You can get by using a 69 x 69-inch square on a 60-inch table,  however the draping is very skimpy.

TIP: Carry an extra roll of plastic table covering for emergencies. It is better to be safe than sorry. You can always use that extra roll at your next party.

You can buy various size plastic tablecloths by the case from your paper supplier. Inquire for a list of various sizes.

You can use plastic for skirting tables. For a round table stand the roll on end and pleat plastic. Use masking tape to tape the plastic to the top of the table. Place a round tablecloth over the table to drape over the top edge of skirting. (See diagram on page 198.)

## DECORATIONS

Decorations are the ginger to the food. Various decorations create a theme party and accent the party mood. Thus, the spirit of the decorations moves the guest to get into the party theme. First impressions are lasting impressions. Decorations accent the taste of the food. If it looks good it generally tastes good. The color scheme has everything to do with both the decorations and the food. Can you imagine the response you'd receive if you served black cauliflower or peach-colored broccoli?

## PICNIC MENUS

**Wisconsin Picnic**
Hamburgers, brats & hot dogs
Potato Salad
Coleslaw
Baked Beans
Deviled Eggs
Fresh fruit
Relishes
Buns & butter
Condiments
Dessert bars
Lemonade & iced tea

**The Big Deal Picnic**
Choice of 3: Chicken, brats, hamburgers or
    hot dogs
Potato Salad
Baked Beans
Deviled Eggs
Fresh fruit
Relishes
Buns & butter
Condiments
Dessert bars
Lemonade & iced tea

**Western Picnic**
Chicken & ribs
Potato Salad
Baked Beans
Relishes
Corn on the Cob
Rolls & butter
Assorted bars
Lemonade & iced tea

Here are some examples of decorations for various theme parties:

### Hawaiian

Palm trees, birds of paradise, hula dancers, Hawaiian tablecloth, seashells, shiny blue tablecloths (for water), ukuleles, grass skirts.

### Caribbean

Tropical tablecloths, seashells, fish-shaped ice sculptures, watermelon carved into a whale.

### Baby shower

Tablecloth with a baby theme (teddies, lambs), watermelon carved into a baby buggy, sheet cake decorated with baby booties.

### Zoo picnic

Tablecloth with animal theme, stuffed animals, stuffed monkey hanging from artificial tree.

### Red, White and Blue

Patriotic tablecloth with star skirting, rocket centerpiece, basket with apples and pineapples, stars, firecrackers and sparklers tied with a bow.

## CENTERPIECES

It is very important to have the right centerpiece for each individual theme party. Some centerpieces are unique while others range from simple to elegant. I generally shop for the materials for the centerpieces. However, if I am pressed for time I have a staff member or a reliable florist to assemble the theme centerpieces. Re-use nonperishable centerpieces to help get your money's worth out of them. Maintain the centerpieces after each use.

## HAWAIIAN PINEAPPLE CENTERPIECE

You'll need a special tray with a cylinder attached in the center. Cut tops off 4 large pineapples. Core pineapples, but leave skin on.

Slide the 4 cored pineapples down onto the cylinder, one on top of each other. Attach an anthurium to the center of the pipe and on the top of the pineapples. Attach 7 anthurium leaves and 8 palms into the 2 top pineapples at random to form palm leaves. Leave the two bottom pineapples plain. Decorate the base with fresh fruit and flowers. (See picture on page 207).

## ROCKET AND STARS FOREVER CENTERPIECE

This is the centerpiece for the Red, White and blue Picnic. (See the diagram and illustration on page 205.) You'll need to create 5 rockets and 3 stars of varying sizes for each centerpiece.

To create the rockets, use cardboard rolls from paper towels, toilet paper, and plastic table cover rolls. Cut one cardboard roll for each rocket to desired length. For the top of each rocket cut a circle out of stiff paper a few inches larger than the diameter of the roll. Cut a slit in the circle from the edge to the center; overlap the edges to form a cone. Glue edges together. Glue the cone onto the cylinder. Let dry about a half hour.

Spray-paint the rockets with silver paint and sprinkle glitter over the paint while it's still wet.

For each rocket, cut a dowel several inches longer than the rocket. Spray-paint the dowel silver. Glue the painted dowel to the inside of the rocket cylinder. Let dry.

Cut stars in different sizes out of stiff paper, two matching stars of each size. Glue a small dowel between each pair of stars, rotating the stars to alternate points. Let dry for a half hour. Spray all the stars and dowels gold

and sprinkle with gold glitter while the paint is still wet.

Spray-paint three wooden curls of stick in gold. (You can purchase wooden curls at the local florist supply company or craft store.)

Cut a piece of styrofoam to fit into a cylindrical glass vase. Cover the vase with glitter to hide the styrofoam. Stick the dowel ends of 3 stars and 5 rockets into the styrofoam in an attractive design.

Place the gold wood curls into the centerpiece at different heights. Twine decorative red star wire (purchased at a local party store) around the centerpiece. Cover your table with a stars and stripes tablecloth, and add a table runner in glittery red fabric. Place the centerpiece in the middle of the table.

## BASKET CENTERPIECE

This centerpiece not only can be used for the Red, White and Blue Picnic but also for an old-fashioned Christmas theme party. Hot-glue silk leaves onto the handle of a basket and around the base. Arrange artificial red apples, grapes and a pineapple in the basket and attach with hot glue to the greens.

## ORGANIZING THE MEGA-PICNIC

There are many plans and organizational skills needed to orchestrate a successful large picnic.

It is a thrill to get a call and book a large company picnic for the first time. After you hang up you may have second thoughts and wonder what you are getting into by saying yes. (Nothing ventured, nothing gained.)

So you proceed and begin to make party plans. Fax your order for the number of tables and chairs, party date and day, and place for the rental contact person to sing his/her name for a confirmation. Schedule the time a day before to set up the tent and chairs.

**Menu**

Brats, hamburgers, hot dogs
Potato Salad
Coleslaw
Pasta Salad
Potato chips
Baked Beans
Relishes
Watermelon
Buns, butter, margarine
Ketchup, mustard, mayonnaise, and relish
Brownies and dessert bars
Lemonade and sodas

Call for the availability of a refrigerated semi truck. It is wise to reserve the truck two months in advance when possible.

Generally a large food vendor you trade with will let you use the company's refrigerated truck if you purchase all the food for the picnic from their company. Arrange for the refrigerated semi truck to be dropped off at the designated party site on the day before the actual party date. This gives you an opportunity to set up 8-foot tables for working space inside the truck.

Once the semi trailer is in place it will not be moved again. So plan in advance where the semi will be parked. Make sure the truck is near the buffet lines and the grill area to minimize running. It may be wise to meet with the driver to insure proper location. Each truck has a back door and a side door. Have separate locks and keys for each. Make sure the refrigerated truck runs the entire night and all through the party.

The driver will deliver all the products needed for the party in the semi at the party site. This helps you cut your travel time. You also can have room in your own refrigerator back at your catering kitchen.

How to set up the refrigerated trailer: Use 2 sets of tables 8 feet each and piggyback the tables to form work space needed. Put like food products together. Be sure all the food to be grilled, such as hamburgers, brat and hot dogs, are the

first items by the back door. You can even store the grills in the truck overnight. Once all the meats are off the truck and located at the grill site, organize trays of food such as watermelon and relishes. Relish trays are ideal for large crowds. All items are ready prepared and set to be arranged on trays.

Arrange coleslaw and potato salad in serving bowls. Purchase presliced and diced onions. Arrange sliced onions on 12- to 16-inch trays. Place diced onions into small bowls. Serve with kitchen tablespoons.

Make sure you carry soap and water for easy cleanup. Wear plastic gloves for scooping up food. Change plastic gloves in between types of food for proper sanitation.

Use a sharp French chef's knife for cutting the watermelon. (Once I had to use a small pocket knife to cut the watermelon when the French chef's knife was not packed.)

Get your bakery company to deliver the buns and desserts the day of the party so they are fresh and not cold from being stored overnight in the refrigerated truck. The buns can be placed on 8-foot tables alongside the truck. Request that the bar desserts be precut so you only have to put them out on the table. There is always an extra charge for this service, but it is worth every cent.

Order a lemonade dispenser and a truck with sodas if the party site does not handle liquid refreshment. Refer to the diagram on page 204 to see how the food trailer is set up. This layout becomes your portable kitchen for the party day.

Run the ramp down from the truck for easy access for setting up and refilling the buffet tables. Set out cold and hot foods no more than 20 minutes prior to the party.

## HOW TO SET UP THE BUFFET FOR A LARGE PARTY

The spoke system is very efficient to serve large crowds in a short amount of time. This system is also called the sunburst layout. (See diagram on page 202-203.) The advantage of using this method for the buffet line is that it saves on equipment. The sunburst (spoke) system serves four buffet lines. Instead of using 16 chafing dishes for the suggested menu use only 8 chafing dishes. This system serves a large crowd fast.

Cover each table with a plastic tablecloth and tape in place. Use plastic gathered skirting to skirt round tables. Cover round tables with tablecloths. Place a large centerpiece on a covered riser. This gives the centerpiece height. Surround the centerpiece with baskets of ketchup, mustard, mayo and pickle relish, and also bowls of diced onions and trays of sliced onions.

When returning to your shop refrigerate open gallons containers of condiments in the cooler.

TIP: Individual packets of condiments should travel in their original boxes. They are easier to carry and will keep the product fresher. Be sure to open and check boxes of condiment packets to be sure condiments are intact. One time I took an unopened case of ketchup packets to the party. To my surprise I found broken ketchup packets. I wiped off the ketchup packets from the top and used the bottom packets. I got by.

## RENTAL EQUIPMENT FOR A PICNIC FOR 1,500 PEOPLE

- 40 x 100' tent
- Sixteen 8-foot tables for buffet
- 2 round tables for buffet
- 4 extra 8-foot tables for silverware, napkins and condiments
- 4 extra 8-foot tables for desserts
- 32 tables for seating
- 250 chairs

If you were not having the picnic at a place with extra seating than you would have to have extra tents, tables and chairs for sitting the guests. If the serving time is 3 hours long you should have enough tables to sit half to two thirds of the crowd at one time.

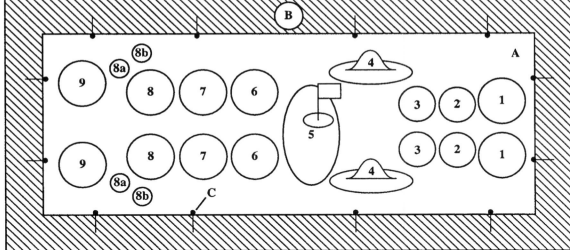

**Ethnic theme picnic: Mexican section**

A. Mexican blankets for tablecloths
B. Skirting to match Mexican blankets
C. Pearl corsage pins
1. Plates (9")
2. Basket with knives
3. Basket with cocktail napkins
4. Tortilla chips in Mexican hats

5. Centerpiece and flag
6. Layered cream cheese taco dip
7. Refried bean dip
8. Avocado salad
8a. Salt
8b. Pepper
9. Mexican wedding cakes

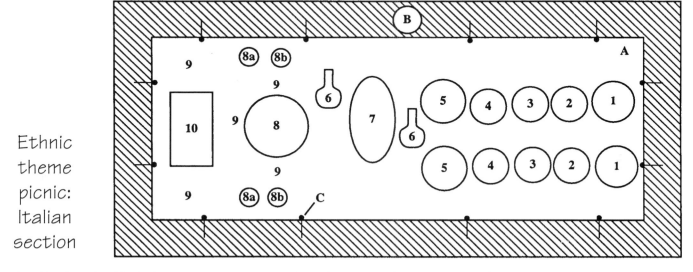

**Ethnic theme picnic: Italian section**

A. Checkered tablecloth
B. Skirting
C. Pearl corsage pins
1. Plates (9")
2. Forks
3. Knives

4. Basket of paper lunch napkins (red, green)
5. Basket of crusty buns
6. Chianti bottles with candles
7. Italian bread with grapes centerpiece

8. Vegetable salad
8a. Salt
8b. Pepper
9. Pasta decoration
10. Italian sausages

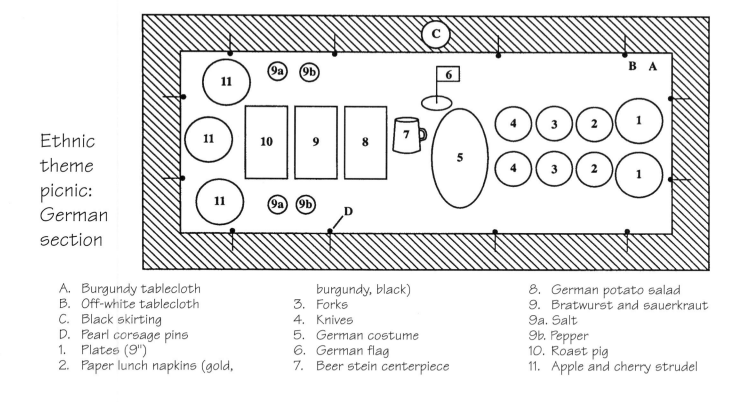

**Ethnic theme picnic: German section**

A. Burgundy tablecloth
B. Off-white tablecloth
C. Black skirting
D. Pearl corsage pins
1. Plates (9")
2. Paper lunch napkins (gold, burgundy, black)
3. Forks
4. Knives
5. German costume
6. German flag
7. Beer stein centerpiece
8. German potato salad
9. Bratwurst and sauerkraut
9a. Salt
9b. Pepper
10. Roast pig
11. Apple and cherry strudel

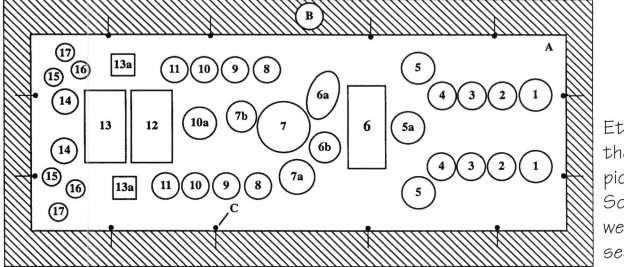

**Ethnic theme picnic: Southwestern section**

A. Tablecloth
B. Black skirting
C. Pearl corsage pins
1. Plates, black (9")
2. Forks
3. Knives
4. Dinner napkins
5. Relishes
5a. Cowboy boots
6. Black Beans Southwestern Style
6a. Centerpiece
6b. Cactus candles and holders
7. Large basket with buns
7a. Cowboy hat
7b. Driftwood
8. Individual butter pats
9. Gourmet mustard
10. Onion slices
10a. Tomatoes
11. Lettuce
12. Tenderloin steaks
13. Corn
13a. Dinner napkins for corn
14. Melted butter
15. Salt
16. Pepper
17. Handi-wipes

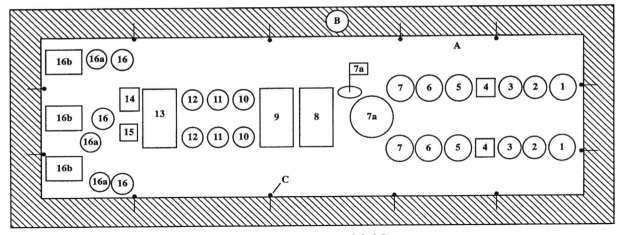

Ethnic theme picnic: Spirit of '76 section

| | | |
|---|---|---|
| A. Tablecloth | 6. Basket of assorted crackers | 13. Colonial chicken |
| B. Skirting | 7. Old Glory Fruit Salad | 14. Uncle Sam sign |
| C. Pearl corsage pins | 7a. Centerpiece and flag | 15. Uncle Sam hat with play money |
| 1. Plates (9") | 8. Calico Baked Beans | 16. Dessert plates |
| 2. Forks | 9. Valley Forge Potatoes | 16a. Dessert forks |
| 3. Knives | 10. Butter | 16b. Blueberry Pan Pie |
| 4. Dinner napkins | 11. Sour cream | |
| 5. Liberty Bell Cheese | 12. Shredded Cheddar cheese | |

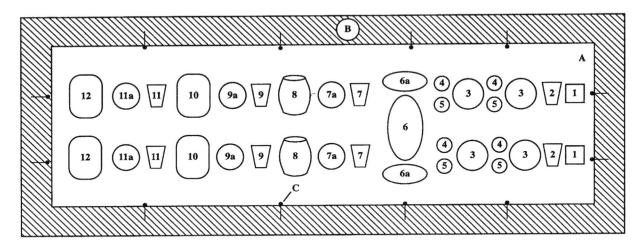

Ethnic theme picnic: Beverage section

| | | |
|---|---|---|
| A. Tablecloth | 5. Sugar | 9a. Ice for lemonade |
| B. Skirting | 6. Centerpiece | 10. Lemonade |
| C. Pearl corsage pins | 6a. Hat | 11. Cups for iced tea |
| 1. Cocktail napkins | 7. Soda cups | 11a. Ice for iced tea |
| 2. Coffee cups | 7a. Ice | 12. Iced tea |
| 3. Coffee | 8. Barrels of soda | |
| 4. Cream | 9. Cups for lemonade | |

190

## Ethnic theme picnic: Beach section

A. Beach towels
1. Plates (9")
2. Basket of forks
3. Basket of knives
4. Basket of napkins
5. Hot dogs
5a. Basket of buns
6. Basket of mustard
7. Basket of ketchup
8. Basket of relish
9. Bowl of diced onions
10. Sand box
11. Basket of potato chips
12. Beach ball
13. Fishnet
14. Seven Layer Salad
15. Fruited Gelatin
16. Seashells
17. Deviled Eggs
18. Dessert plates (6")
19. Dessert bars
20. Soda glasses
21. Sodas
22. Straws
23. Umbrella
24. Beach bum with glasses

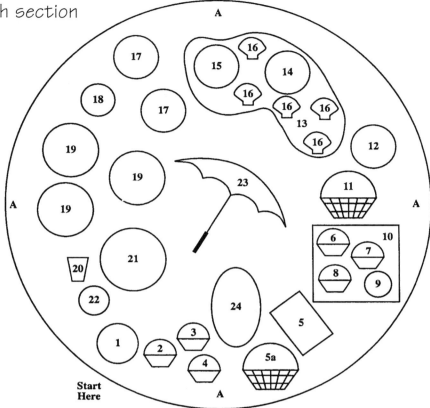

Buffet setup

Inverted V buffet with 3 rounds
1-sided buffet

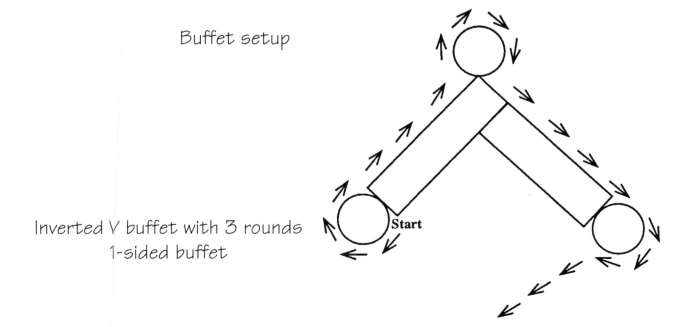

191

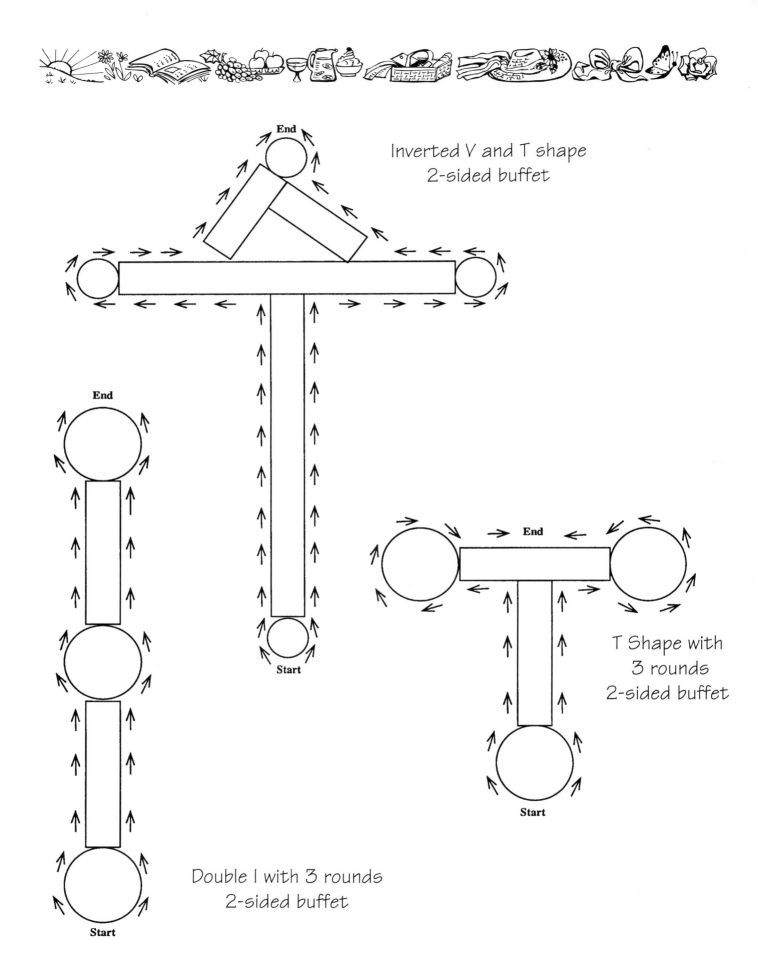

Inverted V and T shape
2-sided buffet

**End**

**Start**

End

T Shape with
3 rounds
2-sided buffet

**Start**

End

Double I with 3 rounds
2-sided buffet

**Start**

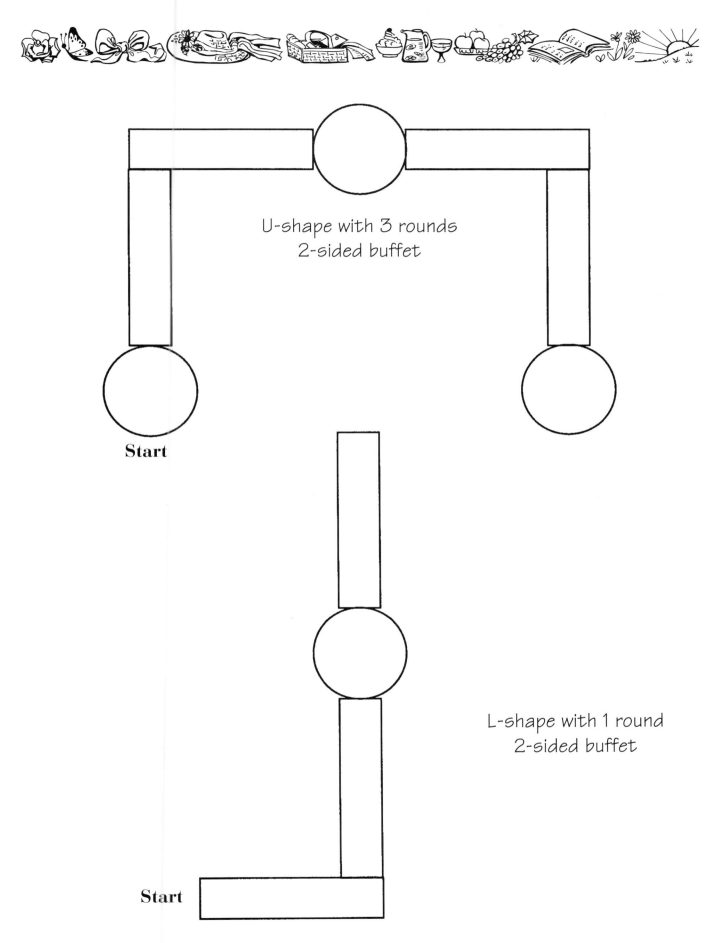

U-shape with 3 rounds
2-sided buffet

**Start**

L-shape with 1 round
2-sided buffet

**Start**

# 2-Sided Buffets

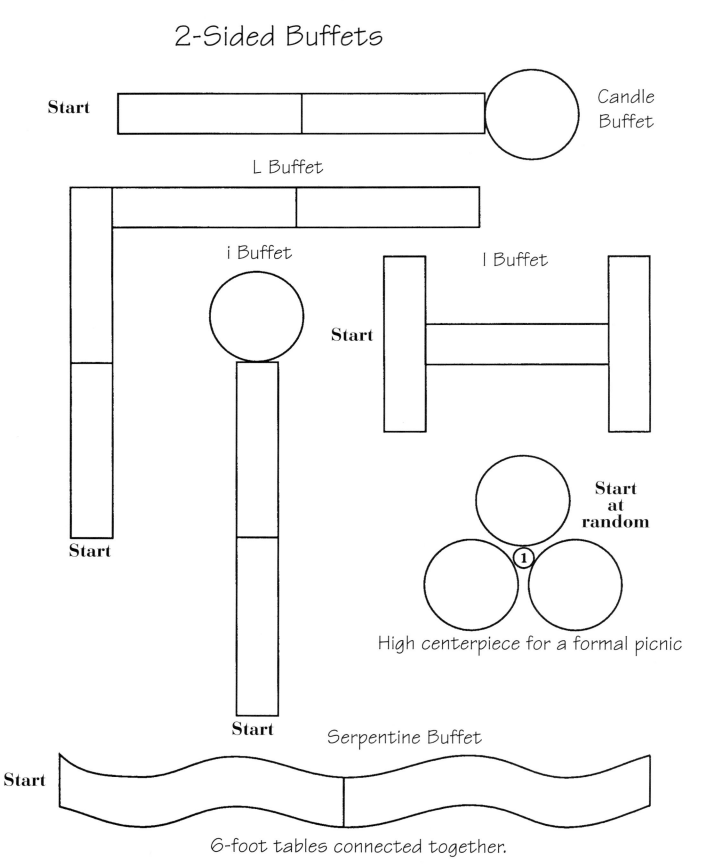

**Start**

Candle Buffet

L Buffet

i Buffet

I Buffet

**Start**

**Start**

Start at random

**Start**

High centerpiece for a formal picnic

Serpentine Buffet

**Start**

6-foot tables connected together.

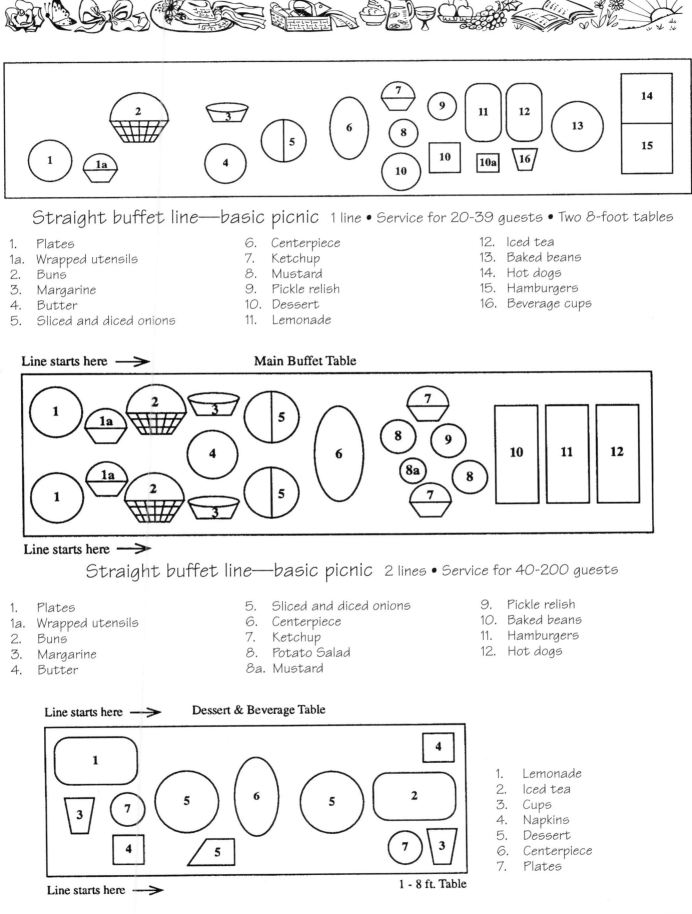

## Straight buffet line—basic picnic  1 line • Service for 20-39 guests • Two 8-foot tables

| | | |
|---|---|---|
| 1. Plates | 6. Centerpiece | 12. Iced tea |
| 1a. Wrapped utensils | 7. Ketchup | 13. Baked beans |
| 2. Buns | 8. Mustard | 14. Hot dogs |
| 3. Margarine | 9. Pickle relish | 15. Hamburgers |
| 4. Butter | 10. Dessert | 16. Beverage cups |
| 5. Sliced and diced onions | 11. Lemonade | |

**Line starts here** ➡    **Main Buffet Table**

**Line starts here** ➡

## Straight buffet line—basic picnic  2 lines • Service for 40-200 guests

| | | |
|---|---|---|
| 1. Plates | 5. Sliced and diced onions | 9. Pickle relish |
| 1a. Wrapped utensils | 6. Centerpiece | 10. Baked beans |
| 2. Buns | 7. Ketchup | 11. Hamburgers |
| 3. Margarine | 8. Potato Salad | 12. Hot dogs |
| 4. Butter | 8a. Mustard | |

**Line starts here** ➡    **Dessert & Beverage Table**

**Line starts here** ➡    1 - 8 ft. Table

1. Lemonade
2. Iced tea
3. Cups
4. Napkins
5. Dessert
6. Centerpiece
7. Plates

195

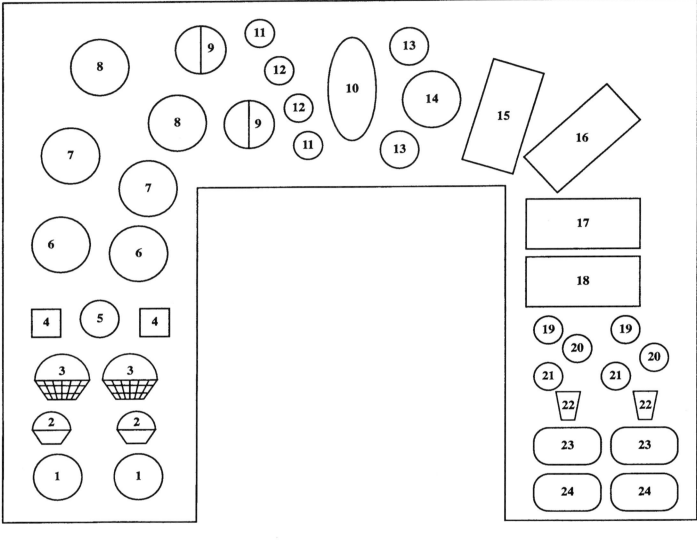

## U-shaped buffet line
### Service for 20-200 guests

1.  Plates
2.  Wrapped utensils
3.  Hamburger and hot dog buns
4.  Margarine
5.  Butter
6.  Potato salad
7.  Coleslaw
8.  Relishes

9.  Sliced and diced onions
10. Centerpiece
11. Ketchup
12. Mustard
13. Pickle relish
14. Sauteed green pepper
15. Baked beans
16. Italian sausages

17. Hot dogs
18. Hamburgers
19. Dessert plates
20. Napkins
21. Dessert
22. Beverage cups
23. Lemonade
24. Iced tea

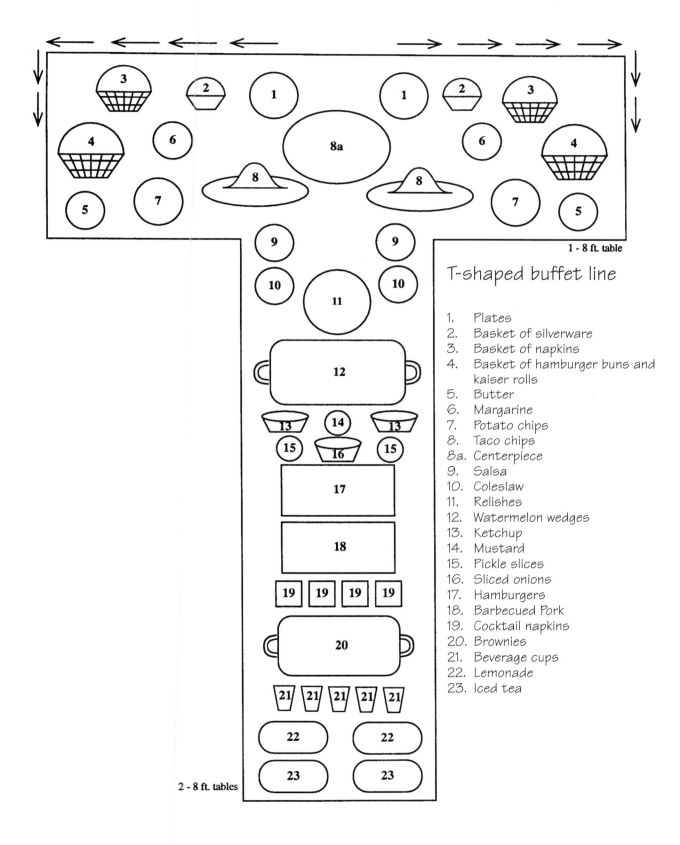

1 - 8 ft. table

## T-shaped buffet line

1. Plates
2. Basket of silverware
3. Basket of napkins
4. Basket of hamburger buns and kaiser rolls
5. Butter
6. Margarine
7. Potato chips
8. Taco chips
8a. Centerpiece
9. Salsa
10. Coleslaw
11. Relishes
12. Watermelon wedges
13. Ketchup
14. Mustard
15. Pickle slices
16. Sliced onions
17. Hamburgers
18. Barbecued Pork
19. Cocktail napkins
20. Brownies
21. Beverage cups
22. Lemonade
23. Iced tea

2 - 8 ft. tables

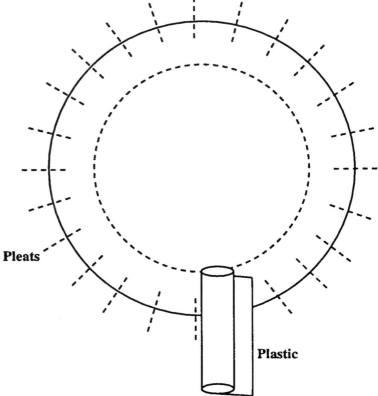

# How to skirt a round table
with plastic table covering on a roll

**Pleats**

**Plastic**

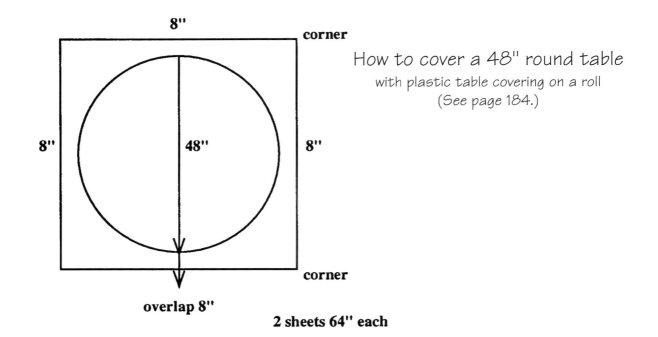

8"

**corner**

8"      48"      8"

# How to cover a 48" round table
with plastic table covering on a roll
(See page 184.)

**corner**

**overlap 8"**

**2 sheets 64" each**

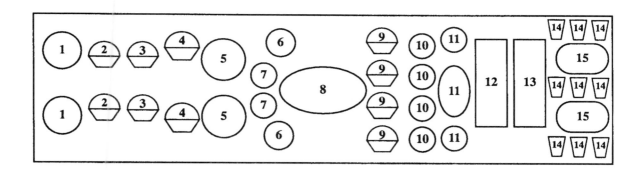

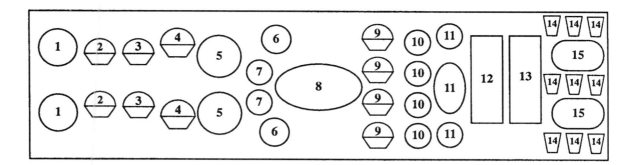

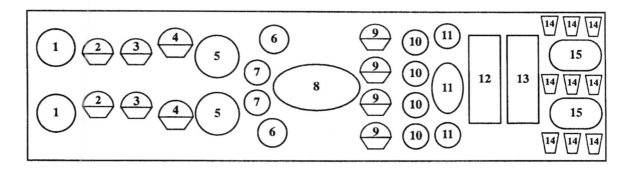

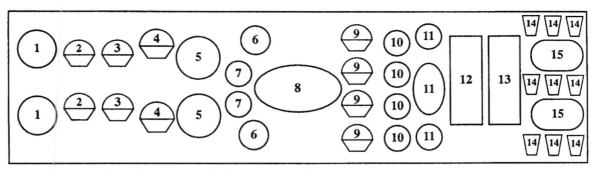

## Multi-lines for 1,000 people 4 lines • four 8-foot tables

1. Plates
2. Forks and knives
3. Dinner napkins
4. Hot dog buns
5. Potato chips

6. Butter
7. Margarine
8. Centerpiece
9. Ketchup
10. Mustard

11. Diced onions
12. Baked beans
13. Hot dogs
14. Beverage cups
15. Lemonade

**Dessert**

**Dessert**

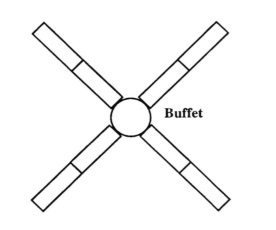

**Buffet**

**Dessert**

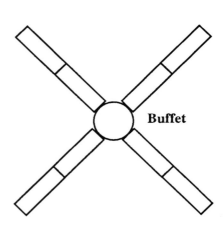

**Buffet**

Mega Picnic for 1,500 people

40 x 100-foot tent

**Condiments**

**Condiments**

**32 8ft. Tables - 250 Chairs**

**Dessert**

**Dessert**

**Condiments**     **Dessert**

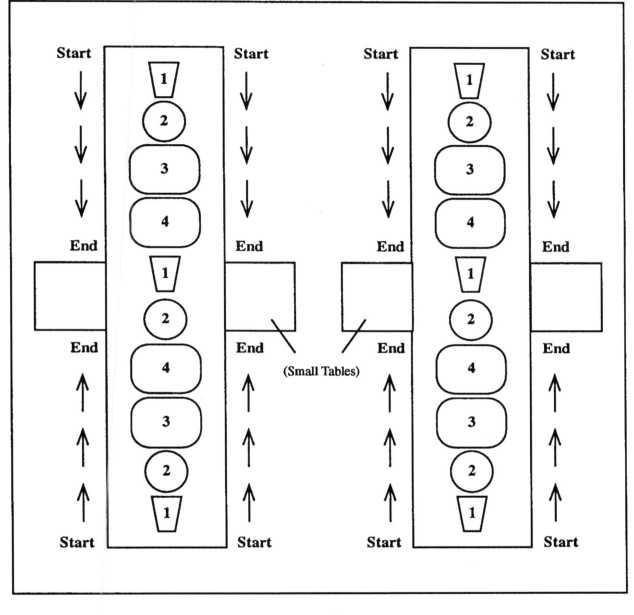

Mega Picnic Beverage Tent   20 x 30-foot tent

1. Cups
2. Ice
3. Lemonade
4. Soda

# Sunburst buffet
## (Spoke method)

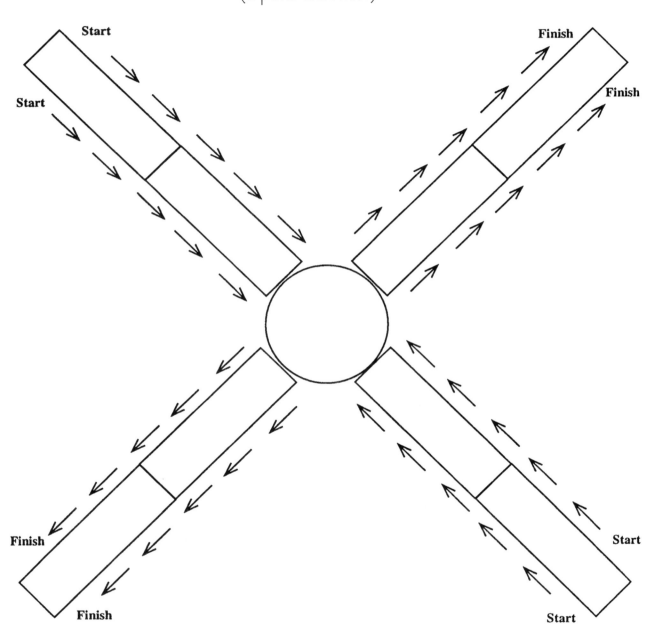

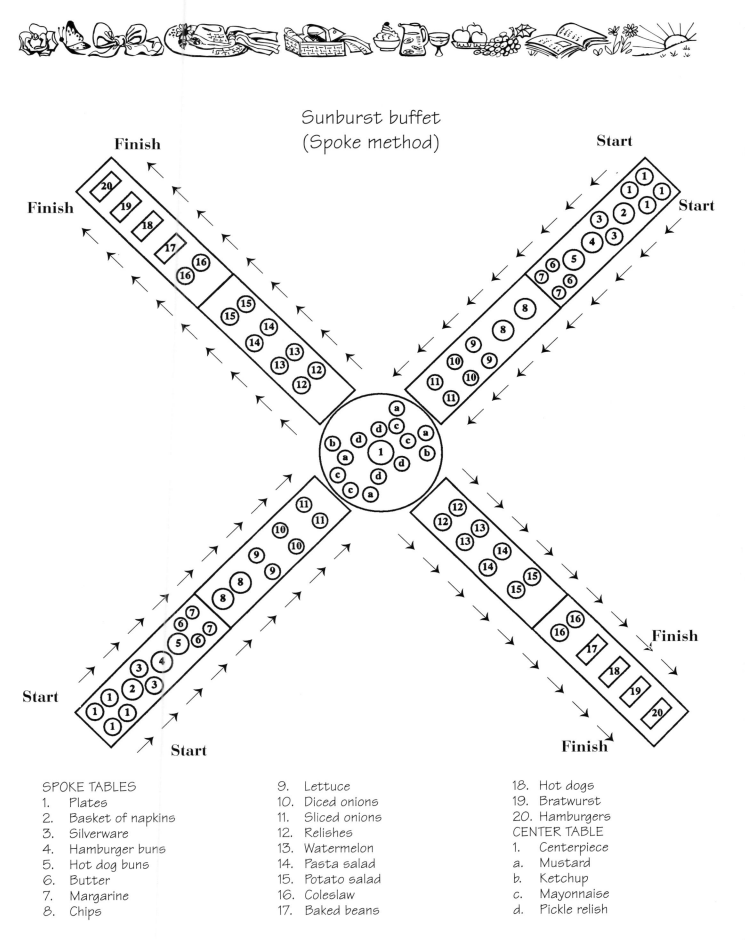

Sunburst buffet
(Spoke method)

SPOKE TABLES
1. Plates
2. Basket of napkins
3. Silverware
4. Hamburger buns
5. Hot dog buns
6. Butter
7. Margarine
8. Chips
9. Lettuce
10. Diced onions
11. Sliced onions
12. Relishes
13. Watermelon
14. Pasta salad
15. Potato salad
16. Coleslaw
17. Baked beans
18. Hot dogs
19. Bratwurst
20. Hamburgers
CENTER TABLE
1. Centerpiece
a. Mustard
b. Ketchup
c. Mayonnaise
d. Pickle relish

203

# How to lay out a refrigerated truck

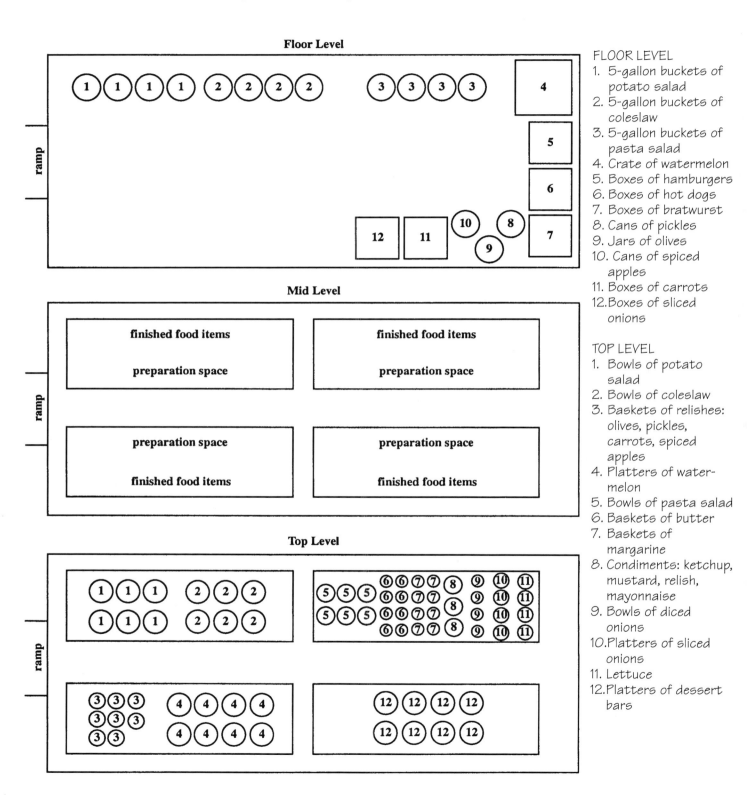

**Floor Level**

ramp

(1) (1) (1) (1) (2) (2) (2) (2)  (3) (3) (3) (3)  | 4 |

| 5 |

| 6 |

| 12 | | 11 |  (10) (8)  | 7 |
              (9)

**Mid Level**

ramp

| finished food items | | finished food items |
| preparation space | | preparation space |

| preparation space | | preparation space |
| finished food items | | finished food items |

**Top Level**

ramp

(1) (1) (1)  (2) (2) (2)  | (5)(5)(5) (6)(6)(7)(7) (8) (9) (10)(11) |
(1) (1) (1)  (2) (2) (2)  | (5)(5)(5) (6)(6)(6)(7)(7) (9) (10)(11) |
                          | (5)(5)(5) (6)(6)(7)(7) (8) (9) (10)(11) |
                          | (6)(6)(7)(7) (8) (9) (10)(11) |

(3)(3)(3)  (4) (4) (4) (4)  | (12) (12) (12) (12) |
(3)(3)(3)
(3)(3)  (4) (4) (4)  | (12) (12) (12) (12) |

**FLOOR LEVEL**
1. 5-gallon buckets of potato salad
2. 5-gallon buckets of coleslaw
3. 5-gallon buckets of pasta salad
4. Crate of watermelon
5. Boxes of hamburgers
6. Boxes of hot dogs
7. Boxes of bratwurst
8. Cans of pickles
9. Jars of olives
10. Cans of spiced apples
11. Boxes of carrots
12. Boxes of sliced onions

**TOP LEVEL**
1. Bowls of potato salad
2. Bowls of coleslaw
3. Baskets of relishes: olives, pickles, carrots, spiced apples
4. Platters of water-melon
5. Bowls of pasta salad
6. Baskets of butter
7. Baskets of margarine
8. Condiments: ketchup, mustard, relish, mayonnaise
9. Bowls of diced onions
10. Platters of sliced onions
11. Lettuce
12. Platters of dessert bars

**1.**

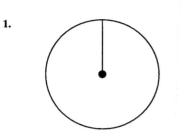

# How to make the
# Rocket and Stars Forever centerpiece
## (page 185)

*Created by Pat Nekola and Lucki Huber*

**2.**

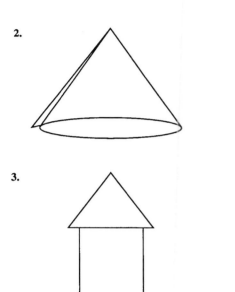

**3.**

Star shapes for the
Rocket and Stars Forever
centerpiece

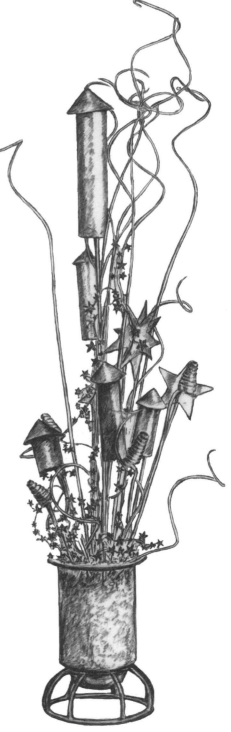

205

# Palm tree centerpiece

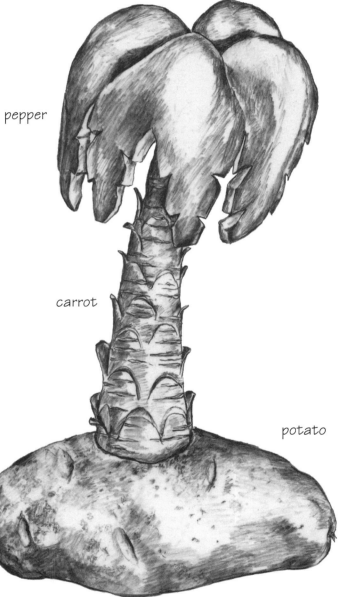

bell pepper

carrot

potato

Cut a slice off the bottom of the
potato so it will not wobble. Cut a
hole in the center top of the potato
just large enough to hold the carrot.
With a sharp paring knife cut scales
on carrot for palm tree effect.
Cut the top off a green bell pepper.
Remove membranes and seeds from
the inside. Cut sides of pepper into
palm leaf shapes. Secure pepper
"leaves" onto carrot "trunk" with a
toothpick.

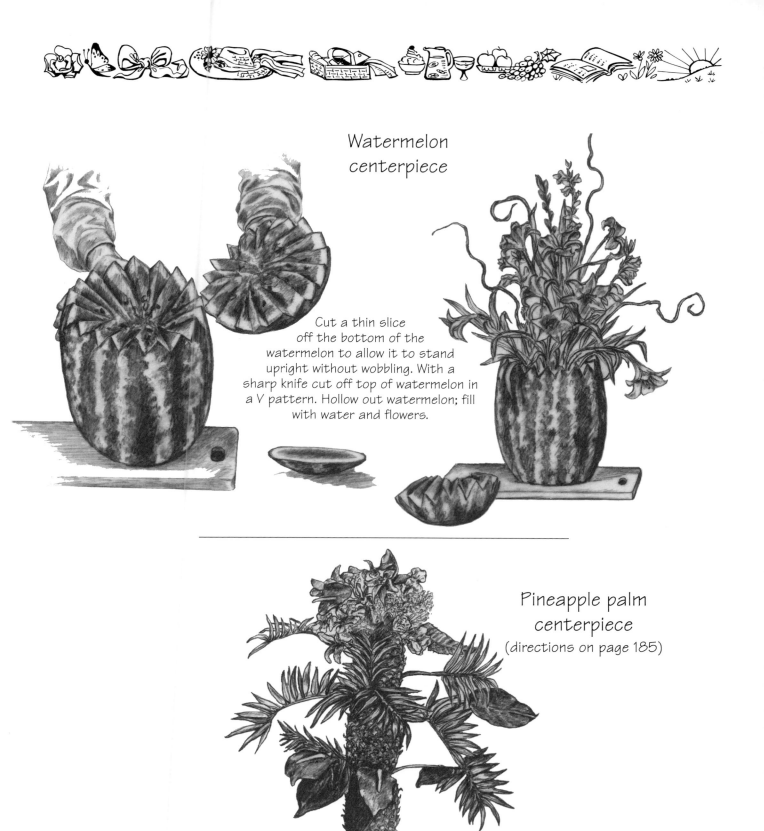

## Watermelon centerpiece

Cut a thin slice off the bottom of the watermelon to allow it to stand upright without wobbling. With a sharp knife cut off top of watermelon in a V pattern. Hollow out watermelon; fill with water and flowers.

## Pineapple palm centerpiece
(directions on page 185)

# Pineapple swan centerpiece

A

Cut a small slice off one side of pineapple to allow it to lay flat.

B

Cut a larger slice off the other side. Reserve the cut section.

C

Hollow out pineapple, leaving a shell about 1 inch thick.

D

Fill pineapple shell with fruit. Cut the shape of the head and neck of a swan out of the reserved piece.

E

Trim the head and neck section.

F

Place head section in body of swan.

Tall flower centerpiece

Flower centerpiece

# Setting Up Shop

Having the right equipment to do off-premises catering is essential. In setting up your business, consider first the three "Cs" of catering: coolers, convection ovens, and countertops.

COOLER (WALK-IN) This should be outfitted with wire racks, NSF (National Sanitation Foundation) approved, arranged at differing heights. The cooler should be large enough to provide plenty of storage. Monitor the temperature with a thermometer and maintain the cooler at 40 degrees. The wire racks must be sanitized (washed down with a mixture of chlorine bleach and water) weekly. The cooler floor should be washed every other day. If anything spills, wipe it up immediately. Make sure all foods are rotated out to prevent spoilage. Diligent care will keep the cooler odor-free.

For each party, label a section of racks with the customer's name and use this designated area to house all the refrigerated foods for that party. Locate the sections by the order of the party on that particular date. For example, if you have the Smith picnic at 11:30 a.m. and the Jones picnic at 12:30 p.m., shelve the Smith picnic's foods closest to the cooler door and the Jones picnic's foods next down from the cooler entrance.

REACH-IN COOLERS come in single- and double-door widths. They contain adjustable shelves. Store bulk refrigerated foods here. For freezer storage, I started my business with a reach-in stainless steel freezer. As your business grows, you may want to add a walk-in freezer.

CONVECTION OVENS In your catering business start-up, you may be tempted to purchase only a single-door convection oven. You will most likely be on a budget, trying to hold down expenses, and will rationalize that your business will initially handle only small parties.

Within the first six months of my business, I had to buy a second single-door convection oven and, within the first year, I had to add a double door-convection oven. I strongly recommend spending the extra money up front and getting a double-door convection oven first.

Convection ovens operate with a rotating fan that circulates the hot air and cooks foods very evenly. They are very well suited for cooking meats. One single door convection oven can hold six half-size pans (4 inches deep) or three full-size pans (4 inches deep). One double door convection oven can hold 16 half-size pans (4 inches deep) or 8 full-size pans (4 inches deep).

For cooking hors d'oeuvres and heating foods in a convection oven, reduce the temperature called for by 50 degrees.

For picnics, you will use the convection oven primarily to heat baked beans and sauerkraut to carry in hot boxes to the picnic site. These will hold in hot boxes for up to four hours. Cover the tops of the pans tightly with foil when heating in a convection oven.

When you are finished using the convection oven, always remember to initiate the cool-down knob. This will disperse the heat.

HOTEL PANS are large rectangular stainless steel pans with a lip around the top edge. You see them used in steam tables on restaurant buffets to hold hot foods. They come in full-size, two or four inches deep, and half-size, two or four inches deep.

COUNTERTOPS must be NSF-approved stainless steel in various lengths. In your kitchen design, you will want to stagger the countertops around the different food preparation areas. Keep a fresh bucket of water and chlorine bleach solution to wipe off the countertops after every food preparation.

SINKS At least two sink setups are required. Generally, a sink with a garbage disposal is directly attached to a commercial-size dishwasher. Here the dishes are rinsed before loading into the dishwasher.

The other necessary sink area is a four-compartment sink with a stainless steel drainboard at each end. Right to left, the first compartment with disposal is used for rinsing pots, pans and other utensils. The second sink compartment contains hot, soapy water. The third sink has clear water for rinsing again. The last sink is for sanitation and holds a mixture of chlorine bleach and water. After taking the pots and pans, etc., through this cycle, they are left to air-dry in dish racks on the stainless steel drainboard.

Each sink will have a grease trap to pick up excess grease. These traps must be cleaned out periodically.

STOVE Six-burner stoves with ovens come in gas or electric. Most caterers use gas because of the lower operating cost. The pilot light must remain lit at all times. Install a stainless steel ventilation hood over the stove according to your local health department specifications.

A rack with wire shelves can be used to store spices and should be set up near the stove.

MIXERS A large commercial mixer on a floor stand is needed for mixing large quantities of food. It has various speeds and needs to be turned off before changing to a different speed during a food preparation. If not, this will be very hard on the gears. After completing a mixing process, turn mixer off and reset to the lowest speed. The next person using the mixer may not look at the speed setting, and upon turning the mixer on, will end up wearing the food. A useful attachment is a grinder which is used to mince cooked poultry for salads or shred cabbage for slaw. It is also good to have a couple of tabletop mixers for the small jobs. These come in four- or five-quart size with various attachments.

BAKING UNIT This stainless steel cabinet with a stainless countertop is used to store baking supplies such as flour and baking soda. Put the small tabletop mixers on the countertop. This unit is your baking area with everything at your fingertips.

TIP: In the summer months store chocolate, coconut and nuts in tightly covered containers in the cooler.

MEAT SLICER This is a must. It is used not only to slice meats and cheese, but also a variety of vegetables such as tomatoes, lettuce, onions, and cucumbers. The meat slicer must be taken apart, cleaned, and sanitized after each use. It will come with an attachment to sharpen the blade. You and your workers must learn to respect the meat slicer. It does not know the difference between a finger and a piece of meat. Check with your local health department to find out what age workers must be to operate both the meat slicer and the floor mixer.

CUTLERY Some caterers sharpen their own knives. I use a knife sharpening service that drops off a sharpened set of knives every two weeks when picking up the used set. This ensures that the cutlery is always sharp. One of the greatest knives to use is the French chef knife, for it chops, dices, and slices. Your collection of cutlery should also include a boning knife and paring knives.

SCALES Much of each party's or picnic's foods are measured out by weight. You will need at least two kitchen scales, each holding up to 25 pounds. Make sure the scale is set at zero before weighing anything. Weigh the empty container and then turn the scale back below zero that many ounces. Then place the container on the countertop and fill with the food to be weighed. This will prevent the pan from tipping and spilling. Weigh the filled container to get an accurate weight of the food only. (See diagrams on page 217.)

COFFEEMAKERS In outfitting your kitchen, you will want to start out with three 100-cup capacity coffeemakers and a 30-cup coffeemaker. (See diagram on page 18.)

MISCELLANEOUS The following is a list of some of the items to include in setting up shop:

Spatulas, metal and rubber
Commercial can opener
Potato peelers
Pots and pans, various sizes
Mixing bowls
Baking sheets
Pastry bags and decorating tips
Pastry brushes
Wire whisks
Colanders
Rolling pins
Measuring cups, liquid and dry
Measuring spoons
Stainless steel quart and pint measures
Meat thermometers and probes
Ladles, various sizes
Scoops
Heat lamps
Towels, washcloths, and aprons
Disposable plastic gloves

HOT BOXES (See illustrations on page 218.) These are insulated boxes for transporting hot or cold foods. Never mix hot and cold foods in the same box. Hot boxes are either front-loading or top-loading. The front-loading hot box comes in a double or single size. The double front-loading hot box comes on wheels. This hot box will accommodate trays up to 18 inches in diameter. Slip baking sheets in on the runners to create shelves on which to place the trays. Hotel pans need no shelves underneath as they will easily slide in with the pan lip resting on the side runners. A single front-loading box will hold three full-size hotel pans.

Top-loading hot boxes are just that. The top lifts off and hotel pans are placed down inside. These boxes come in two sizes: full-size and half-size. The full-size has a handle on each side. A half-size top-loading hot box will hold one full-size hotel pan or two half-size hotel pans, two or four inches deep. A full-size top-loading hot box will hold two full-size hotel pans or four half-size hotel pans, four inches deep, or three full-size hotel pans, two inches deep. After filling the pans with hot foods, cover tightly with foil. This will help insulate the food even more. The front-loading hot boxes will hold more food, but are quite heavy to lift.

Top-loading hot boxes stack for easy storage when empty. Store them with the lids off which will allow air to circulate and prevent any odors from building up inside. The hot box lid has a continuous rubber gasket around the inside edge. Before cleaning the hot box after each use, remove this gasket. Submerge it in hot, soapy water, wiping while rotating. Rinse in clear water and then sanitize. Leave the gaskets off, hanging in a special place in the shop. Reinsert the gasket on each hot box lid at the next use.(This applies to top-loading boxes only; the gaskets don't have to be removed on double-door hot boxes.)

PORTABLE COOLERS In addition to hot boxes, ordinary coolers can be used to transport cold foods. A good size is 14 x 27 inches. You can put nine 12-inch domed round trays in each cooler, filling in the spaces between the trays with ice packs. Portable coolers are great for carrying molded gelatin salads, deviled eggs, milk for coffee, margarine and butter, and extra jars of pickles and olives.

Another conveniently sized portable cooler is 14 x 19 inches. This smaller cooler works well for carrying meat. Because of the weight of the meat, you need to transport it in smaller loads. Fill the cooler completely and lay two flat ice packs over the top of the meat. The meat will stay much colder much longer. Be sure the cooler lids are latched securely. One of these coolers will hold 20 pounds of hamburger patties. To

transport bratwurst, Italian sausage, kielbasa, and other sausages, place chilled, pre-boiled sausages in large plastic food storage bags (do not use garbage bags as they are pretreated with insecticide) and carry in the small portable coolers. Approximately 70 to 80 sausages will fit in one cooler. Most importantly, use the portable coolers to transport only cold foods. Remember to use ice packs in each cooler.

CHAFING DISHES Have 6, standard size. At the picnic site, wrap foil all around the chafing dish sides, extending down to the table top. This will keep the sternos lit, protecting them from any breeze.

BAIN MARIE This is a pair of pans, one slightly smaller than the other. The smaller pan fits on top of the larger one, and act as a double boiler. Use a bain marie to melt butter for corn on the cob and to heat sauces on the grill.

SALAD BOWLS One dozen in each of the following sizes: 4-quart, 5-quart and 6-quart. Some caterers use extra-large bowls and therefore carry fewer to the picnic site. However, the larger bowls do not look as nice on the buffet table. Smaller bowls will not stay out as long and maintaining foods such as potato salad is not as risky. The smaller bowls are more easily refilled and serving spoons will not slide easily into the food.

TRAYS In your shop inventory, you will need one dozen each in 8-, 12-, and 18-inch diameter. The 12- and 18-inch trays are used the most.

SERVING SPOONS Kitchen-sized tablespoons are nice to use for salads. This size serving spoon will also help control portion sizes. With larger spoons, people tend to take more food. Long-handled commercial serving spoons are good to use for hot foods. The handles stay cooler and the spoon will not slide into the food.

TONGS AND SPATULAS Serving tongs come in 6-, 8- or 10-inch lengths. The 6-inch length is used for deviled eggs and relishes.

Barbecue tongs and spatulas used to turn hamburgers are 15 to 16 inches long. Use one set of barbecue tongs and one hamburger spatula per grill.

RISERS Elevating foods on the buffet table will visually create peaks and valleys and accent dimension. A straight, level buffet table is boring to look at. Risers can be all different shapes and heights. For a big and showy display, milk crates covered in pretty tablecloths and laces do well. Mix and match shapes and heights using such things as pillars, salad bowls turned upside-down, and plastic cubes. For a more contemporary look, glue clear acrylic pieces together and leave uncovered. Let your imagination be your guide.

BASKETS AND STRAW HATS These are the most versatile serving pieces. Baskets in different shapes and sizes make attractive holders for breads, cheese, fruits, vegetables, and desserts. Always line the baskets with clean fabric swatches or napkins, and change them after every use. You can even tuck your trays and bowls into baskets. Straw hats are fun. They are great for holding dry ingredients like crackers or rolls. For a Mexican picnic, overlap sombreros filled with tortilla chips. Use cowboy hats as food holders for a Western style barbecue.

GRILL A commercial grill is 2 feet x 5 feet. It comes disassembled for easy transport and storage in the shop. Generally one grill is sufficient for up to 50 people. However, depending on how many different grilled items are on the menu, you may need a second grill. For a picnic of 500, I recommend four grills. Use five grills for picnics of up to 1,000 and six grills for 1,500 to 2,000 guests. The length of serving time also affects the number of grills used at a picnic.

Use a fireplace shovel to move hot coals around when readying the grill for cooking. The best grill brushes for cleaning the grill tops are those made with disposable brush surfaces. After several uses, just remove and replace.

GARBAGE CANS WITH LIDS After grilling, dispose of the used charcoal in galvanized metal garbage cans. Use a shovel for cleanup. A 10-gallon garbage can is a good size. Secure the lids very well and carry the filled cans back to the shop. Some parks have cans especially designated for disposing of hot coals. Check it out. Never place the charcoal-filled cans anywhere in your truck or van but on the uncarpeted floor area. Thirty-two gallon plastic garbage cans with lids are used in the shop and at parties for cleanup.

SMALL TABLES Carry a 4-foot table or a couple of card tables and set up near the grill. Use these as work surfaces on which to place grilling utensils and small coolers.

Other necessary items for grilling should include: small spray bottles to wet down the flames and control the heat, matches or a long-handled butane lighter, and leather welding gloves. (Pages 80-81 have a detailed list of useful items to pack for grilling.) You don't want to over-inventory your equipment, tying up money in items you may only use infrequently. A reputable rental dealer can and should become one of your best business friends. If you need tents, tables, chairs, tablecloths, and skirting, see him/her. The dealer will also supply you with valuable rental information for setting up your picnic. Crunch the numbers, and if it will cost you more to rent the needed equipment than the potential profit you would realize, refer the party to another catering service.

# Supplies to Rent

CHINA
1 Dinner, salad, bread, or dessert plate
1 Cup or saucer. . . . . . . . . . . . . . . . . . . . . .
1 Dinner, salad, or dessert fork . . . . . . . . . . .
1 Spoon. . . . . . . . . . . . . . . . . . . . . . . . . . .
1 Knife. . . . . . . . . . . . . . . . . . . . . . . . . . . .
1 Champagne glass. . . . . . . . . . . . . . . . . . . .
1 Fluted champagne glass . . . . . . . . . . . . . . .
1 Wine or water glass. . . . . . . . . . . . . . . . . .
TABLE LINENS
Tablecloth (white) 69x69". . . . . . . . . . . . . . .
  (white or color) 72" square . . . . . . . . . . . .
  (white or color) 90" square . . . . . . . . . . . .
  52x114" banquet . . . . . . . . . . . . . . . . . . .
  90" round. . . . . . . . . . . . . . . . . . . . . . . .
  (white or color) 108" round . . . . . . . . . . . .
  (white or color) 120" round . . . . . . . . . . .
  (white or color) 132" round . . . . . . . . . . . .

Skirting for buffet, cake, gift and head tables. .
Cloth napkins (white or color) . . . . . . . . . . . .

PARTY ITEMS
Centerpiece. . . . . . . . . . . . . . . . . . . . . . . . .
Candelabra . . . . . . . . . . . . . . . . . . . . . . . . .
Champagne fountain . . . . . . . . . . . . . . . . . . .
Coffeepot (100 cups). . . . . . . . . . . . . . . . . . .
Coffeepot (30 cups) . . . . . . . . . . . . . . . . . . .
Small chafing dish . . . . . . . . . . . . . . . . . . . .
Large chafing dish . . . . . . . . . . . . . . . . . . . .
Sternos. . . . . . . . . . . . . . . . . . . . . . . . . . . .
Small punch bowl . . . . . . . . . . . . . . . . . . . . .
Large punch bowl . . . . . . . . . . . . . . . . . . . . .
Cooler . . . . . . . . . . . . . . . . . . . . . . . . . . . .
Hot box. . . . . . . . . . . . . . . . . . . . . . . . . . . .
TABLES AND CHAIRS
Round table (48"). . . . . . . . . . . . . . . . . . . . .

Round table (60"). . . . . . . . . . . . . . . . . . . . . . . .
Banquet table (8' x 30') . . . . . . . . . . . . . . . . . . . .
Chair, folding (white padded) . . . . . . . . . . . . .
Chair, folding (black metal). . . . . . . . . . . . . .
Chair, folding (tan metal). . . . . . . . . . . . . . . . .
TENTS
20x20' (seats approximately 32). . . . . . . . . . . .
20x30' (seats approximately 48). . . . . . . . . . . .
20x40' (seats approximately 64). . . . . . . . . . . .
30x60' (seats approximately 152) . . . . . . . . .
40x60' (seats approximately 200) . . . . . . . . .
Tent sides. . . . . . . . . . . . . . . . . . . . . . . . . . . . . .
(20-foot lengths)

DANCE FLOOR
Oak parquet (3x3') . . . . . . . . . . . . . . . . . . . . .
Black and white (3x3') (Checkered or any black
& white design) . . . . . .
(**Plywood base required to be put down first if
dance floor is outside on grass. . . . . . . . . . . . .
(Asphalt, if smooth and solid, will not need ply-
wood base)
(There is also a delivery and pick-up fee for
rentals-cost depends on delivery location). . . . .
MISCELLANEOUS
Plastic or paper table covering. . . . . . . . . . . . .
SERVICES
Bartender (hourly fee, 3-hour minimum) . . . . .
Clown (hourly fee, 2-hour minimum) . . . . . . .
Cake cutting/serving fee . . . . . . . . . . . . . . . . .

# Disposable Items

Dinner plates. . . . . . . . . . . . . . . . . . . . . . . . . .
Salad, bread, or dessert plates. . . . . . . . . . . .
Forks. . . . . . . . . . . . . . . . . . . . . . . . . . . . . . . . . .
Knives . . . . . . . . . . . . . . . . . . . . . . . . . . . . . . . .
Spoons . . . . . . . . . . . . . . . . . . . . . . . . . . . . . . .
Dinner napkins (white) . . . . . . . . . . . . . . . . .

Dinner napkins (color) . . . . . . . . . . . . . . . . . .
Fork, knife, & spoon wrapped in dinner napkins
Cocktail napkins (white) . . . . . . . . . . . . . . . . .
Cups (for coffee, soda, tea, or lemonade). . . . .
Wine and champagne glasses . . . . . . . . . . . . .
Stir sticks. . . . . . . . . . . . . . . . . . . . . . . . . . . . . .

As you are researching the catering business and before renting or buying a location and purchasing equipment, you will want to get to know your local and state health departments very well. Be completely informed on all regulations. Once you have done your homework and set up shop, it's time to get organized.

How to weigh food on a scale (page 212)

A
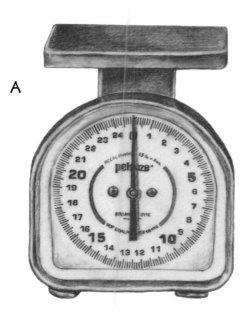

B
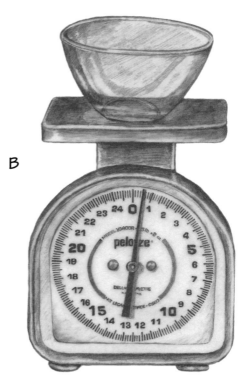

C
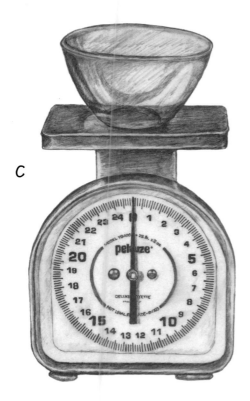

D
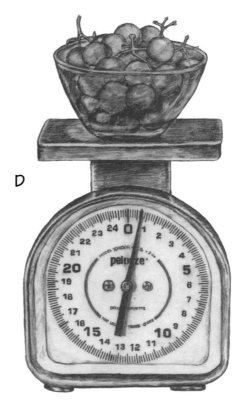

Hot boxes (page 213)

# Organization is the Key

After booking a picnic, securing a deposit and writing up a contract, a caterer's work begins. Make a list of duties for yourself to get the party plans launched and organized. For example, make sure the rental agent has enough equipment available on your picnic date. Line up tent sizes and colors, tablecloths and skirting, the number of tables needed for the guests, and sizes of rental tables. Check that the tables and chairs match.

Confer with the food vendors and paper product vendors. I have included a sample of the Paper Supplies Order Guide that I developed for my catering business. The first column denotes the quantity to be ordered. The second column lists how many items are in a unit. The third column shows the price per unit and the next column breaks down the price per item, followed by the item number and description. Use this type of order guide for food vendors, also. It is smart to have at end of the order guides a list of vendors and their products along with their fax and phone numbers.

If you will be having any entertainment at the picnic, make reservations well in advance. If you're having a bar, reserve a bartender. Gather up the special centerpieces and other decorations necessary for a theme party. Schedule your workers. If you don't have enough trucks or need a refrigerated truck, you will have to make these arrangements.

Sketch a diagram of the picnic setup showing positions of tents, tables, chairs, buffet layout, and entertainment areas. If props are required for a theme picnic, show on the diagram exactly where they go and give a copy to the prop providers. Send copies of this diagram to whomever is involved with the setup.

Make appointments to meet the client and the picnic site manager if there is one. Bring the setup diagrams and go over all the details to finalize the party plans. Leave a copy of the diagram with each person.

For ordering prepared foods and other ingredients, have a master list printed listing all items used in preparing your business's available menu choices. Include lines for the vendor's name, date of order, amounts, and promised delivery date. As the items are received, check them off this order list.

You may assign one or two people to prepare the picnic foods for a small party. This team will be responsible all the way through—from preparation to serving to cleanup.

As your business expands, it gets more complex. Systems become necessary.

On one wall in the shop, you should have a large calendar for the month. Each party should be listed with the client's name, number of guests, and the party time under the appropriate day. This gives the crew an overall view of the month and how it is filling in with bookings. This also helps with scheduling workers. They are able to see at a glance what days of the month are getting busy and be prepared.

We also use a "clipboard" system. On one wall, we have two clipboards. One has a list of the upcoming parties for the following week. The other clipboard has the "To Be Packed Box List" for the current week. This is a per-party list consisting of two sheets: (1) List of grill items, and (2) a list of buffet items. (See the samples I have included in Chapter 4 on page 82.) Each item is checked off and highlighted as it is packed.

On the same wall are clipboards for each day of the week. To each of these clipboards are attached a copy of the party contracts in the

order of their scheduled times, with the earliest party of the day on top. The outside sheet of each of these clipboards is a daily task sheet. This would list not only foods and amounts to be prepared, but also any orders from vendors that need to be made by that day. Any items that needed to be purchased from the local grocery store are also posted on this list. These daily task sheets would be prepared a week in advance.

TIP: Never turn down add-ons to the guest list. If a client calls the day before the party increasing the number of guests, tell the client it is no problem. Do whatever is necessary to accommodate. This may cause you stress at the time, but is good public relations and a client-building must for repeat business. Learn to be flexible.

On the daily task sheets, the head chef should list the total amounts of each food needed for the following day. Under each food category, the client's name and amounts needed for the party are listed. The prep person for each category checks the daily task sheet clipboard, makes up that amount of food, divides it into amounts needed for each party, then places the food into serving bowls, garnishes and plastic-wraps each bowl. Each bowl is placed into a clear plastic food storage bag and tied. The bag is labeled with the kind of food contained, the client's name, and what number bowl out of the total number needed for that particular party. (Example: Potato salad, Jones party, 2 out of 5.) The preparer would then put the bowls, ready to go, into the walk-in cooler in the area designated for that party.

After the client signs the party contract, itemize your copy, listing amounts of each food needed. This is for kitchen use only. At the end of the day, after all the food for the next day's parties is prepared, an assigned worker walks through the cooler with the party contract. The worker should physically touch each wrapped item and check it off. This hands-on step is a valuable double check.

The key person is the head chef. He or she is responsible for overseeing all the parties. On the day before each party, the chef should be given a list showing all the foods and amounts needed, heating times at the shop, loading time, and travel time to each party.

Making lists may sound like a lot of busy-work and I'm sure at this point you may visualize yourself inundated with paper. We have all, at times, experienced the feeling of rebelling against "living life by the list". However, let me emphasize that these lists are important tools in keeping chaos out of catering. Use my systems as guidelines in developing your own lists, streamlining whatever works best for your business. An organized caterer is a successful caterer, minimizing stress and maximizing efficiency.

PAT'S PARTY FOODS
# PAPER SUPPLIES ORDER GUIDE

| Unit | Items/ Case | Price/ Case | Price/ Item | Item # | Description |
|---|---|---|---|---|---|
| ____ | 1,000 | _____ | _____ | _____ | DELUXE KNIVES, White |
| ____ | 1,000 | _____ | _____ | _____ | DELUXE FORKS, White |
| ____ | 1,000 | _____ | _____ | _____ | DELUXE SPOONS, White |
| ____ | 1,000 | _____ | _____ | _____ | DELUXE SOUP SPOONS, White |
| ____ | 1,000 | _____ | _____ | _____ | DELUXE KNIVES, Crystal |
| ____ | 1,000 | _____ | _____ | _____ | DELUXE FORKS, Crystal |
| ____ | 1,000 | _____ | _____ | _____ | DELUXE SPOONS, Crystal |
| ____ | 1,000 | _____ | _____ | _____ | SOUP SPOONS, Formal Heavyweight |
| ____ | 500 | _____ | _____ | _____ | KNIFE/FORK/SPOON PACKETS, Heavy-Duty |
| ____ | 250 | _____ | _____ | _____ | CUTLERY/CONDIMENT PACKETS |
| ____ | 250 | _____ | _____ | _____ | CUTLERY/CONDIMENT PACKETS W/NAPKINS |
| ____ | 500 | _____ | _____ | _____ | PLASTIC SERVING SPOONS |
| ____ | 144 | _____ | _____ | _____ | PLASTIC SERVING SPOON/FORK SETS |
| ____ | 4,000 | _____ | _____ | _____ | COCKTAIL NAPKINS, 10 x 10 1/4" fold - White |
| ____ | 3,000 | _____ | _____ | _____ | COCKTAIL NAPKINS - Red |
| ____ | 3,000 | _____ | _____ | _____ | COCKTAIL NAPKINS - Raspberry |
| ____ | 3,000 | _____ | _____ | _____ | COCKTAIL NAPKINS - Melon |
| ____ | 3,000 | _____ | _____ | _____ | COCKTAIL NAPKINS - Dusty Rose |
| ____ | 3,000 | _____ | _____ | _____ | COCKTAIL NAPKINS - Burgundy |
| ____ | 3,000 | _____ | _____ | _____ | COCKTAIL NAPKINS - Jade |
| ____ | 3,000 | _____ | _____ | _____ | COCKTAIL NAPKINS - Aqua |
| ____ | 3,000 | _____ | _____ | _____ | COCKTAIL NAPKINS - Teal |
| ____ | 3,000 | _____ | _____ | _____ | COCKTAIL NAPKINS - Yellow |
| ____ | 3,000 | _____ | _____ | _____ | COCKTAIL NAPKINS - Gold |
| ____ | 3,000 | _____ | _____ | _____ | COCKTAIL NAPKINS - Navy Blue |
| ____ | 3,000 | _____ | _____ | _____ | COCKTAIL NAPKINS - Black |
| ____ | 3,000 | _____ | _____ | _____ | COCKTAIL NAPKINS - Gray |
| ____ | 3,000 | _____ | _____ | _____ | DINNER NAPKINS 2-ply 15 x 17" (1/8" fold) - White |
| ____ | 1,000 | _____ | _____ | _____ | DINNER NAPKINS 2-ply 15 x 17" (1/8" fold) - Red |
| ____ | 1,000 | _____ | _____ | _____ | DINNER NAPKINS 2-ply 15 x 17" (1/8" fold) - Raspberry |
| ____ | 1,000 | _____ | _____ | _____ | DINNER NAPKINS 2-ply 15 x 17" (1/8" fold) - Melon |
| ____ | 1,000 | _____ | _____ | _____ | DINNER NAPKINS 2-ply 15 x 17" (1/8" fold) - Dusty Rose |

| Unit | Items/ Case | Price/ Case | Price/ Item | Item # | Description |
|---|---|---|---|---|---|
| ____ | 1,000 | ____ | ____ | ____ | DINNER NAPKINS 2-ply 15 x 17" (1/8" fold) - Burgundy |
| ____ | 1,000 | ____ | ____ | ____ | DINNER NAPKINS 2-ply 15 x 17" (1/8" fold) - Jade |
| ____ | 1,000 | ____ | ____ | ____ | DINNER NAPKINS 2-ply 15 x 17" (1/8" fold) - Aqua |
| ____ | 1,000 | ____ | ____ | ____ | DINNER NAPKINS 2-ply 15 x 17" (1/8" fold) - Mint |
| ____ | 1,000 | ____ | ____ | ____ | DINNER NAPKINS 2-ply 15 x 17" (1/8" fold) - Teal |
| ____ | 1,000 | ____ | ____ | ____ | DINNER NAPKINS 2-ply 15 x 17" (1/8" fold) - Yellow |
| ____ | 1,000 | ____ | ____ | ____ | DINNER NAPKINS 2-ply 15 x 17" (1/8" fold) - Gold |
| ____ | 1,000 | ____ | ____ | ____ | DINNER NAPKINS 2-ply 15 x 17" (1/8" fold) - Navy Blue |
| ____ | 1,000 | ____ | ____ | ____ | DINNER NAPKINS 2-ply 15 x 17" (1/8" fold) - Black |
| ____ | 1,000 | ____ | ____ | ____ | DINNER NAPKINS 2-ply 15 x 17" (1/8" fold) - Gray |
| ____ | 25 | ____ | ____ | ____ | TABLECLOTHS DUNI 72 x 72" - Red |
| ____ | 25 | ____ | ____ | ____ | TABLECLOTHS 72 x 72" - Hunter Green |
| ____ | 25 | ____ | ____ | ____ | TABLECLOTHS 72 x 72" - Bordeaux |
| ____ | 25 | ____ | ____ | ____ | TABLECLOTHS 72 x 72" - Bittersweet |
| ____ | 25 | ____ | ____ | ____ | TABLECLOTHS 72 x 72" - White |
| ____ | 25 | ____ | ____ | ____ | TABLECLOTHS 72 x 72" - Black |
| ____ | 25 | ____ | ____ | ____ | TABLECLOTHS 72 x 72" - Yellow |
| ____ | 25 | ____ | ____ | ____ | TABLECLOTHS 72 x 72" - Salmon |
| ____ | 25 | ____ | ____ | ____ | TABLECLOTHS 72 x 72" - Dark Blue |
| ____ | 25 | ____ | ____ | ____ | TABLECLOTHS 50 x 108" - Red |
| ____ | 25 | ____ | ____ | ____ | TABLECLOTHS 50 x 108" - Hunter Green |
| ____ | 25 | ____ | ____ | ____ | TABLECLOTHS 50 x 108" - Bordeaux |
| ____ | 25 | ____ | ____ | ____ | TABLECLOTHS 50 x 108" - Bittersweet |
| ____ | 25 | ____ | ____ | ____ | TABLECLOTHS 50 x 108" - White |
| ____ | 25 | ____ | ____ | ____ | TABLECLOTHS 50 x 108" - Black |
| ____ | 25 | ____ | ____ | ____ | TABLECLOTHS 50 x 108" - Yellow |
| ____ | 25 | ____ | ____ | ____ | TABLECLOTHS 50 x 108" - Salmon |
| ____ | 25 | ____ | ____ | ____ | TABLECLOTHS 50 x 108" - Dark Blue |
| ____ | 144 | ____ | ____ | ____ | BANQUET CANDLES 12" - White |
| ____ | 144 | ____ | ____ | ____ | BANQUET CANDLES 12" - Red |
| ____ | 72 | ____ | ____ | ____ | FUEL - **8 oz.** |
| ____ | 144 | ____ | ____ | ____ | FUEL - **3 oz.** |
| ____ | ROLL | ____ | ____ | ____ | 40" x 300' PAPER TABLE COVER - White |
| ____ | ROLL | ____ | ____ | ____ | 40" PLASTIC TABLE COVER |
| ____ | 40 | ____ | ____ | ____ | 54" SQ. 3 POLYTISSUE TABLE COVERS - White |

| Unit | Items/ Case | Price/ Case | Price/ Item | Item # | Description |
|---|---|---|---|---|---|
| ____ | 40 | ____ | ____ | ____ | 72" SQ. 3 POLYTISSUE TABLE COVERS - White |
| ____ | 1,000 | ____ | ____ | ____ | PLACEMATS, Plain Green |
| ____ | 1,000 | ____ | ____ | ____ | PLACEMATS, Plain Red |
| ____ | 1,000 | ____ | ____ | ____ | PLACEMATS, Red with scalloped edge |
| ____ | 5,000 | ____ | ____ | ____ | ROYAL LACE DOILIES 12" |
| ____ | 1,000 | ____ | ____ | ____ | MOIST TOWELETTES |
| ____ | 1,000 | ____ | ____ | ____ | DISPOSABLE ASHTRAYS |
| ____ | 15,000 | ____ | ____ | ____ | WRAPPED TOOTHPICKS |
| ____ | 10,000 | ____ | ____ | ____ | TOOTHPICKS 2½" Frilled - Ass't. Colors |
| ____ | 10,000 | ____ | ____ | ____ | TOOTHPICKS 3" Frilled - Ass't. Colors |
| ____ | 10,000 | ____ | ____ | ____ | COFFEE STIRRERS, 5" Plastic |
| ____ | EACH | ____ | ____ | ____ | 15" STYRO CONES |
| ____ | EACH | ____ | ____ | ____ | 15" STYRO CONES |
| ____ | EACH | ____ | ____ | ____ | 12" STYRO CONES |
| ____ | 500 | ____ | ____ | ____ | COFFEE MUGS, 7 oz., Plastic |
| ____ | 1,000 | ____ | ____ | ____ | COFFEE CUPS, 8 oz., Foam |
| ____ | 1,000 | ____ | ____ | ____ | LIDS FOR ABOVE |
| ____ | 500 | ____ | ____ | ____ | COFFEE MUGS, 7 oz., Plastic |
| ____ | 1,000 | ____ | ____ | ____ | SM. SODA CUPS, 12 oz. Foam, Queen Anne |
| ____ | 1,000 | ____ | ____ | ____ | LIDS FOR ABOVE |
| ____ | 1,000 | ____ | ____ | ____ | LG. SODA CUPS, 16 oz. Foam, Queen Anne |
| ____ | 1,000 | ____ | ____ | ____ | LIDS FOR ABOVE |
| ____ | 500 | ____ | ____ | ____ | STEMMED CHAMPAGNE CUPS, 4 oz. 2-part |
| ____ | 120 | ____ | ____ | ____ | STEMMED CHAMPAGNE CUPS, 5 oz. Prestige |
| ____ | 500 | ____ | ____ | ____ | WHISKEY/WINE STEMMED CUPS, 5½ oz. - Clear |
| ____ | 1,000 | ____ | ____ | ____ | CUT CRYSTAL TUMBLERS 7 oz. - Juice & Punch |
| ____ | 500 | ____ | ____ | ____ | CUT CRYSTAL TUMBLERS 9 oz. - on the Rocks |
| ____ | 500 | ____ | ____ | ____ | CUT CRYSTAL TUMBLERS 10 oz. - Highball |
| ____ | 1,000 | ____ | ____ | ____ | BEER OR HIGHBALL CUPS 12 oz. - Translucent |
| ____ | 1,000 | ____ | ____ | ____ | BEER CUPS 16 oz. - Translucent |
| ____ | 10,000 | ____ | ____ | ____ | WRAPPED STRAWS |
| ____ | 500 | ____ | ____ | ____ | PLATES 10¼" FOAM COMPARTMENT |
| ____ | 500 | ____ | ____ | ____ | PLATES 9" FOAM LUNCHEON |
| ____ | 1,000 | ____ | ____ | ____ | PLATES 7" FOAM BREAD |
| ____ | 1,000 | ____ | ____ | ____ | PLATES 6" FOAM DESSERT |

| Unit | Items/ Case | Price/ Case | Price/ Item | Item # | Description |
|------|-------------|-------------|-------------|--------|-------------|
| ____ | 1,000 | _____ | _____ | _____ | BOWLS 12 oz. SOUP OR SALAD |
| ____ | 240 | _____ | _____ | _____ | PLATES, 7 1/2" SCROLLWARE - Clear |
| ____ | 100 | _____ | _____ | _____ | DINE-OUT CARTONS |
| ____ | 250 | _____ | _____ | _____ | CAKE (LUNCH) BOXES 9 x 5 x 4" - White |
| ____ | 250 | _____ | _____ | _____ | CARRYETTE CARTONS |
| ____ | 250 | _____ | _____ | _____ | MICRO-COMBINATION TRAYS 16 oz. |
| ____ | 250 | _____ | _____ | _____ | MICRO-COMBINATION TRAYS 8 oz. |
| ____ | 50 | _____ | _____ | _____ | STEAM TABLE PANS FULL-SIZE 4" Deep |
| ____ | 50 | _____ | _____ | _____ | LIDS FOR FULL-SIZE STEAM TABLE PANS |
| ____ | 100 | _____ | _____ | _____ | STEAM TABLE PANS HALF-SIZE 2 9/16" deep |
| ____ | 100 | _____ | _____ | _____ | STEAM TABLE PANS HALF-SIZE 4 3/16" deep |
| ____ | 100 | _____ | _____ | _____ | LIDS FOR HALF-SIZE STEAM TABLE PANS |
| ____ | 50 | _____ | _____ | _____ | SERVING TRAYS 12" Flat (#16) |
| ____ | 50 | _____ | _____ | _____ | DOME COVERS FOR 12" TRAY |
| ____ | 50 | _____ | _____ | _____ | SERVING TRAYS 16" Flat (#15) |
| ____ | 50 | _____ | _____ | _____ | DOME COVERS FOR 16" TRAY |
| ____ | 50 | _____ | _____ | _____ | SERVING TRAYS 18" Flat (#14) |
| ____ | 50 | _____ | _____ | _____ | DOME COVERS FOR 18" TRAY |
| ____ | 50 | _____ | _____ | _____ | CATERING CUPS 16 oz. |
| ____ | 250 | _____ | _____ | _____ | LIDS FOR 16 oz. CATERING CUPS |
| ____ | 100 | _____ | _____ | _____ | SHEET CAKE PANS HALF-SIZE |
| ____ | 100 | _____ | _____ | _____ | LIDS FOR HALF-SHEET CAKE PANS |
| ____ | 25 | _____ | _____ | _____ | SHEET CAKE PANS FULL-SIZE |
| ____ | 100 | _____ | _____ | _____ | ROUND CAKE PANS 9" |
| ____ | EACH | _____ | _____ | _____ | CARDBOARD ROUND 6" |
| ____ | EACH | _____ | _____ | _____ | CARDBOARD ROUND 8" |
| ____ | EACH | _____ | _____ | _____ | CARDBOARD ROUND 10" |
| ____ | EACH | _____ | _____ | _____ | CARDBOARD ROUND 12" |
| ____ | EACH | _____ | _____ | _____ | CARDBOARD ROUND 14" |
| ____ | EACH | _____ | _____ | _____ | CARDBOARD ROUND 16" |
| ____ | EACH | _____ | _____ | _____ | CARDBOARD ROUND 18" |
| ____ | EACH | _____ | _____ | _____ | CARDBOARD HALF-SHEET CAKE |
| ____ | EACH | _____ | _____ | _____ | BOX HALF-SHEET CAKE |
| ____ | EACH | _____ | _____ | _____ | BOX FULL-SHEET CAKE |
| ____ | 100 | _____ | _____ | _____ | DOILIES 4" |

| Unit | Items/ Case | Price/ Case | Price/ Item | Item # | Description |
|------|------|------|------|------|-------------|
| ____ | 500 | ____ | ____ | _____ | DOILIES 12" |
| ____ | 250 | ____ | ____ | _____ | DOILIES 16" |
| ____ | EACH | ____ | ____ | _____ | RUFFLE - White |
| ____ | 50 | ____ | ____ | _____ | SHEET CAKE BOXES 11 x 17x 1" |
| ____ | EACH | ____ | ____ | _____ | RUFFLE - White |
| ___ | EACH | ____ | ____ | _____ | RUFFLE - White |
| ____ | EACH | ____ | ____ | _____ | RUFFLE - White |
| ____ | 100 | ____ | ____ | _____ | BUCKETS 83 oz. (5 lbs.) - Treated Marble |
| ____ | 100 | ____ | ____ | _____ | LIDS |
| ____ | 100 | ____ | ____ | _____ | BUCKETS 165 oz. (10 lbs.) - Treated Marble |
| ____ | 100 | ____ | ____ | _____ | LIDS |
| ____ | 300 | ____ | ____ | _____ | BUCKETS 35 oz. - Treated Marble |
| ____ | 50 | ____ | ____ | _____ | LIDS |
| ____ | 500 | ____ | ____ | _____ | SQUAT FOAM FOOD CUPS 16 oz. |
| ____ | 1,000 | ____ | ____ | _____ | LIDS FOR SQUAT CUPS 16 oz. |
| ____ | 1,000 | ____ | ____ | _____ | SQUAT FOAM FOOD CUPS 4 oz. |
| ____ | 1,000 | ____ | ____ | _____ | LIDS FOR SQUAT CUPS 4 oz. |
| ____ | 5,000 | ____ | ____ | _____ | PLASTIC SOUFFLE FOOD CUPS 2 oz. - Clear |
| ____ | 2,500 | ____ | ____ | _____ | LIDS FOR SOUFFLE CUPS 2 oz. |
| ____ | 2,000 | ____ | ____ | _____ | TART CUPS |
| ____ | 10 | ____ | ____ | _____ | WAXED TISSUE |
| ____ | 30 | ____ | ____ | _____ | TOWELS, ROLL, 2-ply 11 x 10" |
| ____ | 4,000 | ____ | ____ | _____ | TOWELS, SINGLE FOLD - Natural |
| ____ | 96 | ____ | ____ | _____ | TOILET TISSUE, 2-ply |
| ____ | DRUM | ____ | ____ | _____ | POTASSIUM CHLORIDE ICE MELT, 100 lbs. |
| ____ | 6 | ____ | ____ | _____ | LIQUID BLEACH |
| ____ | 100 | ____ | ____ | _____ | PLASTIC GLOVES, 1.25 ml, Med. |
| ____ | 1,000 | ____ | ____ | _____ | PLASTIC GLOVES, 1.25 ml, Lg. |
| ____ | EACH | ____ | ____ | _____ | TOP SCRUB APC/DEGREASER |
| ____ | EACH | ____ | ____ | _____ | OVEN & GRILL CLEANER |
| ____ | 4 | ____ | ____ | _____ | LOTION DISH SOAP |
| ____ | ROLL | ____ | ____ | _____ | ALUM. FOIL HEAVY-DUTY 15" x 1,000' |
| ____ | ROLL | ____ | ____ | _____ | ALUM. FOIL HEAVY-DUTY 18" x 1,000' |
| ____ | ROLL | ____ | ____ | _____ | ALL-PURPOSE FILM 18" x 2,000' |
| ____ | ROLL | ____ | ____ | _____ | ALL-PURPOSE FILM 12" x 2,000' |

| Unit | Items/ Case | Price/ Case | Price/ Item | Item # | Description |
|------|------|------|------|------|------|
| ____ | 100 | _____ | _____ | _____ | GARBAGE LINERS 23 x 17 x 46" 2 ml - Buff |
| ____ | 125 | _____ | _____ | _____ | PREMIUM GARBAGE LINERS 23 x 17 x 46" - Black |
| ____ | 250 | _____ | _____ | _____ | LINERS 18 x 14 x 36" 1.5 ml TRAY COVER - Clear |
| ____ | 200 | _____ | _____ | _____ | POLY BUN PAN COVERS 21 x 6 x 35" - Clear |
| ____ | 250 | _____ | _____ | _____ | WBSKT LINERS 18 x 14 x 36" 1.5 ml - Buff |
| ____ | 1,000 | _____ | _____ | _____ | 12 x 12" POLYBAGS 1.5 ml - Clear |
| ____ | 1,000 | _____ | _____ | _____ | 20 x 24" POLYBAGS 1.5 ml - Clear |
| ____ | 1,000 | _____ | _____ | _____ | 10 x 14" POLYBAGS - Clear |
| ____ | 1,000 | _____ | _____ | _____ | 12 x 20" POLYBAGS 1 ml - Clear |
| ____ | 250 | _____ | _____ | _____ | 18 x 24" POLYBAGS 1 ml - Clear |
| ____ | 200 | _____ | _____ | _____ | 21 x 6 x 35" POLYBAGS - Clear |
| ____ | 1,000 | _____ | _____ | _____ | 7 x 7" FOLD LOCK SANDWICH BAG 1.5 ml - Clear |
| ____ | 1,000 | _____ | _____ | _____ | FOLD LOCK POLY BAGS 6³/₄ x 7" - Clear |

This order form is set up as a sample for your reference. Note that napkins, tablecloths, and such come in a wide range of colors and sizes; make sure you have your own supplier's detailed list of available goods when setting up your own form.

# On the Move

Transporting food to the party site safely is crucial. An incident from an associate's catering career illustrates that point: To save time, 500 pieces of cheesecake were plated up in advance at the shop. They were placed on shelved containers with rollers to be easily rolled in at the party site. The containers were loaded onto the truck. An inexperienced worker neglected to secure them, and to add to the potential problem, the worker also failed to latch the back doors of the truck tightly. He drove off and, sure enough, at the first quick turn, the truck doors swung open and some of the containers rolled out and off the back of the truck. One of the workers ran to the nearest grocery store and bought frozen cheesecakes. He used a small blowtorch to soften them. Another worker phoned back to the shop to have more plates sent over. They managed to re-plate the missing cheesecake slices and got through the party with no one knowing what had happened on the way.

Let's talk about how to avoid disasters like this incident and have a "smooth move."

Designate an area in your shop where all dry supplies (paper products, linens, utensils, etc.) can be stored. Use plastic storage boxes with lids. A good size measures 18 x 23 1/2 x 14 inches. When unused, they can be nestled into each other for convenient storage.

If you have enough of these plastic boxes, pack them with the needed paper products, linen, skirting, utensils, and any other non-food items one to two days before a party. Write the client's name on masking tape and label each box. Using the "General Packing List" (see sample on page 229), check off the items as they are packed. Stack the plastic boxes four or five high, keeping together all boxes for each party. It is very important to arrive at the party site with all necessary items.

TIP: For each party, carry a tote bag, a "catering contingency companion," to the party location. Some of the items you will want to include are extra salad forks, tongs, hot pads, towel, washcloth, serving spoons, food storage bags, a small roll of aluminum foil, paring knife, manual can opener, metal spatula, matches and lighter.

When first starting out in business, you may not be able to afford to buy all the hot boxes you need. The plastic storage boxes can double as hot boxes to carry cold foods. Lay flat ice packs in the bottom of the box. Top with a ribbed towel and put in a domed tray of cold food. The ribbed towel provides traction and prevents the tray from sliding around. In an 18 x 23 1/2 x 14-inch box you can fit three 16-inch round domed trays, stacked atop each other with a towel between each layer.

Rolls and buns are delivered to your shop by the vendor on bread racks. These racks are made of plastic and are lightweight with meshed bottoms recessed to hold the packages of breads. The filled racks are easily stacked. Leave the rolls or buns in their original packages and double-check that your quantities for that party are correct and that the rolls have been pre-sliced. Stack the loaded bread racks into your truck for transport. Remove the breads from their packaging at the picnic site and put into napkin-lined baskets.

Condiments such as brown and yellow mustards, ketchup, pickle relish, and mayonnaise are best served in individual packets. These packets come in cardboard boxes. Be sure to mark any opened boxes with the number of remaining packets. Load the number of needed boxes of mustards, ketchup, and pickle relish into the plastic storage boxes for transport. The mayonnaise packets are carried in a cooler.

To transport beverages, both hot and cold, use insulated beverage containers. Perk regular and decaffeinated coffee at the shop. Fill the beverage containers with boiling water and close with lids to heat the container. After 15 minutes, drain out the water and fill with hot coffee. Be sure and add a "Decaf" label to the decaffeinated coffee container.

For cold beverages, such as lemonade or iced tea, just fill the container with the beverage. Label each container with the client's name and type of beverage. If you take canned sodas, place the needed quantities in the walk-in cooler the day before the picnic to chill. Put in portable coolers and top with ice for transport. Pack ice cubes in the portable coolers, sticking an ice scoop on top inside each cooler of ice.

Pack all the cold foods into double front-loading hot boxes, coolers or plastic storage boxes that have been specially outfitted as previously discussed. All the hot foods go into hot boxes. A day before the picnic, pack all the grill boxes, using the grill section of the "To Be Packed Box List" (see page 82 for sample).

Use a small van for parties of up to 50 people. A larger cargo van will be needed for parties of over 50 and up to 200. The grills come out of shop storage disassembled. The grill legs for each grill are stored in that grill's body. From the back door of the van, stack the grill bodies on top of each other on the van floor on one side of the van towards the front. Lay the grill racks on top of the grill bodies. Stack the plastic storage boxes containing grill items on the grill racks. Put these out slightly from the van's side, leaving a small space in which you can sandwich bags of charcoal. Place the coolers with meats next to the grills in one area. Put the beverage containers on the van floor behind the driver's seat. Load the rest of the storage boxes,

cold foods, bread racks, desserts, and garbage cans. Load the hot foods last.

For larger parties, use a step van. It's very much like a cube van, but with a step on the back. Inside the step van and along each side are tall stainless steel cabinets with doors. They are anchored to the van sides with tie-down straps which hook into the van's sides. Stainless steel runners are along each interior cabinet side. Slide baking sheets in for shelves and use these for all your cold food trays. You do not need these trays to be covered with domed lids; just plastic wrap each tray tightly and bag with a large food storage bag and twist tie shut. Place flat ice packs in back of the baking sheets and along the cabinet bottom. Your food will stay nice and cold. These cabinets are movable, so before anchoring into place and loading, make sure you leave enough floor space for the grills.

After loading the cold foods in the cabinets, wheel out the double front-loading hot boxes. You will need a couple of strong men to lift these into the van. Sandwich them in along the sides of the van near the back and anchor in place with tie-down straps. Put into the van the rest of the storage boxes, hot boxes, coolers, insulated beverage containers, garbage cans, and bread racks. Load the grills last on the same principle as the smaller van. For a mega-picnic (party of 1,000 or more), see pages 199-204.

The van is now loaded and you are on the move to the party location. You want to have with you everything you need to put on a fun-filled, problem-free, and delicious picnic for your client. You also have your "catering contingency companion" as a small backup, just in case. The greatest insurance for a successful picnic is careful attention to the checklists at the shop and teamwork with workers, double-checking each other and all items.

# General Packing List

GROUP:_____ DATE:_____ DAY:_____

SET UP TIME:_____ SERVING TIME:_____

NUMBER OF PEOPLE:_____

AMT. PAPER SERVICE
____ 10½" 3-SECTION DINNER PLATE
____ 9" DINNER PLATE
____ 7" BREAD PLATE
____ SALAD/SOUP BOWL
____ COFFEE CUP
____ COFFEE CUP - 6-oz. FOAM
____ COFFEE MUG - 7-oz. PLASTIC WHITE
____ PUNCH CUP - 9-oz. SQUAT
____ CHAMPAGNE GLASS
____ WINE GLASS
____ FORK

____ DESSERT FORK
____ KNIFE
____ TEASPOON
____ SOUP SPOON

____ TONGS - SMALL 4"
____ TONGS - LARGE 6"

AMOUNT CHAFERS
____ CHAFING DISH/FANCY/SQ./FULL
____ CHAFING DISH/FANCY/ROUND
____ CHAFING DISH/PLAIN/HALF
____ CHAFING DISH/PLAIN/FULL
NOTE: ALL CHAFERS MUST HAVE STERNOS
____ COCKTAIL NAPKIN/COLOR
____ TIE COLOR ____

AMOUNT MISC. SERVING ITEMS
____ CREAMER
____ SALT & PEPPER SHAKER SET
____ SUGAR/SWEET 'N LOW CADDY
AMT MISC. SERVING ITEMS
____ COFFEE POT W/LID

AMT. CHINA SERVICE
____ 10" DINNER PLATE
____ 9" GLASS PLATE
____ 7" BREAD PLATE
____ GLASS COFFEE MUG
____ BEVERAGE GLASS - 9-oz.
____ BEVERAGE GLASS - 14 oz.
____ COFFEE SAUCER
____ WATER GOBLET
____ WINE GOBLET
____ CHAMPAGNE GLASS
____ FORK - DINNER
____ FORK - SALAD
____ FORK - DESSERT
____ KNIFE
____ TEASPOON
____ SOUP SPOON
____ TABLESPOONS
____ SERVING SPOON - SLOTTED
____ SERVING SPOON - SOLID
____ SPATULA
____ CAKE SPATULA
____ CAKE KNIFE
____ LADLE/SIZE ____oz.
____ LADLE/SIZE ____oz.
____ ICE CREAM SCOOP SIZE ____
____ KNIFE/TYPE

AMOUNT MISC. ITEMS
____ SCISSORS W/ MASKING TAPE
____ GARBAGE BAGS
____ PAPER TOWELS
AMT MISC. ITEMS
____ MATCHES/6"PLASTIC BAGS

____ WATER PITCHER

____ SERVING TRAY/LG OVAL

____ SERVING TRAY/ROUND CORK

____ SERVING TRAY/FANCY STAINLESS

____ TRAY STANDS - SIZE ____

____ PUNCH BOWL W/LADLE

____ ICE BUCKET W/TONGS

____ ICE PAN W/LID - CLEAR PLASTIC

____ ICE SCOOP

____ ROLL BASKET/SIZE ____

____ ROLL BASKET/SIZE

____ BASKET/SIZE ____

____ BASKET/SIZE ____

____ PLASTIC SALAD BAR/SM.

____ PLASTIC SALAD BAR/LG.

____ CANDLE HOLDER/TYPE ____

____ CANDLES/COLOR ____

____ CANDLES/COLOR ____

____ CENTERPIECE/COLOR _____

DESCRIPTION _____

____

____ CARVING BOARD W/FOIL COV. SHEET

____ CARVING SET/KNIFE, FORK, STEEL

____ HEATLAMP (TEST BEFORE PACKING)

____ ____ KETCHUP

____ ____ MUSTARD

____ ____ PICKLE RELISH

____ ____ SALT

____ ____ PEPPER

____ ____ SUGAR

____ ____ SWEET'N LOW

____ COLOR BROCHURES/6" PLASTIC BAG

____ EXTENSION CORD W/ DUCT TAPE

____ ELECTRICAL ADAPTERS

____ MULTI-PLUG BAR

____ ASHTRAYS - DISPOSABLE

____ HANDI-WIPES

____ TOWEL W/WASHCLOTH

____ HOT PADS/PAIR

____ APRON W/NAME TAG

____ PLASTIC GLOVES

____ AMOUNT TABLECOVERINGS

____ PLASTIC ROLL/WHITE

____ PAPER/SIZE ____ COLOR ____

____ LINEN/69 X 69 WHITE

____ LINEN/52 X 114 WHITE

____ LINEN/SIZE ____ COLOR____

____ LINEN/SIZE ____ COLOR____

____ LINEN NAPKIN/COLOR ____

____ LINEN NAPKIN/COLOR ____

____ TABLE SKIRTING

____ PINS FOR SKIRTING

AMOUNT PORTION PACKS - PC'S

# Strictly Business

There are many thoughts, goal setting, and planning in order to run a catering business. What are the qualities needed for running a catering business?

**H**—**H**ealth
**E**—**E**nergy
**A**—**A**ttitude
**R**—**R**ight product
**T**—**T**ime

**H**—**H**ead
**U**—**U**ltimate goals
**G**—**G**uidance to success
**S**—**S**tick-to-it-iveness

Many people get into the catering business because they are good at cooking. There are many facets to catering that need to be met. First of all you need to understand that when you start a business from scratch you may not make a profit for 3 years or more. So you need startup money to keep going. If you buy an existing business you will make money but you should get the owner to give you tips on how to run the business so that you do not make a lot of mistakes and lose your customer base. Catering is a service. When you try to sell this service you need to have credibility. A list of satisfied or repeat customers is a plus to get the parties you so deserve.

If you are trying to secure business parties, for example, make up a list of previous satisfied clients that other potential business customers can call for references. Include the company name, contact name, and phone number. Be sure you have permission to use the names of these people and businesses. It is wise to have 6 to 12 references to show that you are capable of doing the job properly. Type up the list on your letterhead and fax or mail it to the potential customer. It is better to fax the information. Call back the potential customer to make sure your references were received.

I can recall my first party vividly. I worked hard at selling myself. I finally got a small party. I had brand new chafing dishes. While I was serving the party a gentleman came up to the buffet line and said those are mighty shiny chafing dishes. My response was sir, we believe in perfect sanitation. He just smiled and walked away.

If you do not know how to sell parties you will have to take a couple of sales classes and get your sales line down.

My first party was for only 25 people. Before the day of the party I went to the home and saw where I would be serving the food so I would have no surprises. The party was a success. I got another party from a guest at that party. Then I tried a party for 100. It was also successful. I just kept on going.

I always said that catering is like a love affair: you keep going back for more. It is an enticing business. You are creating a beautiful party and you are making people happy. You get into all kinds of beautiful homes, city and county parks, fancy halls, and serve many people. While you work hard you love to hear those wonderful compliments on how great the food looks and tastes. The decorations create the atmosphere and when all is said and done you are willing to do almost anything to get another fantastic party. It is you the caterer that people associate the party with.

Catering takes a great deal of planning and organizing. A signed contract is a must so that both the caterer and the customer agree in

writing to what is expected. Then you the caterer must produce. You must think of yourself as an actor putting on a show. The production must go on no matter what happens behind the scenes. If the lettuce turns brown or the desserts are smashed, do not tell the host. Get more lettuce and dessert and go on with the show.

Catering is very stressful. You work under a lot of pressure to serve the party on time. Catering is very heavy work. You cook the food. You load up the food carrying the food in proper containers to prevent spoilage. You unload the food and equipment at the party site. You set up the buffet. You serve and re-pack all the leftover food and equipment into the truck. You return to your shop and you unload the truck. You wash up the equipment and put the leftovers in the cooler. You must have everything you need for every occasion, for there often isn't any equipment at most of your party locations.

You need to be a cool cucumber in front of your host and guests. You must be a party pleaser. You wear a smile and say everything is going just great even though you are struggling with a few details that you are worried about. Be prepared to cover yourself in those emergencies such as forgetting an item. You can run and get the item if need be. I learned in one fast hurry to always do a double touch of all items in your truck going to each party. I had a check-off sheet that helped me get items to the party. I also carried extra serving spoons, tongs, towels etc. in an extra box to be safe. I called it my caterer emergency box. You can bring items back but it is time-consuming to run and get them. I had a chef who used to kid me about loading up and unloading the extra box because it was a rare occasion that I missed something as I became experienced. You may even hold up the party and cause some dissatisfaction.

You can have wonderful food and still not be successful in the catering business. It's you the owner that sells your expertise. People pick up quickly if you are sincere and will produce and follow through. If you spoil the party and do not meet the expectations of the client, the word of mouth will harm you greatly. If you do a great job your repeat list will grow by leaps and bounds. You will get high marks. People will spread the word about how great your food and service are. You must always be consistent and be there for the customer.

After the party is over send a short evaluation enclosed with a self-addressed stamped envelope. (See example on page 238.) Sometimes people will tell you everything was great; they feel uncomfortable telling you in person that they have a few concerns. This evaluation gives them a chance to express their

## TIPS

◆ Many locations will expect you to pay a fee for catering a party in their hall. You will have to tack this fee onto the customer's bill or charge a higher price. Some places ask for 15 percent or as high as 20 percent of your catering bill for using their facility. If you can't recover that cost you may need to turn down that party in order to maintain a profit. Without profit it is a waste of your time.

◆ Get a good-sized down payment—at least half the total bill—on the party before you begin to make party plans. Collect the balance in advance if you can, or on the day of the party at the latest. I have had one bad check in 18 years of business. The gentleman made it good.

opinion. If they really liked everything they will tell you, too. This becomes good material for you to learn how to improve and also to accept compliments. If they are satisfied you can ask the client for a letter of recommendation. I am especially happy when I get an unsolicited thank you letter for a job well done. These letters have helped me greatly to go onward in my catering career.

Personal contact is another great way of securing business. That can be very time-consuming. The telephone is also a dynamic tool for selling. Telemarketing will help increase sales greatly if used properly. Going to businesses and taking a treat to the decision-making meeting also will help secure business. I remember wanting to secure a large Hawaiian party. I sent a beautiful young lady dressed in a Hawaiian costume with a presentation. She got the job on the spot.

Also being very professional and businesslike is a must for success. I recall bidding against ten other caterers for a zoo party. I offered an ice sculpture of an ape holding a banana. I got the party. Just dare to be different.

Be prepared to answer questions from prospective clients as they are planning their event. Here are some questions that may come up—and some that you may want to ask, if the client doesn't ask first.

1. Is caterer licensed? Is caterer licensed to serve alcohol?

2. Does caterer provide a written contract?

3. Does caterer own or rent equipment? If caterer rents, is client charged rental fees?

4. Does caterer have insurance? How much? For what?

5. What is required for deposit? When is balance due? Will caterer take checks?

6. Will caterer be there personally at event? If not, who will, and what experience to they have? Can client meet before event?

7. Is caterer willing to use client's recipes?

8. How is buffet line set up?

9. What are decorations for buffet tables?

10. How are guest tables set up? Can client meet caterer at event site to discuss?

11. What type of table coverings, dishes, linens, etc. will be used? Is there an extra charge for china versus paper?

12. Extra charge for cake plates and forks, champagne glasses for toast? Cake cutting charge?

13. Will caterer place client's centerpiece?

14. Extra charge for use of the grill?

15. Is client charged for guests who don't show up?

16. Do guests get seconds? How much time is allotted for guests to eat?

17. Who provides containers for leftovers? Does client pick up leftovers at event site or caterer's facility? Does caterer issue a waiver of liability if client takes leftovers? (Insurance companies often frown on caterers giving leftovers to clients.)

18. Is client responsible for cleanup and garbage removal?

I began in a church basement and rented a lower level area. I had to put all the equipment into this rented area, which was expensive. However, I got the local newspaper to write an article about my business. When I moved to my second location, a historic building, the

local newspaper wrote another story and took pictures of the building inside and out and also of me. This is good free publicity and is very good for business. I booked parties from that article.

The 100-year-old building was originally a schoolhouse. I gutted out the entire building and made it into a catering service. I am a very traditional person so I decorated the entire place to be homelike. First impressions are lasting impressions so I had the entryway decorated with fruits, breads and quaint decorations to give a good impression. I changed the decorations for each season to create some interest. There was one office on each side of the entryway. Our friendly staff greeted each potential customer. We had a special room filled with pictures of parties, framed letters from satisfied customers, a table with decorated dummy cakes, a buffet setup, china, and paper products. The potential customers were seated at a decorated round table. We gave tastings to show off our wares, and tours through our kitchen facilities.

People were especially fascinated with our quaint old building. The kitchen and loading area were in the back of the building. The space was very workable. The huge windows brought sunlight and warmth into the kitchen during the winter months. Bread or other goodies baking made the kitchen and building smell good when customers came in for appointments. I no longer operate out of that building, but it was a great location.

## SAMPLE LETTER

*Remember to keep letters very short. A customer will not read a long letter. Sample:*

Dear _____ ,

As your company grows, you may be thinking of generating more business. Let Pat's Party Foods catering service assist you in making your plans for your next function. If you have a need for an open house, seminar, a small catered lunch, or a fantastic picnic Pat's will make any event a big success.

Whether you will expect 20 to 2,000 guests, Pat's Party Foods will provide plenty of tasty food worthy of a celebration at your place of business or any other location you choose. Pat's is a full-service licensed caterer with over a decade of experience providing quality group food service. Please let us know how we can be of service to you.

We wish you a successful business year.

Sincerely,


Pat Nekola
Pat's Party Foods

It is a great feeling to start a business and watch it grow. It is truly a most challenging and satisfying experience. You have to be able to stick with your business in good times and in bad times, just like a marriage. Without dedication you will fail. Running a business is not for everyone.

Social catering is cyclical. When you are busy you are pushed hard. There are certain months of the year that you are slow. Weekends are very busy. As your business grows you may be doing 12 to 15 parties on a given day. That takes real skill and organization.

It would not be wise to take a large number of parties at the same time if you are under-staffed and short of equipment. You need a lot of convection ovens and cooler space to do a lot of parties. Sometimes you are better off turning down a couple of parties rather than having a disaster. If at all possible it is a great idea to stagger the parties somewhat. With experience you will learn how do exactly that.

When you first begin your business you will wear many hats. It will consume most of your time. You will work many weekends and holidays. While everyone is having fun you are working long hard hours. Before you begin a business it is wise to have a business plan. Take some classes and make definite plans before you invest your capital. Here are some questions and ideas before you begin a business:

- How would I start and run a catering business?
- Why do I want to run my own catering business?
- Why will customers buy from me? (completeness, convenience, visibility, availability, less expensive, more for the money, reliability)
- What reward do I expect?
- Will I earn a living?

- Will I feel satisfied?
- Will I use my talents?
- Will I take charge and run with this business?
- Will I offer something better to the customer and the community?
- Will I gain recognition?
- Will I be able to be a good boss?
- Do I know the laws in the workforce, and can I follow them?
- What pay is good for my staff and myself?
- Can I keep good records and be a real business person?
- Do I have specific goals and time limits?
- Do I understand how to achieve financial freedom?
- Can I manage, people, equipment, supplies and materials, and money?
- Do I understand the responsibilities of running a catering service?
- Have I considered that having a staff involves recruiting, interviewing, scheduling, work rules, safety, record-keeping, payroll and firing?
- How much capital will it take to purchase equipment?
- Can I prepare and deliver the food and meet health codes?
- Have I thought about financing, start-up capital, operations budget?
- Have I considered financial sources such as bank or home equity loans?

As a manager you must plan, organize, direct, coordinate, control and delegate.

You must have financial and personal goals for your business, a good understanding of the operations of a catering business, and your own philosophy for the business.

The keys to success are attitude, strength, good habits, skills and specialized knowledge.

When you are screening a potential employee you will require an application for

employment, statement of interest and a list of qualifications. At the actual interview give the candidate a practical test, if necessary, and check references. When you interview have a written job description and an interview outline that is prepared ahead of time. Greet the candidate and establish rapport. Explain the position that's available. Ask a lot of questions: listen to the person you are interviewing. Briefly review pay and benefits. Encourage questions from the candidate.

As your business continues to grow you will have a file with a card on each customer; also keep a computer list. Keep in touch with customers. Be aggressive in a pleasant manner. Always stay interested in your customers so they will continue to do business with you. Look for new business at all times. When you have parties you can have business cards, matches or personalized pens available. Give something that a customer can keep on hand in a pocket or a drawer. A person may get your literature and two years later call you. Always keep your name out in the front line. Participate in your community and join the local chamber of commerce. Take an active part in the Chamber. Also join the National Restaurant Association, your statewide restaurant association, and NACE (National Association of Catering Executives). It is important to know what is the latest and greatest. Be creative. Listen to what the customer wants and make sure they are more than satisfied. Go to classes at your local technical college and learn anything and everything about business, management and catering.

Almost every person I talk to starts out a catering service because he or she likes to cook but has little or no business background. As the business grows the owner must manage the business and sell parties. They eventually hire chefs and a large serving staff. I wrote newsletters or special promotion letters to the cus-

tomers. Write a letter of thanks or even offer a small gift certificate to a repeat customer for their next party. Most people are appreciative and interested.

When you receive an order for a new job take the time to write a brief note and thank the customer for selecting your catering service. I always wrote a thank you note after every party. I signed my name on every letter. People are impressed that you took the time to do that for them.

A color brochure is a great selling tool. We live in a world of color. While the initial cost is expensive, the color brochure produced in good taste will help secure many parties. The pictures in the brochure show your work and the writeup tells what you are all about. This brochure will create an image and tell where you are located.

Take pictures of all your parties because a book of pictures also helps you sell parties. Very often the person looking for a party does not always know what he or she wants. The pictures give ideas to the potential customer.

Develop a logo and use it consistently on your stationery and business cards to give you a visual identity. All stationery and business envelopes must be very professional. I use large envelopes with my logo, so the customer receiving the mail could plainly see it came from my catering company. One side has the logo and the catering firm. The words "food and service worthy of a celebration" invited the potential customer to select our catering firm. Our business checks also use the logo. The logo and contacts used for getting your name out in the public eye will help you secure business and grow provided that you satisfy your customers. You may not be able to satisfy every customer all the time but you can most of the time if you work hard at it.

Contact meeting halls and find out how to get on the hall list. Work with the halls to get recommendations. Develop a rapport with the

hall owners and there will be many chances to secure business.

Network with many other businesses such as photographers, entertainment businesses, florists, bakeries, party planners, jewelry shops, and sales representatives from various vendor companies, to name only a few. These people can help you get leads. You work together. This is what networking is all about.

Come up with ideas for promoting your catering business, and implement them. For example you may pitch a tent outside your catering shop. Advertise an open house and invite key businesses to tour your facilities and taste your food. Be sure you get the decision makers of each business to come to your open house.

The best way to get a booking is to ask for it. Many people are afraid of rejection. I always figured if I asked for the party the worst thing they could say is no but if the client said yes I had a job. The more people you ask the more chances you have to secure business. It is a numbers game.

Setting up a business office, in addition to your kitchen facilities, is very expensive but is a must because a well-run office helps the kitchen staff to produce the party. A computer, fax machine, typewriter, desk, file cabinet, and basic office supplies are a must to operate the business. Put all your recipes on the computer and have a recipe file also in the kitchen.

## SAMPLE LETTER

*You can also write a letter introducing a new staff member; this is a good way to keep in touch with your clients. Example:*

Dear _____:

We have just hired a new secretary. Donna is available to answer all your catering questions. Barb, our computer analyst, is presently computerizing all of our business transactions in order to serve you more effectively. Chef Louie and Sous Chef Jack, along with our entire cooking staff and serving staff, work as a team to ensure you that there will be plenty of tasty food attractively presented. Pat is also available to create a special party tailored to meet your needs. Try our picnic theme party ideas with decorations and costumed servers to make a great company gathering.

See you soon.

Sincerely,


Pat Nekola
Pat's Party Foods

Organize the office file cabinet with dividers A-Z for business and A-Z for general customers. Have a file folder for each customer in the file cabinet. Each customer folder will have a name, complete address, work and home phone numbers and a fax number. When I first began my business we did not have a fax machine because most businesses did not own them. Once fax machines became popular I purchased one. I don't know how I ever ran my business without this piece of equipment. I fax the information after the call and then spoke to

---

## EVALUATION LETTER

Dear Client:

The following questions are intended to ensure that you and other customers of Pat's Party Foods will consistently receive fine food, exemplary service, and attractive presentations. Your evaluation, comments, and suggestions would be much appreciated.

Please rate us on the following:

| | | | | |
|---|---|---|---|---|
| Food quality | ___Excellent | ___Good | ___Fair | ___Poor |
| Presentation | ___Excellent | ___Good | ___Fair | ___Poor |
| Service | ___Excellent | ___Good | ___Fair | ___Poor |

What suggestions would help us to serve you better?

_____

_____

Are there other services which you would like us to provide?

_____

_____

It has been our pleasure serving you. It is our hope that we will be able to assist you again soon. Thank you for doing business with us.

Bon appétit!

Pat Nekola
Pat's Party Foods

_____
Customer signature (optional)

them immediately to try to get the party. I also had to buy a computer and ended up with three computers to keep good records. Modern technology is great. Keep the contract and/or invoice with other pertinent information about the party in a folder for each customer. When the customer calls year after year you can refer to the file.

A bookkeeper is a key staff member as your business grows, for you will not have time to keep your books. Always keep your finger in the books to make sure the books are being taken care of properly and that you are not missing funds. Remember it is good record-keeping along with outstanding business management that keeps the business going and growing. Good service and good food are second in line.

An Employee Handbook is important because it lays out what is expected of the employees. It also tells the employee such things as your philosophy about the business, customers, attendance, work apparel, serving apparel, responsibilities, grooming, benefits, work rules, reasons for dismissal. You need to cover yourself in all aspects if possible. You also need to be reasonable in your expectations. I always said if it is something I cannot do or will not do I would not expect that of an employee. I knew every job in my business.

Serving attire—usually black slacks and white dress shirts—is important. Black aprons are appropriate for picnics.

Insurance is a must. Contact your local insurance company to help you set up a plan for a commercial package. Get a policy number and set up a payment program. Liability insurance covers general aggregate, products/completed operations, personal/advertising injury, occurrence, fire, legal liability, and medical payments.

The policy must also cover replacement costs for the building and its contents, and for loss of income in case of a fire.

If you do not own your own building the policy will be different, but you will still need insurance. You will have to have insurance to cover the drivers of your vehicles. Most catering business have a policy called a commercial umbrella. It is a liability coverage and is important for your own protection. Every hall, stadium, and zoo will expect you to have insurance coverage for no less than a half million dollars. Others may expect a million dollars. Remember this may change depending on your location. At any rate find out how much insurance you need to have to do business with various halls.

You buy workman's compensation through a regular insurance company. Some state restaurant associations work in conjunction with an insurance company and you can get a lower rate. If this is available in your state you may want to consider this advantage. Unemployment compensation is paid in taxes to the state and federal government. Find out the regulations and follow them. Also, it is to your advantage to keep very good records. I am very fortunate that I have a very low rate because I have had very few workers collect unemployment compensation. I teach my staff about safety and I enforce the rules.

Discrimination laws—be prepared to know and understand these laws and how to protect yourself if you are ever unjustly accused of this act.

Health regulations. Contact your county health department when you are setting up shop and follow the health codes. The health department will conduct surprise inspections. Cooperate with them and they will be your best business friend. Keep your place clean and neat and equipment in order. You will not encounter problems if you follow the rules.

Keep in mind that you need a food and beverage catering license to cater parties. If

you do not have a license and a competitor turns you in you can be fined heavily and you will be put out of business.

Finally, my advice is to go through all the proper channels. Work for other catering companies and study every phase of the business before you open your business.

If you love people, are creative with high energy, and live to work under pressure and have fun, be a caterer. You can party all the time while making a profit. Actually it is not quite that easy.

Figure your labor costs, food costs, operating expenses such as lights, phone bills etc. Add on at least a 20 to 30 percent profit.

Figure out expenses for every party and be sure you make a profit from each party. If you are going to work this hard you deserve a profit.

Take care of your loyal workers. Keep an open mind to change or adjust to improve your business. Think things through before you act.

Plan your general budget to include unexpected extras such as vehicle repairs and general equipment maintenance.

Make sure you pay all your vendors and maintain all bills. Keep in mind that once every worker is paid and every bill is paid the remainder is yours. You have control and can gain financial freedom with careful planning and hard work.

### JUST CATER IT!

# INVOICE

Directions: _____

_____

Phone: _____ Fax: _____

Date of party _____ Delivery time: _____ Serving time: _____

Contact person: _____

| | DATE COMPLETED | | TERMS |
|---|---|---|---|
| | | | |

| DESCRIPTION OF SERVICES | QUANTITY | PRICE | AMOUNT |
|---|---|---|---|
| | | | |

*Signature* _____

| We appreciate your business! Balance due is | **TOTAL** | |
|---|---|---|

Customer name _____

Address _____

Phone _____ Fax _____

Event _____ Location _____

Date of party _____ Delivery time _____ Serving time _____

Number of people to be served _____

NOTE:  Pat's will guarantee service adequate to feed this number and MUST receive notice 5 days in a advance of the event if additional people are to be served. If fewer people attend, the remaining food will be served as seconds to the people in attendance. No leftovers may remain on site due to the liability involved.

Type of service:     ___ Pickup     ___ Delivery     ___Full service

Style of service:     ___ Buffet     ___ Sit-down     ___ Formal     ___ Informal

Comments _____

_____

| Service to include | Price | Total |
|---|---|---|
|  |  |  |
|  | FOOD TOTAL |  |
| 15% gratuity on food and beverages |  |  |
| Rental equipment _____ |  |  |
| Catering Supervisor for _____hours @ $    /hour |  |  |
| Catering Server for _____hours @ $    /hour |  |  |
|  | SUBTOTAL |  |
|  | Sales Tax |  |
|  | **TOTAL** |  |
| Minus down payment (required to reserve date) |  |  |
|  | **BALANCE DUE** |  |

This agreement is invalid unless signed and returned to Pat's Party Foods by _____ with down payment.                                          (Date)

Customer's signature _____ Date _____
Caterer's signature _____ Date _____